TES Guide to Surviving School Inspection

IMPROVEMENT

91   92   93
18%   23%   25%

95   96   97
45%   35%   40%

G000055452

99 ONWARDS — TO MAKE OUR BEST EVER 45%
5* A*-C BECOME OUR EXPECTED NORM
& EVEN TO REACH BEYOND THIS TO OUR
LONG-HELD GOAL OF 50%

SENIOR STAFF TIME TARGETTED TOWARDS
MENTORING & SUPPORTING NEW TEACHERS
OR THOSE EXPERIENCING DIFFICULTIES

N.B. GM T98/W12 — SUPPORT

Butterworth-Heinemann
Linacre House, Jordan Hill, Oxford OX2 8DP
A division of Reed Educational and Professional Publishing Ltd

 A member of the Reed Elsevier plc group

OXFORD   BOSTON   JOHANNESBURG
MELBOURNE   NEW DELHI   SINGAPORE

First published 1997

British Library Cataloguing in Publication Data
A catalogue record for this book is available from the British Library

ISBN 0 7506 2801 4

Typeset by Avocet Typeset, Brill, Aylesbury, Bucks
Printed and bound in Great Britain

Contents

Acknowledgements

The author wishes to thank Mrs Sylvia Gravensteed, Headteacher, Welsh House Farm Primary School, Birmingham, and Ms Judi Askew, Headteacher, Ridpool Primary School, Birmingham, for their contribution to Chapter 7, and for most helpful discussion about the leadership of schools in the course of inspection.

The author also wishes to thank the staff of Ridpool Primary School for access to examples of high quality planning, and Mr Bernard Clarke, Headteacher, Peers Upper School, Oxford, for his contribution to Chapter 7 and his informative commentary on secondary education in general.

Thanks are also due to Mrs Gill Griffiths, Headteacher, Milking Bank Primary School, Dudley, who gave me the opportunity to study and discuss the school's exemplary development plan, and to Mr Derek Holbird, Headteacher, and his staff, Soho Parish C of E Primary School, City of Westminster, for permission to include a copy of the school's inspection action plan. My thanks to Jackie Holderness, Senior Lecturer, School of Education, Oxford Brookes University, for illuminating and constructive advice.

1
Introduction

In retrospect, people may well come to regard the changes that have taken place in English education in the past decade as the most momentous since the war. The opportunity given to schools to opt out of local government control, the advent of local management of schools (LMS) that has so massively diminished the power of local education authorities, the conferring of large powers on governing bodies, the new rights of parents to more and significantly fuller information about their children's achievement and, theoretically at least, more choice about the secondary schools they attend, above all the establishment of a National Curriculum and a national system of assessment have combined to transform the landscape of education. Some at least of the developments seem to be in contradiction with each other: the freedoms conferred on schools by LMS counterbalanced in turn by demands on them for unprecedented public accountability; parents' freedom of choice frustrated by schools' capacity to select the pupils they want.

But two revolutionary changes are quite unambiguous in their nature and the impact they are having. They are the wide-ranging curriculum that is the entitlement of all pupils of statutory school age and the national system of standardized testing that evaluates how well they are learning it at various stages of their schooling, and even, perhaps, through this chain of accountability, how effectively it is being taught. It is perceived that out of these developments will come the possibility of measuring the value added by schools, of precisely evaluating the quality of achievement, continuity and progression in pupils' education, of identifying both where and when under-performance and regression are occurring and their causes.

The outcomes have not always been what the architects of the legislation may have anticipated or wished for. Governing bodies endowed with much greater powers in important respects, but now bearing also serious responsibility for the state and condition of their schools have not, as expected, rounded en masse on staffs but joined with them in blaming government for a lack of resources. For the most part, parents' responses to the opportunities to require more account-ability from schools have been apathetic, though whether a similar lack of interest will apply to SATs' outcomes is more debatable.

In view of the magnitude of such developments and despite the opposition to them at certain times, and in particular quarters, they have eventually slotted securely into place with relative ease. It is a related innovation, the government programme of school inspection, that has caused notable and bitter controversy and aroused determined resistance on several fronts. Remarkably, it has created, for the first time in a distinguished and impeccable history, an open schism in Her Majesty's Inspectorate.

Despite the scepticism with which it was initially greeted, few schools, given the choice, would now go back to LMS; few teachers would care to deny pupils the entitlement conferred on them by the National Curriculum, though its implementation brought the profession to its knees.

But inspection is a sticking point. Probably nothing has inspired more bitterness, resentment, anxiety, perhaps even fear in the pro-fession. Inspection has caught the wider popular imagination, reached out beyond the educational press to occupy the national media, made Her Majesty's Chief Inspector as instantly recognizable to the public at large as a popular show business personality. There is evidence that many teachers, and especially head teachers, have retired early from the profession rather than face up to the ordeal.

Resistance to inspection – or at least the Ofsted version of it – is widely representative of every educational constituency: parents, governors, LEAs, academics and the teaching profession itself (few people seem to have asked the children for their perceptions, but one certainly encounters those who have been infected by their teachers' anxieties; one has recollections of being met at the gates by pupils, who enquired with a mixture of apprehension and excitement whether we would close the school if what we saw did not satisfy us, of children who insisted that if their work during inspection was not good enough, then their teachers were likely to be sacked!). Teachers, prepared to accept the SATs and even the publication of results, are adamant that inspection must go. They argue for a range of alternatives, for various forms of 'supported' self-evaluation; there are those who still hope that, even now, something may intervene to halt the cycle before it reaches them.

Why has inspection become the ultimate aversion for teachers, a cause of profound anxiety, amounting in some cases to a kind of terror that exceeds anything caused by the rigours of the National Curriculum, annual reports to parents, or even the SATs? Why has the period between the notification and the inspection itself become for many schools a kind of educational Gethsemane during which they begin to doubt their ability to survive the trial? It is important for schools to understand and come to terms with the causes of such anxiety, the general lack of confidence in the process, a feeling widespread among teachers that inspection will prove to be vengeful and unsympathetic. It is a perception shared by many governors and parents. Having identified the causes of such anxiety, whether they are well founded, how far they relate to schools' particular circumstances, staff need to take action to deal with them. People are less likely to show their best if they are debilitated by fear and uncertainty, however groundless these may prove to be. Let us briefly consider, therefore, the reasons for anxiety about inspection, since one of the main purposes of this book will be to help schools deal with them.

Schools have always been accountable in a variety of ways to various constituencies: parents, governing bodies, LEAs and central government. Even the most casual of parents are concerned to know something of their children's achievement and progress, wish to be assured they fit in, are happy, behave well and get all the benefit possible from their schooling.

This is particularly marked at the beginning and end of their education. Parents handing their children over for the first time to the prolonged care and guidance of others, conscious that they will be more formally judged than hitherto in a variety of ways, are anxious to know how they compare with their peers, how they are faring, how the school responds to them and, most importantly, how it is providing for them. At the other end of the cycle as pupils leave school parents are just as concerned; now, especially, about academic success, the quality of which is likely to determine future prospects, opportunities, probably even lifestyle. They will certainly hold the schools responsible, in some respects at least, for the outcomes. Schools, for their part, have always acknowledged parents' rights to be accounted to for the care and education their children received and have been prepared to be accountable in particular ways.

Head teachers have perennially been responsible to managing and governing bodies, and through them to the community at large, for the good conduct and effective leadership and management of their schools. However, few areas of responsibility in schools have been exercised with more flexibility over the years; discharged in a wholly nominal way in many cases; more often conducted on a highly amiable basis as between the professionals – the heads, and their representatives – mediating and interpreting their actions to the compliant amateurs, the governors; rarely conducted in anything but a mutually trusting and supportive spirit. But even the most dominant of heads, exercising subtle control over the most pliant of governing bodies, were kept aware of their accountabilities by articles and protocols which, should they be tempted to forget, could be quickly and effectively invoked.

That old, often gentle and permissive relationship was changing dramatically, of course, long before the Education Act and LMS moved schools to the current situation where governors' powers are immense and their right to accountability from the head is total.

As the powers of governing bodies increased, so LEAs declined and with them the obligation of schools to be as heavily accountable to them as they had been in the past. But old habits die hard; many schools are only now becoming conscious of and confident in their new freedom in this particular respect, especially since LEAs still retain some responsibility and power for monitoring the work and achievement of schools in certain vital respects.

Finally, of course, there is central government, frequently a shadowy figure in the past, the paymaster, content to leave the running of things to the LEAs; now paradoxically in the wake of a great, liberating Education Act, intervening more directly and requiring from schools unprecedented accountability through a series of irresistible measures.

And, of course, with the exception of a few rare periods, there was always formal inspection of one kind or another for some schools.

So accountability is bred in the bones of schools. They are accustomed to judgement, to the need for self-justification. Even in a less urgent past, not a summer came but secondary schools were required to mediate aspects of their public examination results and offer fresh assurances for the future.

But, when all is said and done, though schools, down through the ages, may have accepted and generally sincerely responded to the obligation on their part to be accountable to certain bodies and individuals, it would be quite naive to pretend they welcomed it. After all, it was education that coined the metaphor 'the secret garden', suggestive of exclusivity, and cloistered remoteness, of private rites confined to initiates, of a process cloaked in mystery and obscurity.

It cannot be denied that schools themselves did much in the past to remain aloof, not merely from the public at large but even from those to whom they were nominally accountable. In certain important respects parents were most affected by this. Information about pupils' progress was not always readily accessible nor easily understood; what was given was often restricted, marked by a reluctance on the part of schools to clarify for parents the vitally important matters of what their children were achieving in relative terms, against any set of comprehensible norms, where they stood and how they fared in comparison with their peers, what the true nature and value of their progress was, how compatible their achievement was with their capability.

The failure to be specific about pupils' real attainment, about relative performance, often arose from laudable motives and understandable reasons, a concern to nurture pupils' confidence in their personal potential and to secure parents' support for that, a deep-seated mistrust of the possibility of securing reliable definitive measures especially early on in pupils' schooling.

But, as a consequence, many parents were confused about critical elements of their children's education, and unsure and uninformed, if not deluded, about their competence and capability.

It was not a situation that schools rushed to ameliorate. Their understandable concern, as with all human institutions, to put the best face on things was reflected in relatively harmless but nevertheless conscious measures to gloss examination results, to highlight the best features and play down the least favourable, in a willingness to protect incompetent and under-performing staff. There was a tendency, long maintained, to resist parents' involvement in their children's education, a sense, bolstered in some respects by the professional associations, that the professionals knew best, that delayed the possibility of genuine partnerships. It was not unknown for LEAs, where it suited their particular interests, to collude with schools in rationing information, limiting debate and constraining public accountability.

So, historically, the teaching profession, indeed the world of education at large, has been uneasy about surveillance by that other world outside, and by bodies whose credibility and competence to adjudicate in an arcane and highly specialized area they privately doubted.

Unlike the 'performing' professions – actors, artists, musicians, sports stars, with whom they are sometimes compared – teachers, in the main, do not welcome being observed at their work. They can offer very sound reasons for this. Teaching, they would maintain, is not about histrionics, display, show or virtuoso performance; pupils are unlikely to apply themselves and learn in a theatrical arena. They would claim that teaching and learning, by the very nature of their subtlety and complexity, resist easy quantification, that the sensitive nature of the critical interaction between pupil and teacher is threatened by the presence of detached and alien observers. A possible reflection of this viewpoint is the faltering progress achieved by the national and very costly teacher appraisal scheme.

For the teaching profession the current inspection process represents the most fallible and potentially destructive approach to accountability – to the principle of which, teachers would argue, they are wholly committed.

They claim the inspection process is dangerously flawed and cite these factors as the cause of their anxiety:

- Inspection is conducted, in the main, by total strangers to the school, who are expected, and attempt to form, in a week, a comprehensive picture of a complex and intricate organism, that is likely to have taken arduous and often painful effort over years to build, evolve and refine. (LEA teams inspecting in their own areas do possess a more detailed knowledge of local schools and their particular circumstances; they are generally more welcome by teachers who perceive the likelihood of greater understanding and the sympathy that comes from shared vested interests. On the other hand, those who criticize the inspection process from other perspectives, and wish to see it tightened up, regard local teams as incapable of impartiality when engaged with their own schools. This is reinforced by the private admission of some teams who inspect inside and outside their authority that they pursue for strategic reasons a policy of 'toughness abroad and leniency at home'.)

- The teaching profession asserts that a significant proportion of inspectors is ill-qualified to carry out a task of such complexity. Examples cited include secondary specialists, admirable perhaps in their particular field, but largely ignorant of the intricacies of primary practice and 'converted' in a couple of days' training to inspect in that sector and even to lead primary inspections.
- The extreme difficulty of making accurate judgements about certain issues central to the inspection outcome; the vital matter, for example, of the extent and quality of the progress being made by many pupils.
- The artificial context in which inspections are carried out; the immense strain and tension so debilitating for teachers and their work, the impractically large agenda that inspectors must get through in the week, all combine to make it very difficult for a school to be seen at its best.
- The massive and unproductive disruption caused to the normal life and work of the school.
- The inconsistency in the quality of teams, varying from the highly competent and insightful to the poorly organized and imperceptive, to teams so hastily thrown together that they become acquainted with each other only shortly before the inspection begins.
- The wide variation in practice ranging from the relaxed and permissive to the hectoring and unsympathetic.
- The failure to take account of teachers' perceptions and purposes or to understand their anxieties. Reports, it is claimed, fail to catch the essence of schools, and tend to damn with faint praise; as a generality they are reserved, conservative and uninspired. As one head put it, referring to a 'satisfactory' but notably cautious report: 'Is this really what ten years of my life have been about; is this all they amount to?'
- Most seriously, the inability of the inspection system to take adequate account of the desperately challenging circumstances with which many teachers have to contend and the extent of their success in doing so; the magnitude of the achievement of large numbers of pupils gained against extreme adversity. It is claimed that inspectors long removed from the reality of classrooms, with little under-standing of massively changing pupil and parental attitudes,

especially in socio-economically disadvantaged areas, where scepticism about education is rife (where, for example, it is not uncommon for teachers seeking to encourage pupils to maintain progress and improvement to be physically threatened by parents for 'harassment' of their children) and constrained by the technicalities of the inspection format, are in no position to make proper distinctions between schools, between genuine hard-won and continuing achievement and static but impressive-seeming outcomes.

- It is a model that is punitive rather than constructive, imposed and conducted wholly from outside with the aim of 'catching them doing it wrong', a cumbersome machine set in motion for the sole purpose of hunting down a handful of failing schools.
- The inspection model is essentially a secondary one, incompatible with primary education and practice, focused on management structures and subject-centred teaching more common to the secondary phase.
- The reporting format and prescribed style, the insistence on a 'snapshot' perspective derived from the inspection week alone, excludes animated, wide-ranging, incisive commentary that would reflect the distinctive nature of schools, their catchment areas and circumstances, and take account of 'where they had come from', of the contribution of previous work and effort to current achievement. Such reporting, it is argued, should be underpinned by substantial dialogue between inspectors and teachers that allows for elaboration and justification of the work being done, the objectives pursued and the directions taken by the school.
- The evaluation of the attainment of a whole class in relation to national averages is too difficult to manage, since it seems highly unlikely that inspectors could make even vaguely accurate judgements about so complex a matter in the time available.
- The process is not developmental or creative; it finds fault but does not advise.
- Inconsistent conduct of inspections puts schools in a 'lottery' situation where their fate is eventually determined by the experience, attitudes, preconceptions and even temperaments of particular inspectors.

But despite the sincerely felt rhetoric and the undeniable substance in at least some of the reservations, the real reasons for professional fear of inspection may run deeper and be elsewhere.

After all, there have always been inspections. Many schools have undergone the awesome experience of an HMI inspection. A high proportion of LEAs have implemented their own inspection programmes since the 1970s. Schools could find even the latter, run by familiar LEA teams, harrowing, with individual teachers feeling their chances of promotion could well be adversely affected.

But there are critical differences between such forms of inspection and the Ofsted model.

- In the past, inspection reports were not published to the parents and the community. Until recent years HMI reports were not published at all. LEA reports were handled with the greatest circumspection; in most cases where schools were identified as a cause for serious concern, LEAs responded not by publicizing the matter and requiring accountability and retribution, but by seeking to improve the situation with special support and additional resources. Indeed, the charge was sometimes made that successful schools were 'rewarded' by the loss of resources recycled to rescue the failing.

- Most significantly of all, there was no common format for inspections, so valid comparisons could not be made between schools. In recent years HMI began to publish reports manifestly based on consistent criteria, but their visitations were necessarily so rare that for most people they had the effect of summer lightning – they fell elsewhere and damaged others. The chances of such an inspection happening to one were too rare to be a cause of worry. LEA inspections, on the other hand, tended to be home-spun affairs; in some cases the head teacher, and possibly some of the staff, comprised part of the inspection team. Certainly comparisons could be made with neighbouring schools, but LEAs in the main scrupuously avoided this and the reports themselves were often open to endless negotiation. Where schools fared particularly badly, LEA inspectors and advisers were understandably reluctant to broadcast such a state of affairs whose development they felt some responsibility for in the first place, through ignorance, lack of attention or even, at worst, negligence.

With no nationally recognized criteria for the evaluation of effective education, there was no basis for comparing schools, for establishing any hierarchy of proficiency or even minimal competence. It was quite possible for schools that were failing in the most significant respects to drift on unchallenged year after year, often in areas where pupils were in the most urgent need of a sound education. In fairness, it must be said that the latter situation was anathema to the profession; nevertheless, and probably understandably, it was tolerant of the absence of a general system of accountability whose outcomes would be widely available and capable of being manipulated to provide a basis for comparison and some form of hierarchy of merit.

But the Ofsted inspection process was designed to provide a *system of evaluation* that should be free of the shortcomings of previous models. It is different in certain very important respects and it is the combination of these differences, in the main, that make it such a source of worry for teachers.

- Every school and every teacher in the country will be inspected. It is an inexorable process from which there is no escape. Prior to Ofsted many teachers could have gone through an entire career without ever encountering examination of this kind. For the foreseeable future the competence of every school and every teacher will be rigorously assessed and reported on.
- All schools will be judged according to precise and detailed criteria that make it feasible to broadly compare schools.
- Inspection findings are published to parents by means of comprehensive summaries which, despite their brevity, convey an explicit picture of how well a school has fared. Although teachers are not identified by name in the reports, and despite the best efforts of Ofsted to preserve anonymity, it is possible for parents and others, in certain cases such as small schools or departments, to identify which teachers are being referred to.
- The level of overall performance of schools, phases and departments will be made absolutely clear by reports. Obviously where these are positive schools are being accredited, in a very powerful way in the eyes of the parents and the community. Where the reverse is the case – where schools, departments, phases, subjects or, by implication, teachers are adversely criticized – then the judgement can become a long-term label not easily shrugged off.

- Reports indicate the extent to which schools are 'giving value for money', a judgement usually expressed in a fleeting sentence but one that seldom fails to have a particular resonance for parents.
- Reports in every case set out strengths and weaknesses, a kind of balance sheet from which clear conclusions can be drawn by any audience. This balance sheet is underpinned by commentary on all the factors that contribute to pupils' attainment and progress, to their attitudes, behaviour and personal development.
- In effect, the quality of the school, the level of education it provides for the pupils and the competence of the staff are all disclosed to the world at large. This is as near total accountability as one is likely to achieve. The once secret garden has been well and truly laid open to the public.

In fact, Ofsted judgements will allow for schools to be placed in a hierarchy of merit, with provision for schools to be formally treated as failing or having serious weaknesses. In such cases urgent action is prescribed, with more serious consequences awaiting further failure. In extreme cases it is possible for head teachers and senior staff to lose their jobs. The reports will live with schools for years to come. This is one of the facts becoming unpleasantly clear to teachers: that on the evidence of a relatively brief period, judgements will be fixed as surely as fossils in amber. There is also the daunting fact for teachers that they will be objectively judged before colleagues, that some notion of the worth that detached observers attribute to their professional competence will emerge from the inspection. Indeed, individual performance may be seen to affect the judgement of a whole phase in a particular area or subject, or an aspect of school life.

This therefore is the process, in operation now, for secondary schools for three years, and for primary and special schools for over a year, that has caused so hostile and fearful a reaction from the profession.

Ofsted has taken account of criticisms and has reviewed the inspection process, as it promised, at the outset, it would do. It has acknowledged that, despite the 'successes', there were things to put right and improvements to make. Ofsted described its own concerns arising from their evaluation of the system:

- Inspectors found the framework difficult to apply to primary schools, the handbook repetitive and unwieldy and the Record of

Evidence required by Ofsted over-elaborate and time-consuming. There was criticism of the information provided in the important pre-inspection context and school indicator report (PICSI report); too much of it was open to challenge, out of date or otherwise inappropriate.

- There was probably too much guesswork involved in judgement about achievements in relation to ability and particularly about defining pupils' ability.
- The section on **quality of learning** comprising three elements – progress; pupils' attitudes; and key learning skills – was difficult for inspectors to handle.
- There was clear evidence from inspection reports that **good teaching** was the key to achieving high standards. But teaching was underplayed in the framework.
- Extensive critiques of other aspects of provision and management systems put insufficient emphasis on the evaluation of their impact on standards.

At the same time Ofsted offered a robust defence of the success of the system to date. In an introduction to training materials designed to prepare inspectors for the implementation of the new Framework it was stated: 'To set the changes in context, it is first worth reminding ourselves of what has been achieved so far.

While the inspection system certainly has its critics, the visits made by HMI to schools that have been inspected have given us more encouraging news. It is reassuring, for example, to know that many schools do feel there is a place for external, objective assessment of their work – despite the trauma which inspection brings. The publication of inspection criteria and related advice has proved enormously popular and useful to schools. Inspection is becoming less esoteric than before, and many schools are using the inspection materials for their own development purposes, and not simply as part of their inspection preparation. Schools acknowledge the high degree of professionalism among inspectors and the skill with which they manage inspections. And we already have evidence that schools are improving through implementation of their action plans once the inspection is over.'

Ofsted was confident that the major concerns identified would be dealt with by substantial revisions of the original Framework. These would provide for:

- more value to schools from the inspection process as well as the report;
- clearer, unequivocal reports which would provide useful insights for the school – and, most importantly, a thorough analysis of the school's strengths and weaknesses, without the distraction of too much descriptive clutter;
- justification and exemplification of judgements;
- explicit key issues which would encourage good action planning for improvement.

If schools were to believe they were getting 'value for money' from inspections, then the process itself had 'to be more open and developmental'. Schools wanted inspection to be useful to them; inspectors to be clear about their strengths and weaknesses; to engage in a professional discussion about what they see and to report about the schools as a unique institution. That is, schools needed to feel part of a process 'which offered opportunity for professional dialogue with inspectors; that their priorities, challenges and opportunities were understood; and that their own processes for self-review and development were recognized'. Inspectors were to be required, where possible, to discuss with staff: 'The context of work observed, its purpose and the reasons why work is undertaken in a particular way ... to test hypotheses with staff before judgements are finalized'. They were to take account of the context in which the school worked, its priorities for development, the school's views on its pupils' attainment and its provision.

Ofsted believes that the modifications are providing for a more effective and acceptable inspection system, beneficial to schools for these reasons particularly:

- Because there is no mystery about what inspectors are looking for, schools can take stock for themselves before inspections begin. Staff can use the explicit criteria to analyse how well the school is doing and what needs to be done next in terms of development and improvement. Such valuable review and work can be done whether there is an inspection or not.
- Schools can impress upon inspectors, during the inspection, important facts and information that they need to know and take account of. Such information will enable inspectors to evaluate more effectively and explain their judgements.
- The report provides the school with an agenda for improvement and development and gives the parents a clear indication of the strengths

and weaknesses of the school and how it plans to improve.

Many schools, while prepared to acknowledge that the new framework is likely to lead to a more developmental, as distinct from an exclusively inquisitorial process, are still acutely conscious of the impact and possible consequences of so public an examination. But whatever their apprehensions, schools still have to go through the process. They have to make the best of it, rather than allow themselves to be overwhelmed. They need to get all the benefits possible from inspection, to use it as a source of accreditation for their work and as a platform for future development and success.

This book is intended to help schools do just that – to survive inspection successfully. That most emphatically does not mean 'scraping through' or 'getting away' with it, like a learner driver still ill at ease with the car, who manages to acquire, remember and adequately exercise sufficient of the necessary skills on the day to persuade a still dubious examiner, but remains thereafter no more than a cut above the mediocre. It does mean doing as well as possible those things that make a school effective:

- knowing and being committed to the educational entitlement of pupils and planning carefully and in detail to provide for it;
- having and striving after a vision of what is possible and desirable for them, beyond the National Curriculum and their statutory due;
- having detailed strategies, contributed to and shared by all staff, that will translate aims and objectives into practice, setting out such strategies in policies and guidelines accessible to and usable by all who need them;
- developing a shared and comprehensive understanding by all staff of the characteristics of effective teaching and how it will provide for pupils' learning and achievement;
- providing consistent training to develop teachers' practical classroom competence and skills;
- devising and implementing measures that will effectively monitor and evaluate the quality and success of teaching and learning throughout the school;
- ensuring that pupils achieve as well as they can and maintain consistent and satisfactory progress;
- making an environment that will stimulate, enlighten, comfort and inspire;

- striving for a moral, humane and civilizing ethos.

All of which may seem a tall order merely to survive inspection! In fact most schools strive after such ideals, and making the most of inspection is about describing and demonstrating to the best advantage how they go about doing that.

In practical terms, this will call for:

1 *A recognition of the potentially valuable elements of inspection and an understanding of how they can be used to benefit the school.* These include the following:

- A powerful impetus to corporate working and shared commitment on the part of staff. Few things can draw teachers together more effectively than the requirement to show the school at its best *in everyone's interest.* Few things remind staff more forcefully that the days are over when the teachers could feel free to follow their own line or inclination whatever the policies of the school. Inspection is greatly concerned with accountability and the ways in which it manifests itself. Staff cannot stand outside or above that. Few things are more critical to the success of inspection than unreserved commitment on the part of teachers to the implementation of agreed policies and strategies.
- A reason, clear and acceptable to all, for auditing and stock-taking, for identifying what is successful in the school's practice and the outcomes that substantiate it, for setting down realistic future planning.
- The significant body of analysis, commentary and consultation provided by inspection and the secure platform offered for future development.
- Objective, authoritative affirmation of the school's success and worths.

2 *A thorough understanding of the inspection process.* A remarkable number of schools face inspection either unaware of or misconceiving the form it will take, the manner in which it will be conducted and the ways in which inspections will operate; even, in some cases, the exact purpose of it all. The Ofsted handbooks are central to such an understanding and schools need to take the most painstaking account of

what they say and the guidance they provide. The handbooks, though succinct, are exhaustive. It is essential for schools to construct a broad map of the main contents, and acquire familiarity with them that enables staff to concentrate attention on the areas and aspects most relevant to their particular responsibilities and concerns.

The inspection schedule, Part III of the handbook (the key to producing a report which evaluates the school accurately and informatively), is the heart of the Framework.

The sections of the schedule that deal with teaching, assessment and pupils' welfare will be what matters most to classroom teachers; they may be less urgently engaged by issues of leadership or management, and may take little account, for example, of the sections that provide guidance for inspectors on the organizational minutiae of the process.

For head teachers and senior staff a thorough knowledge of the handbook in general is essential. The main body of advice and suggestion contained in this book is largely determined by the requirements implicit in the handbooks and the guidance they provide about the inspection process. Separate chapters will be devoted to the main areas. Advice will be as practical as possible. Examples of school materials and documentation will be provided.

2

Mapping and responding to the inspection Framework

Schools will find it helpful to construct a broad map of the framework. The main areas are as follows:

Part I of the Ofsted Framework: Inspection requirements

● **The purpose of inspection:**
To identify strengths and weaknesses so that schools may improve the quality of education they provide and revise the educational standards achieved by their pupils.
Schools need to keep this constantly in the forefront of their thinking. This is what inspection is about from first to last and everything else is contributory to it. Whatever else inspection does, it will set out to identify the strengths and weaknesses of a school, to state them clearly and to identify key issues for action.

● **The statutory basis for inspection**
Inspection is required by the Act to report on:

– The quality of the education provided by the school;
– The educational standard achieved by the school;
– Whether financial resources are managed efficiently, and
– The spiritual, moral, social and cultural development of the pupils

● **The inspection outcomes**

Inspection must lead to a full report which:
– identifies the strengths and weaknesses of the school, and
– gives the governing body a clear agenda for the action required to improve it.

The Report will be set out in the following way and will mirror the structure of the inspection schedule:

The Report

1. Main findings
2. Key issues for action
3. Introduction
   3.1 Characteristics of the school
   3.2 Key indicators

Part A: Aspects of the school

4. Educational standards achieved by pupils at the school
   4.1 Attainment and progress
   4.2 Attitudes, behaviour and personal development
   4.3 Attendance

5. Quality of education provided
   5.1 Teaching
   5.2 The curriculum and assessment
   5.3 Pupils' spiritual, moral, social and cultural development
   5.4 Support, guidance and pupils' welfare
   5.5 Partnership with parents and the community

6. The management and efficiency of the school
   6.1 Leadership and management
   6.2 Staffing, accommodation and learning resources

6.3 The efficiency of the school

Part B: Curriculum areas and subjects
7. Areas of learning for children under five
8. English, mathematics and science
9. Other subjects or courses

Part C: Inspection data
10. Summary of inspection evidence
11. Data and indicators

The inspection report is at the heart of teachers' anxiety. It is easy to see why. The end of inspection is understandably greeted with relief, a sense that life is returning to normal (save for those schools who have already decided that inspectors 'must take them as they find them' – an engaging but probably ill-advised approach). But in a very important sense, all the strain of waiting, the hard work of preparation, the draining tension and demands of the inspection week itself are but a prelude to the business still to come: the Main Findings of the report, the Key Issues for Action and the way in which the school, over time, must respond to one, and implement the other. The report is both a judgement of teachers' professional worth and standing and a map for their future work.

Although they will have been well prepared in advance, by the oral feedback, about the nature of the report, its ostensibly clinical and detached treatment of the major issues often comes as a disappointment, even something of a shock to many schools. They tend to be aggrieved not only by the brief, rather terse way in which the main findings and aspects such as pupils' attainment are dealt with, but by the relatively unadorned treatment accorded to matters long laboured over and dear to the school. However, what is perhaps most disconcerting of all, no matter how well schools have done, is the factual, explicit enumeration and portrayal of their weaknesses. Indeed, some schools are so preoccupied with these, especially initially, that they have to be helped to put them in perspective and take proper account of the positive outcomes.

For many, of course, the report is a matter for celebration, enhancing the school's vision of itself and confirming it in the esteem of parents and community. For many more it is likely to be a cause of genuine satisfaction, a platform on which they can base future development. A significant proportion is likely to be disappointed, at least in certain important respects, by the findings; because they appear less than the staff deserve, have failed to catch the essence of the school, seem insubstantial, and something of an anti-climax after so much worry and effort. The good things may seem to be submerged in the adverse comments. As one head teacher put it: 'All the good bits are one liners; all the criticisms are paragraphs – and that is how parents and the public at large will read it and see it'.

But what really makes an inspection report so disconcerting and potentially chastening for teachers is the sheer volume of finely graded judgements that it sets forth. There will be dozens, perhaps even hundreds of these; no area evaluated will pass without an explicit judgement. Elements, aspects, issues will not be described; they will be judged. There has been a tendency with inspection, in the past, especially those conducted by LEAs on their own schools, to describe initiatives and developments from a kind of 'This is one to watch with interest' perspective. So, for example, a school setting out to develop links with the community might have expected to see the initiative both described at some length in the report and praised for its potential value. The Ofsted inspection model does not operate in this way. Initiatives will be referred to rather than described and a judgement will be made on a particular initiative in terms of its contribution to the pupils' learning, attainment and progress.

Schools, therefore, need to bear constantly in mind that inspectors, whichever aspects they evaluate, will make their judgements of them according to the impact they have on educational standards and the general quality of education provided. Particular attention needs to be paid consequently to the criteria against which judgements are made. These are listed in the Schedule (Part III of the framework) for each of the areas for inspection – the curriculum and assessment, leadership and management, pupils' spiritual, moral, social and cultural development and so on – under the heading, 'Judgements should be based on the extent to which...'. Much of the advice offered in the chapters that follow this will refer in detail to these criteria. So, for example, in the chapters on teaching there will be a focus on how teachers can:

● employ methods and organizational strategies which match curricular

objectives and the needs of all pupils;
● use time and resources effectively;
● assess pupils' work thoroughly and constructively and use assessments to inform teaching and so on.

The inspection report has to be in the hands of the governing body within five weeks of the inspection. A summary of the report, incorporating the main findings and key issues for action sections, has to be sent to all parents of children at the school.

Part I of the Framework sets out the procedures that inspectors will follow before, during and after the inspection. It is obviously important that schools are thoroughly informed about these procedures and their implications. They will be dealt with in Chapter 3.

Part I of the Framework concludes with an annex on schools requiring special measures. These are schools judged 'to be failing or likely to fail to give pupils an acceptable standard of education'. Such a report by an Ofsted inspection team would have to be corroborated by HMI. Where such corroboration occurred, the key points for action would be treated as special measures to be implemented by the school over a period of time and supervised by HMI.

Judgements about failing schools are based on the extent to which some or all of a range of particular characteristics are identified as existing there. These characteristics are set out in the Annex to Part I of the Framework. They include, for example:

● 'low attainment and poor progress in the subjects of the curriculum by the majority of the pupils or consistently among particular groups of pupils. This will be evident in poor examination, National Curriculum assessment and other accredited results;
● regular disruptive behaviour, breakdown of discipline or high levels of exclusions;
● a high proportion of unsatisfactory teaching.'

The likelihood of being judged a failing school is something that haunts a remarkable number of schools, most of them wholly secure from the possibility of such an outcome. Such anxiety may be an indication either of how obscure the inspection process remains for many schools, or the limitations of their own self-evaluation procedures.

Of course, there could not be a more dismal or serious outcome for a school. The general advice offered throughout this book should be relevant for schools at risk of failure. Clearly, however, the circumstances of schools in that predicament call for more immediate and urgent action.

A second category of schools requiring particular attention has now been established. These are schools designated as causing concerns because of conspicuous weaknesses in the areas of:

- educational standards achieved;
- quality of education provided, and
- the management and efficiency of the school.

The inspection teams are not directly responsible for making the designation, though they may be well aware, putting the report together, that such an outcome is likely, once their findings are scrutinized by Ofsted. Where the inspection team considers such an outcome likely they will advise the school at the end of the inspection or at the presentation of the oral report; in rare cases, however, a team may not have considered the possibility and the decision does not finally emerge until Ofsted has surveyed the final report.

At this stage I would merely make the following point, especially about schools likely to fail, but also about those in the less dangerous but very unwelcome position of being judged to have serious weaknesses. For schools in such a situation – for example because of regular disruptive behaviour or a breakdown in discipline – then the circumstances are likely to be so blatantly intolerable for everyone that matters have to be resolved without delay, especially in the interests of pupils. The trouble is that in such cases things tend to go from bad to worse in the absence of direct action. Grave shortcomings, whether they be poor discipline, low standards of attainment, high level of truancy, ineffective leadership and poor management, or crumbling staff morale, will not heal of their own accord; they become endemic.

At the heart of the problem for many schools in this situation is a failure on their part not so much to recognize the real difficulties – after all, consistently poor examination results, widespread oppressive behaviour by pupils or ineffectual leadership tend to be inescapable – but to acknowledge them and accept responsibility for them. Indeed, a characteristic of such schools is a tendency to attribute blame elsewhere: to difficult pupils, unsupportive parents, disadvantaged catchment areas, poor central resourcing and so on. The alternative is likely to be too unpalatable to swallow: an acceptance that responsibility for failure lies within the school, or areas of it. Whatever the actual problems – poor planning, a lack of clarity about the curriculum, ineffectual pedagogy, poor departmental organization and control – it is highly likely that in the long run much of the blame can be traced to a lack of resolute and competent leadership, whether now or in the immediate past. A natural consequence of this is a fatal reluctance or inability to face the truth, admit where the weaknesses are and vigorously tackle them. Which is why, in turn, in the case of the majority of failing schools, radical action has to be taken about the leadership and senior management. (The question is sometimes asked, after inspection has revealed the true state of affairs, as to why no one – governing bodies or external agents such as LEAs – has taken action earlier. The superficial answer is that account has not been taken of the various objective indicators now increasingly available. But the real answer is likely to be more complex than that and need not delay us here.)

A commonly held view is that only the immediate replacement by strong, decisive guidance of the poor leadership almost inevitably hiding at the heart of failure is likely to rectify matters, and manage the special measures demanded by Ofsted. I accept that this is likely to be so once the inspection process is complete, since any remaining credibility is likely to have been irretrievably blown away by the findings. But I still believe that few if any schools – and especially primary, for particular reasons – need to have found themselves in such a situation in the first place had they consistently taken some, or ideally all, of the following measures:

- first and foremost to develop an ethos of evaluation, that is, a willingness to be critical and objective about the school's achievements, to decide upon and apply processes for providing reliable information about attainment and progress and for signalling causes for concern. Many of the measures used by Ofsted will serve very adequately for a school's self-evaluation purposes. The value-for-money measures used in inspection could also be referred to periodically. Evaluation measures will often be most useful to a school when applied by an external agent – a head teacher/staff from another school, an LEA/inspector/adviser, especially one with Ofsted training, an educational academic, a reputable consultant – someone who will be able to offer judgement in the knowledge that its essential value lies in absolute detachment. Schools, for their part, must be prepared to accept and act upon such expert external evaluation.

The willingness to face up to such judgements, searching and uncomfortable though they may be, is the first vital safeguard against declining below what is acceptable in terms of professional standards. The very act of taking such action, of initiating external review, is a sign, in itself, of one of the important qualities of leadership, whatever else may be in question.

Equally necessary, however, is a readiness on the part of schools to ensure that other measures are being consistently maintained:

- rigorous and constructive appraisal, with a major focus on teaching practice and classroom management;
- monitoring of staff performance by heads of department and, where feasible in primary schools by senior staff, together with training and support for professional development;
- mentoring provision for newly qualified teachers, for staff new to the school, and for staff assuming fresh or extra responsibilities;
- a consultancy/mentoring service available to the head teacher;
- corporate planning by staff of teaching and learning content, related to subject schemes of work;
- consistent moderation of pupils' levels of achievement and progress, related to national norms on a year group, phase and whole school basis, together with the maintenance of work profile books (see page 233).

Part II of the Framework: Guidance on inspection requirements

This part of the handbook provides guidance for the registered inspector (RI) on the management and conduct of inspections in line with the inspection requirements set out in the Framework. It is structured to reflect the sequence of work by the inspection team before, during and after the inspection. Though this section is of particular concern to inspectors, it is important for schools to take account of it and especially the information about particular aspects, including the following:

- **The code of conduct for inspectors.** The principles that must govern the conduct of inspectors should do much to reassure schools that judgements will be absolutely based on 'sound evidence, carefully weighed, collected from a range of sources and firmly based on the criteria in the inspection schedule'. Judgements must not be premature, idiosyncratic or have any element of bias or pre-conception.
- **The evidence base.** This is a matter of great importance to schools. The handbook states that systematic collection and evaluation of evidence is at the heart of inspection. Inspectors will assemble a record of evidence before and during the inspection. It will comprise:
  - **Data from Ofsted.** This will include a pre-inspection context and school indicator (PICSI) report containing: key performance data about the school from earlier years to enable trends to be identified; information about the social and economic characteristics of the area in which the school is situated and comparative data to help inspectors set the school data in a national context.
  - **The head teacher's form and statement.** This is a minimum core of quantitative data about the school, provided in standard format, together with the head teacher's commentary on the school, which should include a brief description of the characteristics of the school, its pupils, and those features of the area it serves which influence its work. This is a valuable opportunity for the head teacher to make a significant and positive contribution to the record of evidence, to clarify:
    - (i) the school's defining circumstances, the background and experience of the intake, the nature of the community and to give a uniquely informed and honest appraisal of the extent of the educational challenge faced by the school, without recourse to self-justification or recrimination;
    - (ii) what are perceived by the school to be important and positive recent developments and, most especially, plans for the future; where the school intends to place particular emphases

and the reasons for these.

- There will be in addition, of course, opportunity for schools to ensure that inspectors are fully informed about aspects of school life that might, through mischance, pass without due recognition: staff development and training provision, extra-curricular activities, links with parents and the community, recent projects and initiatives, now concluded but influential in relation to teaching and learning.

- **The observation form** (see p. 75). This will be used to record evidence and judgements from observations of lessons and other inspection activities, including examination of pupils' work, analyses of assessment and inspection data and discussion with pupils.

- **The subject profile.** This is a summary which draws together the evidence for each of the core subjects and a set of grades which reflects judgements in these subjects.

- **The school profile.** This is a summary which draws together the evidence compiled by the team of inspectors during inspection and a set of grades to reflect the corporate judgements of the inspection team.

Schools will find it helpful to be familiar with the nature of these documents and to use them and especially the observation form in their preparation for inspection. For example, heads of department and curriculum co-ordinators in any evaluation of colleagues' work could use the observation form as a basis for discussion and feedback, while the profiles can act as a reminder of the criteria against which inspectors make their judgements, and provide a practical format for review of school and subject performance.

The initial contact with the school

In the initial contact, the RI will agree inspection dates, arrange the initial visit to the school, discuss its purpose and negotiate a programme, offer opportunity for an explanatory meeting with staff and for a meeting with representatives of the governing body, discuss the documentation that the school will have to provide and make arrangements for its collection.

The initial visit by the RI

The RI is required to deal with the following matters during the initial visit:

- Outline the practical form the inspection will take, for example how inspectors will carry out observations. This particular matter – whether inspectors will talk to teachers and pupils during the course of a lesson, look at samples of work, expect to have records made available, move about the room, the duration of their stay, whether feedback will be provided at the end of lessons, how often teachers may expect to be observed during the course of a day and for the entire inspection period – is obviously very important to individual class teachers especially.
- Make provision for seeing samples of pupils' work, records, reports and, where appropriate, individual education plans.
- Discuss the PICSI report, offer any necessary advice about the completion of the head teacher's form and statement.
- Explain that analysis of the school's documentation is used to give inspection team members a background to the inspection and to identify particular issues on which the inspection might focus – the nature and quality of curriculum planning, for example.
- Make clear that schools and governing bodies can identify particular aspects they would like the team to focus on, provided it is done within the framework and the inspection contract. Clearly the school will need to respond carefully and thoughtfully to this valuable opportunity to identify perceived strengths, worthwhile developments, aspects identified by them for particular action, future plans and so on.
- Arrange to see samples of teachers' planning, assessment evidence, guidelines and schemes of work, attendance registers and any other evidence the school feels might be of value to the inspection.
- Gather any evidence through discussion with head staff and governors that might contribute to the school profile.
- Arrange for the provision of class and whole school timetables. It is important for schools to remember that such an arrangement provides a guarantee that only subjects timetabled will be inspected; in other words, that teachers cannot be taken unawares; all lessons can be planned in detail as exemplars of good teaching and learning practice.

- Clarify the time and nature of discussions with individual members of staff, especially those with key responsibilities, the issues that will be discussed, the kind of information required, the duration of interviews and so on.
- The samples of pupils' work required and the arrangements for receiving and reviewing them.
- Any arrangements for visits to pupils in pupil referral units (PRUs), by a member of the inspection team, where appropriate, or for visits to partner secondary schools where feasible, and requested by the school, to consider liaison arrangements and provision for curriculum continuity.
- Arrangements for the parents' meeting and for dealing with the parents' questionnaire.
- Arrangements for the delivery to the school of the oral report of the inspection findings. This report is provided to the head teacher, and members of staff he/she may wish to be present, and subsequently, almost invariably on the same day, to the governing body. The oral presentation usually takes place about a week after the end of the inspection. It is important for schools to remember that at this particular stage the inspection report has not been written in its final form, but that the findings conveyed to the school and governors are, in effect, the final outcomes, and will not be different in any significant respect from the published report.

Almost without exception, inspection teams will have begun to feed back, where appropriate during the inspection, clear intimations of their findings to heads of departments, subject, year and phase co-ordinators and to all staff holding posts of responsibility. It is also usual for the RI to convey to the head teacher at the end of the inspection a strong sense of the inspection findings (so that, in a sense, the oral report, though greatly amplified, should contain no surprises).

Again, almost without exception, RIs and heads arrange to meet briefly, usually before the beginning of each school day, to liaise about the progress of the inspection, to resolve differences or mis-understandings, to ensure that the school is having the fullest possible opportunity to present all the evidence and information that it wishes to.

The RI will take the opportunity on the occasion of the initial visit to be shown round the school, to meet teachers and pupils, to become familiar with the site and to gain first impressions of the school that will contribute to the construction of a background for the team.

Schools will hardly need to have the importance of this initial visit highlighted for them. Apart from ensuring that the practical management of the inspection is carried through smoothly and therefore as constructively as possible for the eventual outcome, the occasion, though officially 'preparatory' and therefore not a legitimate opportunity for 'inspection', marks the first vital step in the relationship between inspection team and the school. It may well contribute significantly to the formulation of impressions about the environment, ethos, relationships and efficiency of the school. Teachers would be well advised to think of the occasion as part of the inspection process.

During the inspection

During the week inspectors will collect the evidence on which the judgements that constitute the report will be made. They will do this through:

- the inspection of teaching, and pupils at work, in classrooms and other areas;
- discussions with pupils, for example to assess their understanding and knowledge of different subjects and their attitudes to work and their life at school;
- hearing pupils read;
- the scrutiny of a representative sample of pupils' work;
- discussions with staff, especially those with management responsibilities;
- the scrutiny of teachers' plans, records of National Curriculum tests and teachers' assessments, details of any assessment undertaken on entry to nursery or reception classes, or to a PRU, and other measures or indicators of attainment and progress used by the school or PRU;
- the scrutiny of statements of special educational needs, annual reviews and individual education plans;
- with the agreement of the appropriate authority and wherever possible, visiting a small sample of schools where dual registration or re-integration of pupils attending a PRU is taking place.

Part II of the Framework concludes with an account of post-inspection activity. This includes information about:

- the oral report to the head, relevant staff and the governing body;
- provision for feedback during the inspection to the head, individual staff, class teachers, senior staff and staff with particular areas of responsibility;
- the purpose and nature of the report. In this respect it is important for schools to take particular account of what the handbook says about this matter:
  - The 'Main findings of inspection' and the 'Key issues for action' are particularly important sections of the report. These sections, which constitute the summary of the full report, draw out the key judgements about the school and leave the school without any doubt about the issues which need to be tackled in order to raise the educational standards achieved and why the inspection team has identified them.

The report must concentrate on evaluating rather than describing what is seen and focus on the educational standards achieved and the factors which impact on standards and quality.

Part III of the Framework

The inspection schedule and guidance on its use

This is the central part of the handbook, the most important for the inspection process and the most influential in terms of the eventual outcomes. More than any other this must be at the heart of a school's preparation. It is very important for schools to understand the structure of the schedule and to understand that the format of the inspection report will mirror it exactly. Now let us look at the main components of the schedule.

1. The **context** consists of:
   - characteristics of the school, that is, a concise factual statement about the characteristics of the school and its pupils and the area it serves (the school is invited to contribute to this);
   - a brief statement of the main aims and priorities of the school, including any targets set by the school;

- key indicators which summarize the attainment of pupils at the end of each key stage, together with comparative performance data where these are available.
2. The two main parts of the schedule are the **outcomes** and **contributory factors** (see Table 2.1).

Context

3.1 Characteristics of the school

Outcomes

	4.2	4.1	4.3
Educational standards achieved	Attitudes, behaviour and personal development	Attainment and progress	Attendance

Contributory factors

	5.2	5.3	5.1	5.4	5.5
Provision	The curriculum and assessment	Pupils' spiritual, moral, social and cultural development	Teaching	Support, guidance and pupils' welfare	Partnership with parents and the community

	6.2		6.1	6.3
Management	Staffing, accommodation and learning resources		Leadership and management	The efficiency of the school

Table 2.1

The outcomes are about the educational standards achieved by pupils as exemplified in:

- attitudes, behaviour and personal development;
- attainment and progress are of main importance in this group;
- attendance.

The contributory factors are those elements which contribute to the outcomes. They are divided into two groups, the first of which is *provision:*

- the curriculum and assessment;
- pupils' spiritual, moral, social and cultural development;

- teaching is of main importance in this group;
- support, guidance and pupils' welfare;
- partnership with parents and the community.

The second group of contributory factors come under the umbrella of *management* and include:

- staffing, accommodation and learning resources;
- leadership and management are of main importance in this group;
- the efficiency of the school.

The Ofsted Framework deals with the **outcomes** and **contributory factors** of the schedule under Part A: Aspects of the school. Part B comprises curriculum areas and subjects. Part C is about inspection data. In this chapter we shall focus on Parts A and B. The subjects will, however, inevitably be referred to in various ways throughout the book.

The **contributory factors** will be dealt with in separate chapters throughout the book. The first priority of inspection is to ascertain the educational standards achieved by pupils, to assess what pupils know, understand and can do, and the progress they are making. Everything that follows is tied to that: teaching, the curriculum and assessment, the quality of spiritual, moral and social education, the leadership and management of the school, the way in which the school manages the curriculum areas and subjects.

It is very important for schools to have a clear view of the vital distinction drawn in the schedule between the **outcomes** and the **contributory factors** to them. The **contributory factors** will be judged on the *impact* they have on **outcomes**.

Teachers, however, are likely to view these two elements from a very particular perspective. For them the **contributory factors** – teaching, the curriculum and assessment, leadership and management and so on – are likely to be of prime, immediate and lasting concern since they are essentially about *professional performance*. Succeeding chapters therefore will be concerned with these, since they are the means by which effective **outcomes** can be powerfully influenced.

Part A: Aspects of the school

Educational standards achieved by pupils

Let us begin, however, by looking at **outcomes**: the educational standards achieved by pupils at the school, in terms of: attainment and progress; attitudes, behaviour and personal development; and attendance (subsequent numbering relates to inspection schedule numbering).

4.1 Attainment and progress

This, as we have said, is the main focus of inspection. As the inspection Framework states: the main priorities of inspection are to assess what pupils know, understand and can do – that is to say, their attainment – and to evaluate their progress. Judgements will be based on the extent to which:

- the attainment of pupils at the end of nursery education or by five in reception classes meets or exceeds expectations for their age;
- the attainment of pupils at 7, 11, 14 and 16 years meets or exceeds national standards, particularly in English, maths and science;
- students by 19 years achieve or exceed two GCE A level passes or equivalent (e.g. advanced GNVQ) and leave school with qualifications relevant to the next stage of education or training or employment;
- pupils with special educational needs progress as well as or better than expected;
- the attainment and progress of minority groups of pupils is comparable with others in the school;
- the school sustains high levels of attainment or is improving.

This concentration on pupils' attainment against national expectations, on the assessment of standards of attainment in comparative terms, on the precise evaluation of pupils' progress against previous attainment, is possibly one of the most disconcerting features of inspection for schools, especially primary schools. However, had the inspection cycle never been initiated, schools would have found in the SATs an instrument of accountability more potent than anything – including public examination at secondary level – they had previously encountered. This is so simply because the SATs now provide a chain of standardized information – and, indeed, a capability to predict future attainment – running across the entire statutory period of education, and soon to include the pre-school stage as well. It will be possible to track pupils' standardized attainment in the core subjects and in literacy and numeracy across four key stages.

It has always been accepted by teachers that the education pupils receive from their first days in school has repercussions for their academic success as adolescents; hence the marked emphasis over the past three decades, with the advent of universal INSET, on the desirability of continuity between the primary and secondary phases and the realization that effective transition from one to the other is essential to pupils' continuing cognitive development and attainment. But the implementation of continuity has never quite matched the wish for it. SATs in their turn will make imperatives of intentions. Individual class teachers – especially in primary schools – have always been accountable, in important respects, to their colleagues, for the attainment of the pupils they transfer; whether it has been a reception class to middle infants, or a fourth year junior class to the first year of the secondary school. Generally such transition was accompanied by some evidence of attainment; reading and mathematics test results, either standardized or set by teachers themselves; evidence of achievement in spelling, tables and handwriting. Increasingly through the 1970s and 1980s most secondary schools looked for some evidence of experience and understanding in science and, in rare instances, of an initial acquaintance with a modern European language. The transfer of such information was often attended by disagreement and some resentment between sectors about the amount of information that should be passed on and how it should be treated.

There was an attitude prevalent among many teachers, often inspired by the best motives, that children should be allowed a fresh start, from class to class and phase to phase; that what they had done or achieved before should not be allowed to influence their new teachers' thinking and response. Indeed, there are still secondary schools which insist they will start all new pupils off at Level 3 in each of the core subjects, give them 'a level playing field' and allow them 'to find their own place'. But this, of course, simply will not do any more.

Pupils, whether it be convenient for schools or not, now come and, so far as we can tell, will continue to do so, with their own accredited records of attainment, like soldiers with field marshals' batons in their knapsacks, the significance of such levels increasingly clear to them and their parents. The pupil who leaves year 7 having attained a Level 3 in mathematics has recorded a statement about his capabilities that will have implications for those who teach him in year 9. The pupil who comes into year 7 at the exit point of Level 4 in English is staking an undeniable claim to a good GCSE outcome a few years later. In plain terms, the advent of the SATs means that the teacher in year 8, teaching a mixed ability class in science, needs to be clearly aware of the level descriptions that apply to individual pupils and be demonstrably catering for them in terms of learning provision, the ways in which pupils are grouped, the matching of task to pupil attainment, the provision for differentiation; she will need to look for outcomes that reflect ranges of ability. Similarly, a year 4 teacher needs to be able to demonstrate that pupils who achieved Level 3 in core subjects at the end of Key Stage 1 are being adequately challenged in cognitive terms, while the needs of pupils in the same class who represent attainment across the levels prior to that are also being satisfactorily provided for. In relation to pupils' attainment, therefore, schools need to be concerned about the following matters:

- where pupils are in terms of current attainment, especially in the core subjects, and within the common framework established by National Curriculum level descriptions;
- whether it is possible for teachers to look back across a continuum of recorded attainment and determine the extent to which progress is being satisfactorily maintained;
- the establishment of baseline measures of attainment at entry to statutory education and at the ends of key stages. The SATs' outcomes represent a major contribution to this development. Schools and LEAs have devised various measures in relation to baseline assessment at entry to mainstream education;
- the construction of learning tasks that are as precisely matched as possible to pupils' levels of attainment in the core subjects especially;
- organization within mixed classes to provide for widely varying levels of attainment;
- the value of particular systems of organization, e.g. setting to provide for varying levels of attainment;
- the use of current levels of attainment as predictions of future academic attainment;

● the familiarization of early years teachers and support staff with national expectations – desirable outcomes – of the attainment of pupils at the end of nursery education, or by five in reception classes.

While inspectors may regard the outcomes of SATs as the most concrete evidence available to them of pupils' attainment before national secondary examinations, and an indicator of what pupils should or could be achieving across the phases, they will pay no less attention to the extent to which high, average and low attaining pupils, including those with special educational needs, progress as well as or better than expected. Those judgements will influence to a crucial extent the overall judgement of the school. In making judgements inspectors will look at evidence extending over periods of time, derived from standardized test outcomes, teachers' records, profiles of work, and from the progress pupils are making in individual lessons and sequences of lessons. This is one of the elements of inspection about which teachers tend to be most sceptical. They are not always willing to accept that the progress pupils make over briefly observed periods such as single lessons can be reliably measured – an understandable reaction when one remembers that inspectors will often be observing classes of over 30 pupils for lessons lasting little more than half an hour. In fact where individual lessons are concerned inspectors will be looking for evidence of what pupils have learned; this in turn will involve them in relatively simple questions, for example:

● Did all the pupils, or most of them, learn what the teacher set out to teach them, bearing in mind that there are likely to have been different targets for particular groups?
● Was the learning/progress that pupils achieved sufficient in the light of the evidence available about their current levels of attainment? Clearly some broad judgements may be involved here!
● Were there individuals, groups or particular minorities for whom progress was manifestly inadequate?

Inspectors will pay particular attention to the attainment and progress of minority groups of pupils and how these compare with other groups within the school. These may include pupils with special educational needs, very able pupils, those with marked learning or physical disabilities, pupils at different age levels within classes, pupils under five in mainstream classes, pupils from different ethnic backgrounds and cultures, and those for whom English is an additional language.

In assessing attainment and evaluating progress, inspectors will pay close attention in both primary and secondary phases to reading, writing, speaking and mathematics to establish how well developed these are and the extent to which they contribute to pupils' learning across the whole curriculum.

How may schools respond to inspectors' concern about pupils' progress? As we have suggested elsewhere, they need to treat the matter as a very high priority and employ certain strategies themselves for evaluating pupils' progress. These would include:

- analyses of SATs and public examination results and of any standardized testing regularly applied within the school to establish pupils' current levels of attainment and to identify individual strengths and weaknesses for development and correction;
- the use of all forms of standardized testing to establish a continuum of information about pupils' progress;
- the use of information gained from standardized testing to make predictions of pupils' future attainment;
- consistent formative assessment in relation to specific elements of the core curriculum identified as part of school assessment policy;
- the use of pupils' profile books to maintain a consistent record of pupils' attainment and progress, about which pupils and parents will have opportunity to comment at frequent and regular intervals;
- marking of work that enables pupils to recognize where they are making progress and to focus on areas for development, accompanied by support from teachers in relation to these aspects;
- systematic consultation between teachers and individual pupils about pupils' progress, about areas for improvement and development and strategies for dealing with them;
- detailed school policies for the development and support of pupils' competence in literacy;
- regular evaluation by sampling of pupils' progress in individual lessons or sequences of lessons;
- evaluation of progress and attainment in all topic, project and course work;
- regular evaluation of the progress made by pupils in minority groups;

- consideration of the value and feasibility of setting quantitative targets for improvement in the core and other subjects at school and key stage level and monitoring progress towards such targets (this is a process calling for care and detailed planning in the setting of targets that are appropriate and feasible).

4.2 Attitudes, behaviour and personal development

The focus of this section is concerned with how pupils respond to school in terms of their attitudes to learning, their behaviour and their values and personal development.

Inspectors will base their judgements on the extent to which pupils:

- show interest in their work and are able to sustain concentration and develop their capacity for personal study;
- behave well in and around the school, and are courteous and trustworthy and show respect for property;
- form constructive relationships with one another, with teachers and other adults, and work collaboratively when required;
- show respect for other people's feelings, values and beliefs;
- show initiative and are willing to take responsibility.

Inspectors must evaluate and report on pupils' response to the teaching and other provision made by the school, highlighting strengths and weaknesses as shown by:

- their attitude to learning;
- their behaviour, including evidence of racism;
- the quality of relationships in the school, including the degree of racial harmony, where applicable;
- other aspects of their personal development, including their contributions to the life of the community.

This particular educational outcome/standard – attitudes, behaviour and personal development – is obviously linked to the contributory element of pupils' spiritual, moral and social development. Both these areas will have one section – or 'paragraph' in Ofsted speak – allocated to them in the report, in common with other aspects inspected; but it is probably safe to say that the impression they make upon inspectors may well have implications beyond a single comment and affect their perceptions of other elements of the life of a school. So, for example, in circumstances where unruly or oppressive behaviour predominates, inspectors are likely to find themselves focusing with particular thoroughness upon the nature of equal opportunity, the quality of monitoring and the decisiveness of leadership.

In certain situations this aspect of a school may create for inspectors the greatest difficulty in making balanced and assured judgements. An inspector's business is to make judgements about the educational standards achieved by pupils and the impact upon these of the various elements that make up a school. To do this they rely upon a wide range of evidence, upon their own careful observations and upon the application of clearly defined and overt criteria. Inspection is not about speculation, conjecture or recourse to inspectors' personal beliefs or preconceptions. Inspectors are there to report what they see and what evidence tells them about the state of things as they are and the outcomes for pupils. They will report on pupils' attitudes, behaviour and personal development according to the same rules of judgement.

Nevertheless, they may be called upon to exercise particular caution and sensitivity in coming to conclusions about various contingent aspects of school life; for example the quality of discipline, or of teaching itself, in situations where pupils' behaviour and attitudes are a cause for concern. There are likely to be occasions – for instance where teachers are working with larger than usual proportions of difficult-to-manage pupils – where teachers may exercise degrees of restraint and tolerance, a readiness to avoid direct confrontation, to turn a 'blind eye' to certain behaviour, action that may seem to be ill advised or indecisive to an observer, however acute or experienced. Such strategies and responses on the part of teachers may be determined by complex circumstances at particular times, by awareness of pressures and strains on individual pupils' lives, not always immediately obvious to the uninformed outsider.

This is not any argument for permissive responses by inspectors, for inappropriate sympathies or imaginative flights of fancy on their part; but it is a reminder that, on occasions, the reaching of the end of a lesson without damaging confrontation, with the majority of pupils applying themselves for most of the time, may represent a positive achievement on the part of the teacher. Where and when teachers are obliged to adopt particular containing or conciliatory strategies in classrooms to maintain working contexts and an ambience of study and learning, to get the best from pupils, then schools must ensure that the nature of such approaches and the reason and justification for them are made clear to inspectors from the outset of inspection. That is not in any sense to advise special pleading, to expect the application of different criteria or variations upon them or to introduce the notion of extenuating circumstances. To do that would be to invalidate the inspection process. But it does imply that the school should make sure that inspectors are informed properly about circumstances likely to have large and challenging consequences for teaching and learning, that they themselves may not have experienced recently.

In making judgements about such situations, fortunately relatively rare, but increasing, we are driven back more than ever to the inspection criteria against which outcomes are assessed. Let us consider them here only briefly, because they are referred to elsewhere in contributory factor 5.3: Pupils' spiritual, moral and social development.

Do pupils show interest in their work? Are they able to sustain concentration and extend their capacity for personal study?
Whatever the circumstances of pupils' personal lives, however difficult and chaotic these may be, this criterion is concerned with the conditions that schools create to nurture engagement in learning. Positive responses from pupils, a readiness to apply themselves to tasks and to persevere through difficulties are dependent in the long run, and to a considerable extent, on the quality and relevance of what they encounter in classrooms, and the nature of their interaction in learning terms with teachers.

The following are always likely to be decisive factors in determining the quality and extent of pupils' learning and their readiness to commit themselves:

- carefully planned lessons, and, especially, effective and well-timed presentation by teachers;
- as good and precise a match as possible of task to pupil capacity and development;
- the quality of the learning tasks themselves. This is probably, ultimately, the most crucial element of all and one to which teachers need to devote particular planning care. Where there are genuine problem-solving elements, where pupils have opportunity for some success and progress is obvious, where the content relates, in some

degree at least, to existing awareness and previous experience, where resources and equipment are appropriate and accessible, where teacher and, ideally, other informed adult support is available, then it is likely that engagement and perseverance in learning tasks will be more readily secured. In such circumstances it will be easier, too, for teachers to entertain high expectations about pupils' response and behaviour. In relation to this criterion schools will find it helpful to review and pay attention to the following:

- routines for the beginning and ending of lessons, the briskness))) and punctuality with which they are commenced;
- a code of conduct about classroom behaviour, familiar to all pupils and systematically enforced; the provision for swift response to serious infringement of the code of behaviour, and support, where necessary, for teachers who have to provide that response;
- the corporate development of strategies in relation to effective teaching;
- the provision of appropriate and adequate resources;   TEAM MEETINGS
- the development of banks of 'model' or effective lessons;   ETC
- strategies for positive reinforcement of pupils' response and behaviour and acknowledgement of success on their part;
- the organization of group work that provides opportunity for pupils to exercise initiative, responsibilities and leadership.

How well do pupils behave in and around the school? Are they courteous and trustworthy? Do they show respect for property? Do pupils form constructive relationships with teachers and other adults, and do they work collaboratively when required?
Some head teachers have expressed the viewpoint that unless these aspects of school life are established on a sound footing, it is difficult for teaching and learning to be as effective as they could be. They cite, for example, the fact that unchecked misbehaviour in class by individuals or groups not only prevents the culprits from learning, but impedes and obstructs the learning of others. More seriously, such behaviour, unless swiftly and demonstrably dealt with, can be contagious, an incitement to other pupils to emulate what they witness.

Not all misbehaviour, and not by any means the most damaging, will be overt and easily detected. Much highly inappropriate behaviour, including bullying, harassment and racist conduct, potentially a cause of great unhappiness and fear for some pupils, occurs in subtle and insidious ways. Because of its nature it can endure for protracted periods and surprise teachers when eventually detected.

Schools may find it helpful to review and implement, where possible and necessary, the following measures in relation to the issues raised by this criterion:

- maintaining a constant emphasis upon the value and importance of the individual through:
  - the establishment of codes of behaviour, familiar to all, and designed to protect the rights of all pupils;
  - consistent acknowledgement and commendation of care and concern displayed by pupils for each other;
  - a focus in assemblies, school events and occasions, and in particular subjects – history, RE, literature and drama – upon the rights of individuals to fairness, justice and proper treatment in all aspects of their lives;
  - making clear that bullying and harassment are serious social disabilities that cannot be tolerated in the school community;
- the establishment of sanctions against oppressive behaviour, making their purpose clear to pupils and their implementation explicit, when and where bullying occurs;
- encouragement of pupils to confront bullying and racist behaviour immediately it occurs;
- helping pupils to understand that disclosing information about bullying and oppressive behaviour is a positive social action;
- ensuring that all school staff provide positive exemplars for pupils in their relationships with and treatment of each other and of the pupils themselves;
- encouraging parents to convey to staff their perceptions of general conduct and behaviour in the school, and to make practical contact where they have reason for anxiety;
- ensuring that the parents of pupils whose behaviour is giving cause for concern are involved from the outset in corrective action;
- giving pupils as much opportunity as possible to assume some responsibility, on occasions, for the care and support of younger pupils;
- giving pupils a sense of ownership of the school by making them responsible for care and maintenance of particular materials and artefacts;

- delegating responsibility to particular staff for the monitoring of pupil behaviour and conduct and for co-ordinating the implementation of school codes of behaviour and measures;
- reviewing existing measures for monitoring behaviour in classrooms; intervening and supporting where teachers may be experiencing difficulty;
- reviewing on a regular basis pupils' perceptions of behaviour in school, and the degree to which they feel comfortable and secure in the school environment.

Do pupils show respect for other people's feelings, values and beliefs?
The development of their capacity in this area will clearly be significantly dependent on the lead provided by schools and the exemplars offered to pupils. The promotion of interest in other cultures and other faiths, and acknowledgement and respect for their rituals and festivals, will all contribute to a climate of regard for differing beliefs. The curriculum itself will make a critically important contribution to the development of pupils' sensitivities in relation to the beliefs, attitudes and social and cultural traditions of others. Literature, poetry and drama can powerfully enlarge pupils' horizons and extend their understanding of other traditions, their values, qualities and splendour; history can help them understand and admire the human struggle for freedom of belief and tolerance of diversity, and enable them to recognize and reject forces and beliefs hostile to humane and civilized behaviour. But to be truly effective such teaching has to find practical expression in the positive ways that pupils are encouraged to live out their lives in school.

Do pupils show initiative? Are they willing to take responsibility?
From the very beginning of their education pupils need to have opportunity to exercise responsibility; there are few things to which they will respond more enthusiastically and positively. It is an aspect of behaviour, once established and accepted, that will powerfully cultivate pupils' positive self-concept and their perception of the contribution they can make to the affairs of others and the wider world.
   Schools need to consider how pupils are given a chance to be responsible and exercise initiative in:

- the management of their classroom, the carrying out of

administrative routines, the care and conservation of materials, the promotion of a class spirit and ethos;
- the care of the larger school community;
- the care and support of younger pupils and those who need particular help;
- the care for 'strangers within the gate', those who are new, visitors or people unfamiliar with the ways and routines of the school.

Schools need to review how the curriculum is being used to encourage pupils to express feelings and emotions, to appreciate the value of sensitivity and concern for others, of peaceful and harmonious behaviour, and to question and reject violent and destructive behaviour.

In the long run, of course, it is the extent to which schools are themselves wholly representative of civilized, outgoing and enlightened living that will significantly support pupils' acceptance of wholesome values and their growth to mature and positive adulthood and citizenship.

4.3 Attendance

The inspection focus will be on the level of pupils' attendance and its effect on attainment and progress.

Judgement will be based on the extent to which:

- pupils' attendance exceeds 90 per cent and they come to school and lessons on time;
- although the framework deals with attendance very briskly, it is one of the factors that could contribute to a school being considered as requiring special measures. In such cases there would be poor attendance by a substantial proportion of pupils or by particular groups of pupils, or high levels of truancy.

Patterns of attendance

Problems with attendance are something that schools are either likely to suffer from or have no difficulty about at all. There is seldom an in-between, though exceptions do arise in schools where attendance is otherwise satisfactory. These include:

- seasonal fluctuation in attendance in some areas;
- a tendency, reported by some schools, for parents to remove pupils

for additional short breaks and holidays, usually abroad;
- particular groups of pupils, or even whole classes, whose attendance is in marked variance from the rest of the school.

Poor attendance and, to a lesser extent, poor punctuality are very serious matters, of course.

- They disrupt pupils' education and progress, sometimes to a degree where the loss is irretrievable.
- They provide a bad example for other pupils and can create confusion and uncertainty in pupils' minds and a lack of confidence on their part about the school's priorities and intentions.
- Poor attendance and punctuality that go unchecked may similarly raise misgivings in parents' minds about the management and efficiency of the school and, most seriously, about the nature of its concerns for pupils' protection and welfare.
- Pupils who are consistently, or even irregularly, absent or who truant may well be placing themselves in serious physical or moral danger.

Schools need to take the following formal measures in relation to attendance:

- follow official guidance for recording and reporting attendance;
- systematically follow up any unauthorized absence, and require explanation from parents or carers;
- establish measures, where necessary, to improve attendance;
- provide support for pupils who have had a prolonged period of absence, both in moral and psychological terms, but also in helping them to make up ground lost in their academic studies as swiftly and effectively as possible.

It is vital that schools' systems actually monitor patterns of attendance and act immediately where poor attendance begins to show itself. This is an area where some schools, otherwise efficient and well managed, allow themselves to become casual, for whatever reason.

Where attendance becomes irregular in areas of schools or on the part of particular groups of pupils, then schools should strive to establish whether there are specific reasons for this. If it is conspicuously done then schools have to take radical action, involving parents, employing appropriately both support and sanctions, creating reward systems, and securing the support of the LEA. But in such cases schools also have to appraise the curriculum provided and the ways in which it is delivered; the relationships within the school, between pupils and pupils, and adults and pupils; the quality of the learning environment and the nature of the accommodation; provision for pupils' welfare; the ethos and atmosphere; the opportunities for pupils to achieve success; the provision made for advice, guidance and counselling for pupils; the quality of sporting, cultural and general extra-curricular provision and the school's relationships with parents.

That being said, it is important to stress that many good schools continue to fail with attendance despite heroic efforts on their part. In such cases they are often contending with circumstances beyond their control. Schools in such situations must inform inspectors very fully of the facts, the possible causes, the steps they take to monitor and follow up absenteeism, the measures they implement to improve matters and their further plans for future action.

Schools should ensure:

- that the requirements for recording and reporting attendance are met;
- that unauthorized absences are followed up;
- that systems are in place to monitor attendance and to identify causes of patterns of poor attendance;
- that measures to improve attendance are devised and implemented;
- that where necessary the help of the LEA is sought;
- that parents are involved in the school's attempts to improve attendance.

A checklist for action
Inspectors will take account of the following evidence:

Before the inspection
- the head teacher's form
- the PICSI report

During the inspection
- scrutiny of registers

- observation of lessons should record the total pupils present
- discussions with staff and the education welfare officer.

Part B: Curriculum subjects and areas

This part of the inspection handbook's outline of the schedule deals with the subjects of the curriculum.

- For children under five, inspectors will evaluate the main areas of learning: linguistic and literacy; mathematical; scientific and technological; creative and aesthetic; physical; human and social; moral and spiritual. The evaluation will focus on pupils' attainment and progress; teaching and other aspects of provision which make a significant contribution to what is achieved; and pupils' response.
- English, mathematics and science. For these subjects the report must include evaluation of:
  - pupils' attainment in relation to national expectations or standards, drawing on evidence of what pupils know, understand and can do by the end of the relevant stage;
  - progress made in relation to pupils' prior attainment;
  - pupils' attitudes to learning;
  - any strengths and weaknesses in teaching and other aspects which contribute to the standards achieved in the subject;
- Other subjects. The report must include evaluation of each of the aspects indicated above where there is sufficient evidence.

This section of the schedule is dealt with in a handful of pages. But their significance for the outcome of inspection could not be greater. It is here that a majority of judgements will be made. As we have said elsewhere, this emphasis on subjects can come as something of a shock to primary schools not generally accustomed to having curriculum content defined so uncompromisingly on a subject basis. A key phrase is 'what pupils know, understand and can do' – in other words, knowledge, an understanding of key ideas and concepts, and a command of vital skills by the end of the relevant key stage. This is about a prescribed and sequentially delineated curriculum – however much some may argue about the chances of exactly defining that – with clearly defined national norms and levels of attainment. Schools cannot opt for alternatives to these; teachers must be masters of the

National Curriculum orders and the means by which they can be most effectively taught to pupils.

Inspectors will make judgements about what pupils know, understand and can do in subjects, in every lesson. They will gauge pupils' attainment and progress, the response they make, the extent to which planning is in line with National Curriculum requirements and the degree of compliance with statutory requirements.

Throughout the chapters that follow we shall stress the need for schools to focus constantly on pupil attainment, on how well they are doing, on what they know, understand and can do by the end of the relevant stage. This, of course, calls for a systematic process of monitoring and evaluation, of regular formative assessment. Where once inspectors and advisers may have made judgements about educational provision on the basis of the quality of a school environment, they will do so largely now by inspecting pupils' attainment and progress, and the quantity and quality of work they achieve.

Particular attention will be paid to the *progress pupils are making*. Teachers, of course, have been traditionally concerned with this: whether there was reliable evidence that pupils were doing things better and more competently than they had done at previously recorded intervals. From time immemorial teachers have been in the habit of referring pupils to earlier work in acknowledgement of what has been achieved since, or as a spur to greater effort. Many schools can be confident that it is a matter likely to reflect well on them; public examinations and SATs' outcomes increasingly suggest consistent improvement in pupils' attainment; most schools, struggle though they might to implement the National Curriculum and get assessment right, can at least demonstrate positive pupil response to their systematic monitoring of progress and development. Where, for reasons and causes outside the control of teachers, pupils are generally unlikely to match national averages, it will be especially important for schools to be able to show that teaching, assessment and monitoring are contributing to regular and genuine improvement of standards. To be able to do so would be a source of major credit for schools. Nor, of course, can schools accustomed to high attainment on the part of pupils be complacent about the issue of progress. They too need to be able to show an upward trend in pupils' work generally; though theoretically, of course, there may be finite limits to what can be managed in this respect.

It is important therefore for schools to consistently gather evidence of pupils' progress across as wide a subject front as possible. This will be most evident in pupils' daily recorded work, and by reference to their assignments in various aspects of the curriculum. Schools, however, will also maintain samples and profiles of individual performance. We refer later to what seems a particularly effective way of doing this. Pupils themselves need to be constantly encouraged to identify and reflect, through reference to their work, on the progress they perceive themselves to be making.

In every lesson observed inspectors will take account of pupils' attitude to learning, their response to what is being presented by teachers. We have referred to this in the section on educational standards achieved by pupils, that relates to their attitudes, behaviour and personal development (see page 38). We pointed to the obvious there, the strong link between the quality of teaching; choice of teaching methods and organizational strategies; learning environment; and the nature of pupil response. Quite clearly pupils are more likely to become immersed in tasks, to seek solutions to them, to want to resolve problems and difficulties, where teaching has been absorbing, where assignments engage and intrigue them and have some relevance to their interests and enthusiasm. Learners will have the confidence to tackle new work and unfamiliar tasks where:

- they are aware and assured of the skills they have at their disposal;
- they have regular experience of engagement with well-matched, meaningful learning tasks pitched, in cognitive terms, within reaching distance, the much quoted 'zone of proximal development';
- teachers and informed adults are available to support them through this process of striking out into deeper water, in learning terms;
- their learning experience helps them to draw conclusions from trial and error, from negative outcomes; in other words, where they are being helped by being involved in the solution of meaningful problems;
- their ability to recognize false or mistaken conclusions and 'go back to the drawing board', to devise new approaches and strategies, is cultivated; where they are capable of saying, 'that model would have been better if ...' or 'I can improve that painting or piece of writing if ...', or 'that conclusion must be mistaken because ...';

- they are inspired to pursue, individually and collectively, further lines of study and are equipped with the skills and resources to do so.

Some of the qualities that inspectors will look for in terms of pupil response – a readiness, for example, to persevere through obstacles of difficulties – will certainly be dependent on the nature of the tasks they are required to do, but in important respects they may also emerge simply in response to teacher expectations. If one were to risk generalizing about aspects of education, this matter of pupils' readiness to persevere with tasks, to get as much as possible from them, especially at times of setbacks and difficulties, might be an issue that one would select. Despite strong arguments to the contrary, expressed by secondary schools in particular, especially in connection with preparation for examination and course work, I shall risk suggesting that at certain parts of Key Stages 2 and 3 many pupils tend to give up in the face of difficulty or obstacles more readily than they should be permitted to, and would cite as evidence the quantity – let alone the quality – of some completed work. Whatever the case, inspectors will certainly focus on pupils' attitudes to the proper completion of work and to seeing assignments through.

Finally, in evaluating each subject inspectors will focus on strengths and weaknesses in teaching and other factors which contribute to the standards achieved in the subject. Ofsted has made it clear that it regards teaching as the central and most important contributory factor to the educational standards achieved by pupils. Throughout inspections the quality of teaching will be rigorously evaluated and constantly reported on. We deal with teaching in Chapters 4 and 5.

In relation to subjects the report will make judgements about:

- strengths and weaknesses in teaching subjects;
- teachers' knowledge and understanding of their subjects;
- the expectation teachers have about what pupils can do;
- the methods and organization used in the teaching of subjects and how appropriate these are;
- how effectively pupils' work is assessed and how these assessments are used to plan further work;
- the effectiveness with which homework is used to extend pupils' knowledge and attainment in subjects;
- the effectiveness with which resources are used to support pupils' learning in subjects;

- pupils' attainment in the subject overall;
- relative strengths and weaknesses across different aspects of the subject – that is, across different attainment targets;
- variations in attainment among pupils of different gender, ethnicity or background;
- the quality of provision for pupils with special educational needs;
- the nature of pupils' progress in relation to their prior attainment; whether all groups of pupils progress as well as others of similar prior attainment.

Inspectors will concentrate in particular on the following aspects:

- attainment and progress;
- pupils' attitude to learning, their behaviour and personal development;
- teaching.

These aspects will be referred to in some detail throughout the chapters that follow.

Part C: Inspection data

Part C in the inspection handbook's outline of the schedule deals with inspection data. This section is concerned with the summary of the inspection evidence and includes statistical information about pupils, teachers and classes, financial data and the parental survey.

Preparation for inspection: a checklist for action

Schools can take stock before the inspection begins; indeed, it is a valuable thing to do whether facing inspection or not. The Framework defines the important aspects of a school's structure and life. The criteria on which inspectors base their judgements can be used by schools to evaluate the areas on which they wish to focus at particular times.

- In their preparation and evaluation schools can usefully refer to the main sources of evidence used by inspectors. These are set out in the frameworks at the end of each section of the schedule.

- From the outset of the preparation phase schools can begin to amass, in as succinct a form as possible, information to be presented to inspectors about important aspects of school life. This would apply especially to areas at risk of receiving less attention than they deserve, e.g. extra-curricular activities; provision for pupils to complete homework in school; relationships with the community. *(REPORTS)*

  WORK EXPERIENCE REPORTS *PARENT'S COMMENTS*

- Some of this information can be usefully assembled by pupils in the course of their work: maps of the school; descriptions of areas such as wild gardens, resource centres, libraries, history, nature and geography trails about the school, biographies of staff.

- Staff need to be fully aware of what the inspection process is about, how it will be carried out and how it will directly affect them. They need to have a thorough understanding of the inspection handbook that relates to the school, i.e. primary, secondary or special. It will be helpful for staff to have a 'map' of the handbook's most important features. They need to focus particularly on the areas that will most affect them personally.

- Help all staff to become familiar with the inspection criteria and to relate them to their work and any special responsibility they hold.

- A knowledge of the Schedule is particularly important in relation to teaching and learning. The school should secure and read some copies of inspection reports. This will provide an insight into the form inspection takes, what inspectors look for and are concerned to find out, and will help teachers appreciate the predominant emphasis on evaluation and judgement. Note that comparisons are often made between key stages.

- Schools will find the use of the Inspection Resource Pack invaluable to their preparation. This material, available from Ofsted, is intended for inspectors, but is generally very helpful.

- While only a very small minority of schools are judged to be failing or to have serious weaknesses, it is worth considering whether any aspect of the school might qualify as a source of major concern, e.g. excessive absence in an area of the school or consistently disruptive behaviour on the part of a particular group. Schools concerned about particular weaknesses might find it helpful to secure an external viewpoint.

- Know precisely what the PICSI is saying about the school and make sure this objective evidence can be reconciled with your own views and perceptions. Take particular note of statements about pupils' attainment in a national context.

- Ensure that the head teacher's statement provides a succinct, impartial but convincing view of recent school developments and, even more importantly, of your vision and practical plans for the future.

- Help all staff to become familiar with the Observation Form (see page 75). Consider ways of using it in advance of inspection on a departmental basis, in the process of curriculum co-ordinator monitoring; encourage teachers to apply it for self-evaluation of their practice.

- Be clear about what the RI will do, discuss and require on the occasion of the first visit. Prepare staff for a 'walkabout' by the RI.

- Decide with staff and governors whether there are particular aspects of school life and organization that you wish the inspection team to focus on. Be clear why you want to do this and make sure there is substantial evidence to support any claims you make.

- Decide in advance with the Chair of Governors and any other governors involved which matters can be most profitably discussed by them and the RI on the occasion of the initial visit.

- Make sure from the outset that all staff are quite clear about the distinction drawn between outcomes and contributory factors (see Table 2.1), and that the latter will be judged on their impact on outcomes.

- Make sure that children under statutory school age in mainstream classes are being provided for in accordance with the requirements set out in the Schedule. Refer to the DFEE/SCAA publication 'Nursery Education: Desirable Outcomes for Children's Learning on Entry to Compulsory Education'.

- Remember that inspectors, in their observation of lessons, will consistently focus on:
  - pupils' attainment and progress;
  - pupils' attitude to learning, their behaviour and personal development;
  - the quality of teaching.

Pupils' attainment and progress: a checklist for action

Inspectors will take account of the following evidence.

Prior to the inspection:
- National Curriculum assessments, both test results and teacher assessments;
- PICSI report giving comparative data;
- any other evidence of attainment provided by the school, including entry profiles or baseline assessments;
- value added analysis of the progress made by pupils in a year group based on prior attainment and the outcomes of diagnostic tests;
- previous school records.

During the inspection:
- teacher assessments and records;
- observations of pupils at work;
- scrutiny of samples of pupils' current and earlier work, including records of National Curriculum assessments and other teacher assessments;
- analysis of individual education plans, statements and annual reviews for a sample of pupils;
- discussions with pupils and staff.

In relation to attainment and progress, the report will make judgements about:

- attainment in the school in relation to national standards or expectations;
- attainment in English, mathematics and science;
- attainment in other subjects or areas inspected;
- relative strengths and weaknesses among subjects;
- significant variations in attainment between pupils of different gender, ethnicity or background;
- trends in attainment over time;
- how well any targets set or adopted by the school are being met.

The school should consider the following action where necessary:

- Provide, through subject co-ordinators and heads of department, any statistical evidence bearing upon what pupils know, understand and can do in subjects.
- Evaluate attainment at key stages and in public examinations, match them against school expectations based on diagnosis of work and prior attainment, determine to what extent the school is sustaining high levels of attainment or is improving and construct an overarching statement of attainment in the school.
- Ensure that information from SATs, teacher assessment and diagnostic testing is being used to identify pupils' levels of attainment and that learning tasks are being matched to those.
- Consider the establishment of baseline assessment measures at entry to statutory schooling and at the beginning of each key stage. Use these to gain a measure of value added to pupils' education.
- Use statistical information on individual pupils' attainment, allied to teacher assessment to set targets for future attainment.
- Review the ways in which classroom organization and management, and methods of grouping, reflect the range of need and development in mixed ability classes and provide for it.
- Ensure that early years teachers and support staff are familiar with national expectations in relation to the attainment of pupils entering the statutory stage of education.
- Review strategies for evaluating pupils' progress.
- Identify pupils who are failing to make satisfactory progress in main areas of the curriculum, analyse the reason for this and review development and support programmes.
- Identify any minority groups who are failing to make satisfactory progress and diagnose the possible causes of this. Set up measures to correct the situation.
- Analyse progress of pupils with special educational needs (SEN).
- Review strategies for improving levels of progress, including those which directly involve pupils. Evaluate their effectiveness.

Curriculum areas and subjects: a checklist for action

In relation to this section inspectors will take account of the following evidence:

- **English:** inspectors will draw on evidence of the contributions made by other subjects to pupils' competence in reading, writing, speaking and listening.
- **Mathematics:** the report will draw on evidence of the use of numbers in other subjects.

Inspectors will judge subjects on attainment and progress; pupils' attitudes to learning, their behaviour and personal development and teaching. They will do so in the context of National Curriculum requirements and in terms of subject links to National Curriculum orders. The focus on subjects will be maintained, whatever the form they are presented in – discretely, through projects, topics or themes. Inspectors will base their judgements about subjects to a significant extent on the evidence forthcoming from observation of teaching and learning, and the work that goes on in lessons. But they will also take careful account of teachers' records, assessment results, displayed work, portfolios, reports and discussions with teachers and pupils.

Schools are recommended to review and, where necessary, act on the following:

- Teachers need to be as informed as possible about what pupils 'know, understand and can do', in all subjects. This underlines the importance of working to programmes of study and detailed schemes of work.
- Monitor school systems for assessing pupils' attainment, not merely at end of key stage or at intervals such as annually or termly, but regularly through formative assessment, especially in the core subjects.
- Keep regular records and evidence of pupils' progress. Make pupils conscious of the importance of progress.
- Note the importance of evidence of progress where pupils may fall below national expectations.
- Don't allow pupils' successful attainment in relation to national expectations to obscure the importance of ensuring they are maintaining adequate progress as well.
- Consistently evaluate the nature of pupils' response to lessons and subjects. Implement strategies for doing this effectively: monitoring of pupils' work habits; monitoring the quality and quantity of work outcomes; lesson observations and reports back to teachers by senior

staff; formal reviews with pupils; monitoring of quality and extent of pupils' self-initiated study and investigation.
● Evaluate strengths and weaknesses in subjects; subject co-ordinators and heads of departments to lead on this, using observation of teaching and learning, assessment of pupils' attainment, samples of work, outcomes in national examination and SATs, standardized testing within the school.
● Review the provision for differentiation.
● Review the attainment and progress of pupils with special educational needs.
● Review the attainment of more able pupils.
● Review the adequacy of resources for each subject and of additional classroom support provided.

Attitudes, behaviour and personal development: a checklist for action

In relation to this aspect of school life inspectors will take account of the following evidence.

Before the inspection:
● the school prospectus and other information given to parents;
● discussions at pre-inspection meetings with head teacher, governors and parents;
● scrutiny of the completed parents' questionnaire;
● the school's policy on behaviour and discipline.

During the inspection:
● observation of pupils at work and play;
● discussion with pupils, teaching and support staff;
● scrutiny of records of behaviour and sanctions, including exclusions.

Schools may find it helpful to review and consider the following:

● the ways in which the school's policy for spiritual, moral, social and personal education, and its implementation, contribute to the development of positive behaviour and attitudes on the part of pupils, and to their personal development;
● the degree to which inspectors' judgements of behaviour may have repercussions for their perceptions of other aspects of school life;

- the ways in which inspectors can be helped to an informed under-standing of the contexts and circumstances of pupils' lives outside school;
- the general quality of pupils' behaviour in the school, and the measures taken to monitor and respond to it;
- the strategies adopted by the school for managing and improving unacceptable behaviour;
- the role of the curriculum in promoting good behaviour;
- the role of the curriculum, and the general life and environment of the school, in developing pupils' capacity to respect the feelings and values of others.

Attendance: a checklist for suggested action

Inspectors will examine the following evidence:

- the head teacher's form;
- the PICSI report;
- scrutiny of registers; sampling of registration periods;
- observation of lessons to record totals of pupils present, alongside numbers on class registers;
- discussions with staff and education welfare officer.

The inspection report will make judgements on the following matters:

- how attendance compares with the 90 per cent benchmark;
- the extent to which pupils come to school and lessons on time.

Teachers may find it helpful to refer to the following answers given in reply to teacher enquiries in the TES column 'An Inspector Writes'. I have amended some answers where I feel it necessary to do so in the light of new Frameworks.

Q   What can we do to prevent our head from panicking to such an extent before and during inspection that all our work and achieve-ments are undermined?

A   To answer this question without either over-dramatizing the situation or treating it too lightly, I would need to know something of the school and, not least, the personalities involved. My advice is offered with that reservation.

It would be unusual for even the most competent or sanguine of heads not to manifest in the course of an inspection at least some anxiety. But a head's readiness to assume responsibility and provide encouragement for colleagues to ensure that they and the school are presented in the best light would more than atone for any uncertainty she or he had unwittingly generated.

But when a head's anxiety reaches a level where the staff's morale is harmed, then we are considering a failure of leadership. I suggest you consider the following strategies, bearing in mind, of course, that they will need to be modified according to the school's circumstances.

- Acting as a senior management team, or, indeed, as a whole staff in the case of a small institution, persuade the head of the value of drawing up together a list of your positive achievements as a school, identifying the contribution of individual teachers, including the head.
- Decide how you will communicate such information in interviews with inspectors and how you ensure that individual contributions taken together represent a coherent picture of the school.
- In the same way, identify what you regard as shortcomings. Decide what can be done in the time available and find sensible justification for what you are obliged to leave undone. In discussion with the head, stress constantly the need for staff to speak with a unified voice, to emphasize the positive and to resist the temptation to blame individuals.
- As a senior management team, together with the head, establish precisely your roles and achievements, your responsibility for colleagues and how these are discharged. In this context, pay part-icular attention to the head's role and emphasize, diplomatically but firmly, the importance to you all of her/his leadership and support.
- Determine as a staff the support you need and discuss with the head how this can be provided.
- Involve the governing body in this process.
- Seek the involvement of the school's adviser or relevant member of the LEA.

Some people will take the view that circumstances such as these, where uncertain leadership is jeopardizing the interests of staff and pupils, are not most effectively dealt with by protracted action or overly diplomatic behaviour. Consider, before you take radical action such as involving governors or LEA in complaints procedures, that your current view of the leadership you receive may be less jaundiced once the inspection is over.

If you do decide to take action, first try telling the head openly of your concerns. It may be sufficient to encourage a re-appraisal of his or her style of leadership. Remember that recourse to an official body has to be preceded by advice of your intentions to the head. Once action is taken it may be too late to go back.

Q How often will teachers be seen during inspection? Will inspectors offer feedback to teachers after lessons? Will they provide feedback for the head? If not, there seems a danger that misunderstandings may be created that are difficult to change later, rather like a job interview where interviewers' doubts are not made explicit, so the candidate has no opportunity for justification.

A At least 60 per cent of an inspection is devoted to classroom observation, so teachers must expect quite intensive visiting, as individual inspectors seek information. This means that in an average primary school a teacher might expect to be 'observed' at different times by four or five inspectors, for anything from six to eight or nine single-period sessions. I have heard of an extraordinary case of teachers receiving 13 visits, which certainly seems excessive. Subject teachers in secondary schools can expect to receive anything between three and six visits for the subject. Many teachers understandably find this very demanding, particularly because they can never be quite sure when inspectors will visit. In the light of that, any assurance that inspectors try to allow teachers at least some time free of their attentions, and avoid having more than one of their number in a room at a time, is likely to be cold comfort. But at least teachers can be sure that an accumulation of evidence from so many lessons will provide a balanced view and that the subjects observed are the ones they themselves have timetabled and prepared for.

The handbook states that 'feedback' meetings should be seen as part of the inspection. This provision applies to the head, to heads of departments, curriculum co-ordinators in relation to work and achievement in their particular subject, and to individual teachers about their classroom practice. However, while consistency of approach is seen as the very essence of Ofsted inspections, there appears to be some evidence of variation in practice emerging in this matter of feedback. Some teams seem to avoid debriefing class teachers about lessons because to do so for some, when timetables make it impossible for all, might create misunderstandings.

Some schools are prepared to supply cover to release teachers for such discussions. If class teachers request feedback about lessons in general, as distinct from immediate information about each one, then inspectors, in general, arrange for this at mutually convenient times during the inspection. Inspection teams, by the end of the week, will provide, for heads of department and subject co-ordinators, a broad overview of achievement and standards in their curriculum areas.

The registered inspector is required to provide an opportunity, soon after the inspection, for the head, and any staff invited by her, to discuss the main findings and issues for action. Inspection teams are happy to offer broad, general feedback to the whole staff on such an occasion.

Such feedback and discussion, together with the pre-inspection meetings, and opportunities for staff to provide details of their lesson planning, should ensure that teachers' work is properly represented and that it is understood and fairly evaluated according to substantial evidence.

Q   I am a GP with little knowledge of education apart from what I have gained from reading my parents' copy of the TES. I am becoming aware, however, of the considerable stress that inspections are causing for teachers. Whatever inspections achieve, do they justify such a threat to teachers' health and well-being?

A   Your viewpoint will be sympathetically received by many people in education, where there is a feeling that the trinity of National Curriculum, SATs and now, most potently, inspection may be causing unprecedented apprehension and stress for teachers.

I shall try to comment on what is a serious and complex issue by briefly saying what inspection is, what it seems likely to achieve and whether in the end the outcomes justify the anxiety and even grief that it may cause for some people.

Inspection is intended to evaluate, as authoritatively as possible, against accepted criteria, the quality of education provided by schools, the extent to which it satisfies pupils' statutory entitlement and how effectively the pupils are enabled to become competent, informed, intellectually curious, spiritually aware and morally and socially responsible.

Schools' leadership, management, efficiency, curriculum structures and planning, teaching, ethos, discipline, pupils' welfare provision, relationships and communications are rigorously analysed.

The process is a very open one. The Office for Standards in Education has published highly detailed handbooks supported by other literature, informing schools of what to expect and what to prepare for. Schools are informed of their inspection as long as a year in advance and at least a couple of terms. It is not wholly unlike the situation of the student who knows what she is likely to encounter in an examination and may use previously completed coursework as part of her response.

What might inspection, at best, achieve? It should provide an informed analysis of a school, comprehensive and more detached and reliable than even the most effective self-evaluation systems. Its supporters would claim that for this reason inspection is an essential part of any evaluation of education and that to dispense with it would be rather like confining medical diagnosis merely to external or superficial symptoms.

Inspection will establish whether pupils' education entitlement is being received. It will affirm an effective school and good teachers. There seems to be some evidence that inspection helps many teachers be more confident about their skills and capacity; revitalized and assured about their work.

Intentionally or not, inspection can unite staff who may have lacked a common purpose, help them to appreciate their interdependence and the value of mutually supportive corporate effort. It can redefine targets and identify programmes for educational development. It may well provide an impetus in schools for genuine debate about the practical implementation of educational ideas, about the nature of good practice, about the essence of teaching and learning, issues that sometimes have been obscured in rhetoric or cloaked in coyness. It may well be that inspections, publicly reported as they are, will enable people outside education to appreciate more fully the nature of teachers' work and achievement and, probably more than most public services, the extent to which they make themselves accountable.

But, of course, there is the more sombre side of things. Inspection is a tough business. It deals with weaknesses, shortcomings and omissions. The sheer size of the enquiry it imposes upon schools is formidable. Most daunting of all, it identifies failing schools to the world at large. It is the notion of this that perhaps most of all haunts teachers, quite without foundation for the overwhelming majority of them.

There are educationists who strongly reject such public labelling, likening it to the futility of attempting to improve children's performance by ritual rebuke before their peers. Others argue that, in the absence of a formal inspection system, failing institutions can go undetected for years, shortchanging generations of young people. Certainly anyone with experience of seriously failing schools is likely to agree that they are dismal places for all concerned, and the quicker they are transformed the better. But the inspection process has not been set up to identify a relative handful of failing schools. To have put in place so elaborate a structure for a relatively straightforward task would be clearly unacceptable. The purposes of the inspection process are wider than that.

How much stress is inspection causing? I have no statistical evidence to refer to, but there is little doubt that this rigorous and inescapable process, fallible (no matter how hard we try), basing judgements largely on a short period of time before making its judgements public, and inevitably encouraging comparisons between schools, can be for many people a very demanding and harrowing experience: 'What I found devastating about it was that it disposed of 10 years of my life in a few pages of rather drab prose,' said one head.

For some the stress and anxiety may be damaging, even unbearable, and there are those who will argue that it is neither acceptable nor profitable to put people in such a situation. Equally, however, it is argued that the relative few who are overwhelmed by the notion and business of inspection would, anyway, not be able easily to sustain the strains likely to be created by the severe demands of contemporary education.

The fact is that the teaching profession is probably more resilient, more aware of its achievement, more confident about its quality and corporate strength than it has ever been. I believe it is secure enough to take external evaluation and use it for the purpose of further development.

Many years ago, reviving the inspection process for an LEA, I tried to persuade a group of heads to take part in an experiment in which they would form teams from their staffs to inspect each other's schools. They were too diffident to do so. I believe the current generation of teachers has the confidence to undertake the business of inspection for themselves, and have at hand worked out and generally agreed principles and processes, as exemplified by the handbooks for the inspection of schools, that would help them to do so.

When teachers can see inspection in this light as an instrument to be used for their own professional development and to enhance the education of the pupils they teach, undesirable stress and anxiety will be eliminated or reduced to manageable proportions.

I am adding a brief postscript to this answer, which appeared at the beginning of the inspection process. It is now clear that in primary schools especially – where, as I have argued elsewhere, the burden falls most heavily – inspections have proved a massive strain for many teachers. I hope that some of the advice given in this book may help schools to contend more confidently with the matter. It may be helpful, however, for schools in the course of their preparation for inspection and the long build-up to it to secure for staff as a body professional advice about the effective management of stress. In the long run, however, I keep on returning to the advice I often offer teachers: few inspectors, however skilled and experienced, will have your direct and immediate day-to-day knowledge of the management of contemporary schools and the classrooms delivering and assessing the National Curriculum. Trust in your hard-earned experience.

Q   In a recent column you were confident that schools did not need to be anxious about inspectorial partiality and prejudice. How do you square that with a situation where an independent inspection team's judgement that a school was failing has been overturned by HM Inspectors? And what compensation would you suggest for the distress caused to the staff and the damage done to the school's reputation in the community?

A   What I claimed was that the Office for Standards in Education has put in place particular measures to ensure that inspectoral judgements are not affected by prejudice or partiality.

But even the Ofsted safeguards are not proof against human fallibility. It is inevitable that inspectors will sometimes make errors of judgement. And even then there are ways of correcting or minimizing these, through the registered inspector's responsibility for oversight of team members' conduct and judgements; through opportunities available to schools to present evidence that would countermand apparently mistaken judgements, and, in extreme cases, through appeal to Ofsted. But most differences of opinion are not serious enough to require that. They are soon resolved and quickly forgotten.

The judgement that a school is failing is a different matter, probably the most serious charge that can be levelled against a school and one that is bound to have unpleasant connotations for staff. That it is a judgement not lightly made is clear from the regulations and safeguards with which Ofsted hedge it about, the requirement that it has to represent the collective view of the entire team, the need for validation by HMI and not least the requirement that it be based on substantial evidence of conspicuously poor performance in important aspects of pupils' education and welfare.

Consequently, it would be both unlikely and difficult for teams to allow prejudice or partiality to be any part of the basis of such a serious judgement. It is therefore hardly surprising that the number of 'failing' judgements requiring reversal by HMI is tiny, a small fraction of 1 per cent at most, a couple of schools out of hundreds inspected each term.

But, as you imply, all this is little consolation for the school involved, where there seems to have been a considerable inspectoral misjudgement. Of course, such an experience would be a harrowing one for the staff, a dreadful blow to morale and confidence. There is no compensation of the kind you possibly envisage, save the official assurance that the original judgement was mistaken.

However, in the strictest sense, there should be no damage done to the school's reputation in the community, since the report does not technically exist, and will not be received by the governing body, until HMI have validated the judgements.

What the school will have had is an oral summary of the main findings, for governors, and a general oral briefing, for the head and staff. Such information is confidential until the written report is formally received by the governors, so the parents, and the community at large, should have no knowledge of any judgements until that time.

But it would be quite naive to hope that such diverting news would remain confidential for long. What can a school do to protect or salvage its reputation and inform parents and the community of the true state of affairs? Parents, of course, will all receive a summary of the report with the proper information. But I believe it would be wise for the governing body to issue a press statement, or at least ensure that local papers carry a piece, setting out positive aspects of the report and the issues for action, and emphasizing that there are no causes for concern and no call for special measures.

Q We are still confused and worried about the final outcome of our inspection. We have just received oral feedback from the RI. He indicated that the school is not failing, but may be judged as having 'serious weaknesses' arising from the quality of teaching and standards in a number of subjects, including English and maths at Key Stage 2. What are the implications of 'serious weaknesses'? Why do you think the RI is still undecided? We are reluctant to push for a decision in case we tip the balance the wrong way.

A Ofsted has been identifying and taking action on serious weaknesses for over a year in primary schools and for longer in secondaries. As distinct from failing schools, or schools likely to fail, where pupils are judged to be receiving an unacceptable standard of education, and where special measures have to be swiftly implemented, schools with serious weaknesses represent a new category, about 8 to 10 per cent, that are judged to be acceptable at the time of the inspection, but which need to be watched.

Ofsted regards a school as having serious weaknesses when one or more of the following factors exist:

- unsatisfactory or poor teaching and learning in more than a quarter of lessons;
- unsatisfactory standard in four or more subjects and particularly in the core subjects across the whole school or in a key stage;
- standards of pupil behaviour and conduct that cause concern;

- a level of attendance below 90 per cent;
- more than five exclusions in primary or 25 in secondary;
- a school not giving value for money.

Schools that fall into the category of serious weaknesses will be formally visited by HMI six months or longer after the inspection, to ascertain whether they are showing clear signs of improvement.

There may be further visits, but at any time, even at the first visit, a school which is judged to have made 'too little progress' or to have deteriorated would then be regarded as failing and be subject to special measures. HMI would publish a report to that effect.

Obviously, then, serious weaknesses would not be a welcome judgement, and I can sympathize with your instincts to soft pedal the matter with RI in the hope that it may all blow over, rather like a nervous patient hoping the doctors will forget the most ominous symptoms.

But it would be most unwise to do that. You need to clarify the matter immediately because, should the worst come to the worst, your action plan will have to be constructed round the important improvements that have to be made, and you may need to secure support and advice to help with their implementation before the visit of HMI.

The decision about 'serious weaknesses' will be made by Ofsted when they consider the RI's report. However, in seeking to clarify the matter you may well help him to reflect and review the critical issues in a way that is ultimately favourable to you.

Q I assume that the head teacher's personal statement is regarded as very important. But what should be said and how much space should be devoted to it?

A Ideally the statement will point the way, like signposts, to the vital defining characteristics of your school. I have seen this splendidly achieved in a couple of sheets of A4; others have needed three times as much space. You will probably want to say something, briefly, about these things:

- the distinguishing features of your curriculum, particular emphases and the concerns that give rise to them; the elements beyond the

statutory, designed to enrich and illuminate pupils' experience. Remember to refer the inspection team to the school development plan for information on the major structures and processes, the organization, staffing, planning, resourcing, school-governor partnerships that underpin it all;
- the things that form the ethos of the school and give it identity as a community, committed to the fullest possible development of the pupils – something of the spiritual, moral, social and cultural dimension;
- the main arrangements for pupils' physical welfare, safety and well-being.

Heads will want to give inspectors a feeling for the community in which the school is set and the vital partnerships with parents. I have no doubt that whatever the challenge of the former and the circumstances of the latter, you would want to convey a sense of their worth and importance to you, the ways in which you seek to interact with them and the manner in which they impact on the education of the pupils.

Above all, and this is where I suggest the main emphasis of the statement should lie, you would want to write of your vision for the future of the school, and the pupils and community it serves, for the plans you and your staff are putting in place, how they grow from existing developments and achievements and the means by which you hope to realize them.

The inspectors' understanding of your school can only be enlarged if something of the pride and joy you feel in it comes through your statement as well as the inevitable concerns and difficulties.

Q   You have said, more than once, that you do not believe it possible for primary schools to teach the full National Curriculum at Key Stage 2. Does this mean that some inspectorate views are already formed before inspections take place? If so, is the Office for Standards in Education setting schools up to fail and have you made up your minds about the likely quality of teaching in some subjects in advance of inspection?

A   This is a bit like one of those medieval theological disputes about predestination and free will, where it is impossible to reconcile opposing viewpoints. In this case, because I firmly believe it is unlikely that many primary schools, staffed and resourced as they are at present, can manage to teach all the programmes of study to the full range of pupils' ability, does it mean that judgements on this issue are pre-determined and unshakeable? Does it suggest, in fact, that inspectors' judgements generally may be skewed because of their private convictions? I know that some schools, at least, believe it to be so. If they are right, then it is a most serious matter since some inspections would be, in effect, something of a lottery, dependent upon the personal, perhaps impenetrable, whims of individual inspectors.

I am confident, however, that it cannot be so because the inspection process requires all judgements to be based on manifest and verifiable evidence. This does not deny inspectors the right, indeed the obligation, to make judgements; it simply requires judgements to be made within a generally recognized framework.

Inspectors, like everyone else in education, hold all kinds of ideas and convictions about schooling. Such opinions are likely to lead to certain expectations about outcomes in specific circumstances – some of them unpalatable, perhaps, such as the probability that many children in severely disadvantaged socio-economic situations may consistently fail to exceed, or even match, national norms in terms of achievement.

But convictions about possibility or probability do not preclude us from being converted by evidence to the contrary. That seems to be the essence of inspection: enquiry according to generally accepted criteria, to establish true states of affairs, based on substantial, if not irrefutable, evidence against which speculation and supposition can be modified.

I am sure, therefore, that anxiety on the score of inspectorate partiality is probably groundless, since prior opinions and personal beliefs have to be subordinated to the evidence inspection provides.

Q We are a primary school, due for inspection in the spring term next year. Will we be inspected according to the new Ofsted Framework and, if so, are there important changes that we should prepare for?

A You will be inspected in line with the current framework. The new Ofsted Framework, handbook and inspection guidance will be published and on sale in mid-October, but will only become operative for schools being inspected from the summer term 1996 onwards.

Ofsted says the new Framework should make inspection more manageable for inspectors and more worthwhile for schools by contributing more effectively to their strategies for improvement and development.

In practical terms, the main differences from current practice include:

- Inspection will be even more focused on four main strands: standards of achievement; quality of education; efficiency; and spiritual, moral, cultural and social development. The evaluation criteria have been reformulated as benchmarks or standards of good practice. In order to ensure that the essence of an individual school is captured, only significant features, the strengths and weaknesses, will be reported. These criteria will provide a clear basis for inspection judgements and obviously will repay careful study by schools.
- According to Ofsted, the 'standards of achievement' section has been extensively overhauled and retitled 'attainment and progress'. Judgements about attainment are to be based on national standards or expectations of what children know, understand and can do in relation to National Curriculum requirements. Judgements will be based on the extent to which pupils' attainment meets or exceeds national standards. An important inclusion is a judgement on pupils' progress in relation to prior attainment. Attention will be paid to how well a school's curriculum provides effectively for all pupils, whatever their background, age, or capability.
- Particular emphasis will be given to attainment in English, maths and science. Significant variations in the attainment and progress of different groups of pupils will be highlighted.
- Greater attention will be paid to provision for equal opportunities and special educational needs.
- There is no longer a discrete section on the quality of learning. The new emphasis will be on the quality and effectiveness of teaching, the children's response and attitudes to it, their attainment and progress.

These, in essence, are some of the main changes. But what cannot yet be known are what the true changes to the spirit and nature of the inspection process will prove to be. Will they, in the end, result in a greater emphasis on those aspects of children's achievement and progress implicit in test outcomes? Will an increased focus on achievement in the core subjects have consequences for the time and attention given by schools to the broader curriculum and the foundation subjects? We can only wait and see.

Appendix 2.1: The Record of Evidence

The RI puts together a **Record of Evidence (ROE)** which incorporates, in summarized form, all the relevant evidence accumulated by the inspection team. The full Record of Evidence is set out in the Ofsted Inspection Handbook.

The ROE:

- sets out the evidence in a form which assists inspectors in compiling the report;
- provides a material basis for judgements made, in the event of legal dispute;
- exists as a source of information for Ofsted's quality assurance procedures;
- provides information that may contribute to a national evidence base about the education system.

The ROE is made up of the following elements, together with any working notes collected and retained by the RI.

1 Data from Ofsted
This will include the PICSI, which provides performance data about the school over a number of years and contributes to the identification of trends; data and information about the socio-economic circumstances of the school's catchment area; comparative data, about attainment for example, which enables inspectors to treat and apply school data in a natural context.

2 The head teacher's form and statement
This comprises a body of significant quantitative data about the school. The data is provided by the school in line with detailed Notes of Guidance from Ofsted. This information, together with required school documentation, stipulated in the handbook for inspection, provides an important framework for inspection judgements and for the inspector's pre-inspection review.

2A The head teacher's form
The head teacher's form will provide information about the school in relation to areas and aspects of the following kind:

Pupils, school and community
- ethnic groups;
- pupils with special educational needs;
- school meals;
- attendance;
- excursions;
- route taken by secondary school pupils.

Standards of attainment from assessment and examination results.

The curriculum
- teachers' time and its distribution.

Staffing and organization
- qualified teacher staff;
- unqualified teachers;
- teaching staff list and details;
- teaching staff turnover;
- support staff.

(This section calls for extensive information about the deployment of staff, especially in secondary schools.)

Finance
This includes reference to **income**; additional funding for SEN and ethnic minority pupils; Grant for Education Support and Training (GEST) and other grants; income from facilities and services; and to **expenditure**, including staff costs, supplies and services and premises of special facilities.

2B The head teacher's statement
The head teacher's statement is made up of:

- a **personal commentary** and
- a **questionnaire** relating to the school's financial administration and policies, procedures and provision for health and safety.

The **commentary** gives the head an opportunity to put the data in the head teacher's form into a context and to document features and characteristics of the school that s/he feels will contribute to and enlarge the inspectors' understanding.

The head is free to decide on the content and emphasis of the commentary, but is encouraged to consider the following items as a minimum:

- the nature of the school intake: pupil attainment on entry, their backgrounds and ethnic composition;
- any recent significant changes;
- the main educational and financial priorities, and any targets set by the school, especially in relation to attainment. It is suggested that consideration be given to a commentary on factors which have in the recent past, or continue to have, significant implications and repercussions for the school's work and achievement. Such factors, it is suggested, might include: changes in the character of the school, brought about by re-organization, for example; characteristics of funding; substantial or significant changes in staffing or senior management; the impact of accommodation.

3 The school profile

This is a summary of the evidence compiled by the inspection team during the inspection, together with a series of grades based on their corporate judgements. The school profile comments on aspects such as: **educational standards achieved** (attainment and progress; attitudes, behaviour and personal development; attendance) and **quality of education provided**. This involves teaching, the curriculum; assessment; pupils' spiritual, moral and social development, support, guidance and pupil welfare (partnership with parents and the community; the management and efficiency of the school; staffing, accommodation and learning resources; the efficiency of the school).

The inspectors' commentary in the profile of each aspect is comprised of:

- pre-inspection commentary;
- issues for inspection;
- summary of evidence and findings of strengths and weaknesses.

Grades are scored in the following ways:

Grade 1: Excellent.

Grade 2: Very good, favourable, well above average, promotes very high standards and quality.

Grade 3: Good.

Grade 4: Satisfactory, broadly typical, average, promotes sound standards and quality.

Grade 5: Unsatisfactory.

Grade 6: Poor, unfavourable, well below average, promotes very low standards and quality.

Grade 7: Very poor.

4 The subject profile and judgement recording form

This is a summary of the inspection evidence compiled by inspectors in relation to each subject inspected, together with a series of grades based on their collective judgements.

The inspectors' commentary in the subject profile is based on:

- evidence of attainment in the subject in relation to national standards;
- evidence of pupils' progress in relation to poor attainment;
- evidence of pupils' attitudes to learning;
- evidence of strengths and weaknesses in the teaching of the subject;
- evidence of strengths and weaknesses of planning in the subject and in assessment procedures;
- the contribution of the subject to pupils' spiritual, moral, social and cultural development;
- evidence of the contribution made by leadership/co-ordination/management of the subject to qualities of provision and educational standards achieved in subjects;
- evidence of quality of resources and contribution to educational standards achieved in subjects.

5 The observation forms

This is the A4 form on which inspectors' observations of lessons are recorded. They require purely factual information on the year group(s), the subject, teacher status, pupils present, observation time, type of lesson – class, group, etc., – and involvement of support staff.

Inspectors briefly describe the context of the observation and then write short notes of evidence on:

- the quality of **teaching**;
- the nature of pupils' **response**;
- levels of pupil **attainment** in relation to national expectations;
- the degree of pupil **progress**.

A space is available for any other evidence the inspector considers significant in the context of the lesson: presence and contribution of support staff; nature of accommodation; provision, quality and use of resources; application of technology and so on.

All four main areas are scored on a seven-point scale.

Appendix 2.2: Soho Parish School: Ofsted action plan

Introductory notes

1 Where a month is specified, the end of the month is the intended deadline.
2 Following the evaluation of each part of this plan, the results will feed into the school development planning process.
3 Abbreviations, explanations, etc.

SMT	School senior management team.
WCC/LEA	Westminster City Council/local education authority.
Steering Gp	Governors' Ofsted steering group, comprising chairs of all governors' committees.
JDs	Job descriptions.
PTA	Parent teacher association.
Cover	Cost of a replacement teacher, e.g. for a training day.
EY	Early Years.
Inset	In-service training.
Committees	The governors' working committees – Finance, Fundraising, Policy and Curriculum, Building, Staffing.
GEST	Grant for Education Support and Training, which the school receives each year in addition to delegated budget.
EWO	Education Welfare Officer.
LDBS	London Diocesan Board for Schools.

The following excerpts are taken from the Soho Parish School Ofsted action plan.

ACTION	SUCCESS CRITERIA	Timescale for completion 95	96	97	98	PERSON RESPONSIBLE	WHO IS INVOLVED	WHO MONITORS	HOW MONITORED	RESOURCE IMPLICATIONS	EVALUATION
1.1 Employ consultants to advise on curriculum leadership and systems to support delivery	1 Report received and decisions taken		JULY			CHAIRMAN	STEERING GROUP	STEERING GROUP	Receive report	Consultant's fees (in 2.1 meetings)	WCC LEA team carry out follow up to inspection in 1996 and report back to governors
	2 SMT meet consultants to define appropriate systems		JULY			HEAD	CONSULTANT SMT	CHAIRMAN	Keep in close touch with progress	Consultant's fees (in 2.1 meetings)	
	3 Systems implemented		SEPT			HEAD	STEERING GROUP	STEERING GROUP	Head's reports	Training time	
1.2 Restructure senior management team and clarify brief	1 Appoint two senior teachers to join SMT		MAY			HEAD	HEAD, DEPUTY 2 SENIOR STAFF	CHAIRMAN	Receive report and see minutes	One scale point on salary scale £1300 p.a.	Questionnaire to SMT and staff on results of changes
	2 Draw up terms of reference for SMT		JUNE			HEAD	SMT	CHAIRMAN	Receive report and see minutes	Meeting time	
	3 Review and revise job descriptions of Head and SMT clarifying monitoring and evaluation roles		DEC			HEAD	HEAD DEPUTY	CHAIRMAN	Receive report and see minutes	Interview cover £60	

1 Ensure that School Management Gives Clear Leadership about the Curriculum and the Systems which Support its Delivery

SOHO PARISH CE PRIMARY SCHOOL
OFSTED ACTION PLAN
JUNE 1995

ACTION	SUCCESS CRITERIA	Timescale for completion 95	96	97	98	PERSON RESPONSIBLE	WHO IS INVOLVED	WHO MONITORS	HOW MONITORED	RESOURCE IMPLICATIONS	EVALUATION
1.3 Produce Teaching and Learning document incorporating systems for planning, delivery, assessment, monitoring, evaluation and review	1 Review Subject Managers' job descriptions and use of non contact time	DEC				HEAD	SUBJECT MANAGERS	STAFFING COMMITTEE	See job descriptions	£110 cover	Peer discussions
	2 Clarification and agreement on the processes which support teaching and learning		MARCH			SUBJECT MANAGERS	CONSULTANT SMT	CHAIRMAN	Receive draft and progress report	Meetings LEA's Advisers' Time	LEA School Achievement Team to assess in autumn 1996
	3 Subject policies amended to include changes		MAY			HEAD		POLICIES COMMITTEE	Receive draft and progress report		
1.4 Undertake planned management training	1 Head's appraisal cycle actioned	SEPT		SEPT		R Dix-Pincott WCC LEA	WCC & LDBS	STAFFING COMMITTEE	Minutes to Governors' Meetings	£800 over 2 years for cover and appraisers	Annual Review
	2 Development of cohesive management team	MAIN FOCUS				INSET MANAGER	SMT	VICE CHAIRMAN	Receive Inset updates	£800 for training in 1995/96	End of year staff inset questionnaires

1 Ensure that School Management Gives Clear Leadership about the Curriculum and the Systems which Support its Delivery

SOHO PARISH CE PRIMARY SCHOOL
OFSTED ACTION PLAN
JUNE 1995

ACTION	SUCCESS CRITERIA	Timescale for completion				PERSON RESPONSIBLE	WHO IS INVOLVED	WHO MONITORS	HOW MONITORED	RESOURCE IMPLICATIONS	EVALUATION
		95	96	97	98						
1.5 Review use and general effectiveness of external consultants	Terms of reference for advisers including reporting format		JUNE			CHAIRMAN	CONSULTANT GOVERNORS HEAD	POLICIES COMMITTEE	Receive proposals	Meetings	Consult LEA School Achievement Team
1.6 Review systems of communication within the school	Widely understood and effective system of communication operational		APR			HEAD	SMT GOVERNORS PTA, HEAD & STAFF	STEERING GROUP	Feedback	Meetings, software (in 2.1.2)	Positive questionnaires

1	Ensure that School Management Gives Clear Leadership about the Curriculum and the Systems which Support its Delivery

SOHO PARISH CE PRIMARY SCHOOL
OFSTED ACTION PLAN
JUNE 1995

3

The management of the inspection process: before, during and after

This chapter is concerned with the practical management by schools of the inspection process: what needs to be done in preparation, dealing with the inspection period itself, and subsequently implementing the action plan and responding to the implications and outcomes of the total experience.

The appendices attached to the chapter provide an outline of the process, a checklist of the business to be carried out by the RI, including all dealings with the school and the chair of governors and the parents' meetings agenda, and parents' questionnaire, together with the procedures and protocols of the governor body meeting.

However meticulously a school has prepared since receiving notice of the inspection, the messages signalled by the first formal requests from Ofsted for information come as a powerful reminder to teachers of the implications of inspection.

- Judgements will be made; weaknesses and strengths will be identified.
- Parents will be invited to comment on the school, on their children's

attainment and progress, on the help and guidance they receive, on the information the school provides, on the extent to which the school involves them. They will be encouraged to raise any relevant issues they may wish.

- There will be intensive observation of teachers in their work; they will be accountable for their teaching, for the achievement and progress of their pupils, for other responsibilities they bear as co-ordinators, senior staff, mentors to colleagues, managers of budgets and as providers of INSET.

- The school will be keenly scrutinized and judged on the value for money it provides.

- There will be a detailed report, summarized for parents and widely available – a form of public judgement accessible to peers and colleagues.

It is the realization of such possibilities that begins to work upon the imagination. It creates for many staffs a tendency to identify and magnify every possible shortcoming and an almost irresistible temptation to change and transform the school, to attempt to put everything right, amend every omission, and put in place every requirement that inspection may make.

Nothing could be more ill-advised. Schools need first to take control of the situation by putting inspection in a proper perspective. They need to hold constantly before them what the purpose of inspection is: to identify strengths and weaknesses so that schools may improve the quality of education they provide and raise the educational standards achieved. Inspection is not a process of pretence, a game of bluff and counter-bluff; such a perception and approach by those involved on either side would undermine the whole process, rob it of its value and be unlikely to do much good to anyone.

Such an approach would also probably fall apart at the first serious challenge. The inspection process was always intended to be developmental and constructive, though the first model clearly did not always succeed in being so, with unwelcome consequences for some schools. But the new framework and schedule and, equally importantly, the constructive spirit in which they are to be carried out, represent genuine attempts to make inspection a positive instrument for school improvement and development. But the process will be dependent to a considerable extent on the capacity of schools to respond to it in particular ways. It will be helpful to bear the following things in mind before you make a plan of preparation and campaign:

- Resist the clichés and the preconceptions about inspection that are bred by anecdote and hearsay and base your preparations on Ofsted's very clear guidance.
- Remind yourselves from the outset that your school, in common with all human, dynamic institutions, is not perfect and never will be. It has its shortcomings, its weaknesses, its areas that have to be put right and its aspects that require development. It will be so with all institutions, whether they be great offices of state, religious foundations, military services, private sector companies, even Ofsted itself, for whom growth, change and development are essential conditions of their existence. All of them will have reasons for concern, areas of uncertainty, causes for regret, fears of failure, issues they would prefer, at a particular time, to go unscrutinized. But equally, without exception, they will be able to present a balance sheet that tells of perseverance, success and achievement, that in the majority of cases surpasses the shortcomings, the mistakes and the things left undone. This is particularly true of the overwhelming majority of schools.

Schools need to look at inspection from this perspective, to seize upon it as a means by which all that is worthwhile and valuable can be accredited and acknowledged and shortcomings can be identified, not for punitive purposes, but to put them right as quickly as possible. Treat inspection first of all as a public accreditation and then as a platform for future development.

- Resist absolutely the tendency to become obsessed with what you perceive to be wrong with the school. That will exaggerate anxiety, distort perceptions, depress staff and inhibit positive action. Your school will be in a state of development, grown out of previous stages and working to a plan for the present and the future – tenuous though that plan may be in some respects. Inspection offers the opportunity to describe that process of development, to give an account of where you are, what has influenced you to date and to set out your plans for where you are going, presented with all the clarity, justification, objectivity and optimism possible.

● Teachers are in an unprecedented position in terms of their practical knowledge of contemporary educational development. They, often to a far greater extent than the majority of people who inspect them, are informed from personal experience about the complexities of managing schools under LMS, of implementing the National Curriculum, of managing prescribed assessment, of working to achieve the extensive teaching changes that post-14 education is bringing about. That is not to imply that schools should insulate themselves from accountability behind barriers of complacency or assumed superior knowledge, but that they are in a position to speak, explain and clarify from a basis of hard-won insight. The education establishment has to be prepared, indeed eager, to take account of the perceptions of teachers who help pupils to positively bridge the gap between homes that are often blighted and their schools, who make partnerships with sceptical and disillusioned parents, strive to create racially, culturally and socially harmonious communities, have succeeded in teaching the National Curriculum to a remarkable extent in the face of severe constraints, have significantly enhanced pupils' public examination performance, and raised the levels of pupils staying on at school and entry to higher education.

● Inspection will provide you with an action plan that can be treated as an agenda for the future, and with a body of objective, detached consultation that would have proved extremely expensive had it had to be commissioned by you.

A vital part of your preparation for inspection will be the creation of a common consciousness and acceptance of these issues among staff and the whole school community. This will not be done by merely insisting that it should be so. Some of it will grow in the process of preparation, much through reference to teachers' personal experience and success, and what is already being achieved by the school.

Preparing for the inspection

The form this takes will depend to a significant extent upon the nature and size of the school and its current state of development. The implications for the head and staff of a secure, well-established three-teacher rural primary school are obviously going to be very different in certain critical respects from those attaching to the management of a large comprehensive school located in a decaying urban estate. But certain immutable features and concerns will be common to both. There are matters that all schools must provide for: the quality of education the pupils receive and the standards they achieve; spiritual, moral, social and cultural development; proper value for money; appropriate safety, care and welfare.

In making a plan, take particular account of the time available to you. In many cases this will be as long as a year, seldom less than two terms. It is understandable for schools to devote most, if not all, of that time to preparation, but in the long run that may well be counter-productive. Protracted preparation can encourage unnecessary and undesirable attempts to overhaul and change everything, create excessive workloads for staff, disrupt sensible and natural plans for development, ferment an atmosphere of strain and tension at the expense of freshness and enthusiasm, and foster ultimately unhelpful initiatives such as the manufacture of curriculum schemes of work that cannot possibly be fully assimilated or successfully implemented by staff in the time available. So it is critical to establish at the outset what are the essential things requiring attention and action; what is desirable and what is feasible. It may well be, for example, that the initial audit or survey carried out by most schools preparing for inspection throws up a deficiency in terms of health and safety that has to be dealt with immediately, inspection or no, while attractive suggestions for the extension of a piece of hitherto neglected waste ground into a natural wild area, ideal for a range of curricular study, has to be shelved for good practical reasons.

The following plan is offered as a basis upon which schools can build. They will adapt it as they wish in line with their particular needs and current stage of development.

Stage 1

Inform the whole staff about the probable time available to you, prior to the inspection, and arrange a first meeting for the purpose of providing them with essential information. Take the opportunity to offer reassurance about the purposes of inspection (it may be useful to refer to some of the points made earlier in this chapter), and assure staff that preparation will be realistic, systematic, and sympathetic to their needs and to the constant demands of their everyday professional obligations. Now begin the first stages of your preparation. If the size of the school requires it, work initially with your senior management team; for a large secondary school this may be six, seven or eight people, for a primary the head, deputy, key stage co-ordinators and perhaps a couple of senior post-holders.

For many primary schools, especially very small ones, the mention of senior management teams is likely to evoke hollow laughter. In some cases a head teacher will not have a deputy to call upon. Obviously in such cases the burden of preparation will fall heavily on the head teacher. However, it may make planning easier in some respects. In such cases heads are likely to involve colleagues fully from an early stage. They may also need to seek outside advice – from LEA advisers, from fellow heads and so on – more quickly than larger schools would.

Essential to your initial planning is a thorough analysis of the inspection Framework and schedule (see Chapter 2) so that the senior management team is thoroughly informed of the form the inspection will take, its intentions and purposes and the ways in which inspectors will carry it out.

Stage 2

Now make a first survey of the school in the context of inspection – a kind of broad 'state of the nation' review. Set some concentrated time aside for this. Some senior management teams may decide to devote a weekend to the purpose.

Make the survey by matching your present development plan with its aims, objectives and priorities – and perhaps the previous one with its achieved objectives – together with a broad evaluation of all subjects and main school aspects, commissioned from heads of departments, curriculum co-ordinators and relevant post-holders, against the main aspects of the inspection schedule. For many schools, preparation for inspection is marked from the outset by anxiety about the development plan itself. In the light of forthcoming evaluation it may suddenly seem limited by contrast with the encyclopaedic examples comprised of minutely detailed responsibilities, timescales and expenditure over three, four or even five years produced by some schools. Planning teams must be determined to keep this matter in perspective.

Effective school development plans set out clearly and economically priority aims with related objectives in those areas of curriculum development, pupil progress, achievement and welfare, staff development and training, management and administrative efficiency, the introduction of necessary initiative, the maintenance and extension of equipment and resources, and the care and development of the school fabric, on which it is intended to place particular emphasis in the current financial or academic year. Timescales for implementation, executive responsibility and planned expenditure are documented, together with evaluation measures and success criteria. The development plan sets out in similar fashion, but in much broader detail, intentions for the following two years. The planning of subject co-ordinators and heads of departments usually contributes significantly to the school development plan.

In your first analysis of the school's circumstances, do not expend energy or time on the state and format of your development plan. That can be attended to later, as your preparation may call for revised analysis of some of your current plans.

Simply identify how far your objectives and intentions for the forthcoming year and your broad objectives for the following two years, however documented, match up with the two major elements of the inspection framework, i.e. the aspects of the school and curriculum areas and subjects. Review the rationale underlying your planning, why it was that you decided on a particular focus, why certain areas were emphasized by you at the expense of others, why you have made some items a priority, delayed others and, apparently, shelved some indefinitely. Search carefully for any areas where, unwittingly, you may be infringing or neglecting mandatory obligations, e.g. provision according to the new code of practice for special educational needs, any aspects of health and safety, the requirements of religious worship or education, the monitoring of attendance, particular aspects of National Curriculum subjects – provision for information technology, for example.

Go on in this way to complete the first survey against the main components of the inspection schedule, e.g.:

Attainment and progress
- attainment overall in relation to national standards;
- attainment in the core subjects and other subjects/areas inspected;
- progress in relation to prior attainments.

The curriculum and assessment
- planning and content of curriculum and contribution to educational standards;
- areas of learning for children under five;
- provision for personal and social education;
- extra-curricular activities;
- procedures for assessing pupils' attainment.

Leadership and management
- the contribution of all those with management responsibilities, including governors, head teacher and staff, to education and achievement of pupils;
- compliance with statutory requirement.

The efficiency of the school
- financial planning;
- efficient financial control and school administration;
- effective use of staff accommodation and learning resources.

There are other sources which schools might find it helpful to turn to as reference points against which their initial survey of the current state of their affairs could be matched. There is the list of characteristics commonly associated with effective schools derived from extensive research and school inspection findings. These include the following: professional leadership; a learning environment; concentration on teaching and learning; monitoring progress; purposeful teaching and a learning organization. They are set out in Appendix 3.4 in an extract from 'Key characteristics of effective Schools', a report by the Institute of Education, London, for Ofsted.

The school and subject profile judgement recording forms referred to in Appendix 2.1 outline the criteria against which inspectors make their judgement. These will provide a comprehensive basis for a school's initial survey, an insight into the issues that inspectors will concern themselves with in relation to the main aspects of inspection and a valuable aide-mémoire for staff throughout the period of preparation. Some schools still use the extensive school and subject judgement recording forms from the first inspection handbook. These are no longer used by inspectors in compiling Records of Evidence, but still make a useful reference point.

One cannot stress too much the need for schools to treat the handbooks, the inspection criteria, the proclaimed characteristics of effective schools and similar checklists with the proper caution one reserves for any statement of the ideal. A superficial reading of them is likely to send schools into a state of sharp depression, simply because they reflect aspirations and visions of ideal institutions that none of us is ever likely to see realized. It is vital that schools remember this and keep the handbooks and similar commentaries in proper perspective as authoritative guidelines and goals to be aspired to. What schools must hold fast to are their development plans. These, together with the aims, objectives and strategies they incorporate, are the vital points of reference against which their surveys and reviews must be made, their progress measured and related to the handbooks. As we have said, the initial survey will be quickly conducted. It is not a full audit, but an exercise to compare how the school's current state of affairs matches up to the Schedule. It is certain that your main objectives for the coming year and your broad intentions for successive years, however ambitious they may be, will not match all that the Schedule sets out. That, after all, is nothing less than a picture of the ideal school. What the survey will do is alert you to:

- any marked imbalance within the development plan: an excessive emphasis, for example, upon special educational needs at the expense of essential resourcing in particular subjects;
- a failure to focus on critical areas over a long period of time, e.g. the professional development of staff;
- the aspects of teaching and learning where attention and review need to be concentrated;
- the critical relationship between your planned expenditure and the development plan: whether, to take an example, plans to extend and improve the quality of early years provision is underpinned by planned expenditure on staffing, resources, equipment and training;
- a need to reflect on the extent to which you are providing value for money: again, to take an example, whether the expense incurred by the introduction of 'reading recovery' or French in the upper part of Key Stage 2 is justified by measurable outcomes and the possible repercussions for other areas of the curriculum;
- the areas of school life that do not suggest a need for urgent or extensive action and attention.

This initial survey has now provided the school with an agenda for action. The aspects identified by it will be those on which your preparation will be largely focused.

Stage 3

Now plan a detailed audit of all the aspects you have identified. This will be in effect a mini-inspection, a shadow exercise of what the school will face within a year. Despite the understandable reluctance of many teachers to undergo the trial before it becomes absolutely necessary, the benefits of such an exercise are clear:

- It can be confined to those areas the survey has identified as requiring attention.
- Planned to cover the main areas of inspection, it will provide a vital insight into areas of strengths and weaknesses, and highlight any issues calling for urgent attention.
- It will provide for all staff a valuable experience of something close to the process of inspection, whether that arises from observation of their teaching or consideration of their responsibilities as senior staff, heads of departments, year leaders, subject co-ordinators and so on.

Careful consideration needs to be given to the form of the audit. Its purpose is clear: to help the school prepare as thoroughly as possible for inspection. There would be little point or value in forcing staff to endure such an exercise unless it were to leave the school informed about what needs to be done and help teachers to feel better prepared, equipped and more confident. Your survey will have identified the areas that need auditing or inspecting, and those that seem secure enough to be left alone. Certain aspects must be included, simply because they can only be evaluated by objective review, some of it probably externally provided. These aspects would probably include:

- classroom management and teaching performance;
- the general management, leadership and efficiency of the school;
- spiritual, moral, social and cultural development.

Members of staff can make a valuable contribution themselves to the audit; subject co-ordinators or heads of department, for example, can provide a broad survey of their subject areas, related to planning, achievement, areas for development, resources, INSET provision and so on. This has the value of involving staff from the outset, providing a natural opportunity for a shared review with colleagues and a relatively comfortable rehearsal of aspects of the inspection process.

When you have established the nature, emphasis, and duration of the audit, decide who will be responsible for it, and how far it will replicate inspection. Schools may decide to conduct all or most of such surveys themselves. Such audits can be effectively done by LEA advisers, who may well be familiar with the school and have a professional attachment to it, by head teachers and staff drawn from other schools, by college of education staff or by combinations of all of these. In the case of smaller schools, such audits may well be completed in a day or so or by one or two outside people.

Decide at this initial stage upon any particular responsibilities that senior staff will carry in connection with the inspection itself. These might include, for example:

- the co-ordination of governor involvement;
- the organization of essential INSET;
- the preparation and training of administrative and support staff;
- monitoring and maintaining the overall quality of the school as a learning environment;
- the overseeing and support of teacher morale;
- the management of financial matters.

It may be that one senior member of staff assumes responsibility for co-ordinating the overall management of inspection preparation, a kind of chief of staff, who is accountable to the head teacher.

Clearly in much smaller schools, as we have already pointed out, the whole responsibility will fall on the head teacher, supported mainly perhaps by a deputy. In such cases heads may legitimately look for further assistance from members of the governing body and from their own LEA advisory and inspectorate staff.

Inform the whole staff of plans for the audit and describe its purpose and form in detail. Take the utmost care to help them understand and accept its constructive nature; they may be assured, for example, by a decision to confine analysis and feedback of observed lessons by an outside observer, or co-ordinator or head of department, to the teacher, the observer and the head alone.

Stage 4

As soon as the audit is complete, relate it to the findings of the initial survey. Out of this, establish what your priorities for action need to be. Give all staff an opportunity to contribute to this process. Resist imposing upon yourselves an impossible or unrealistic plan of campaign. There will be areas of your work and practice that you are unlikely to be able to change significantly or usefully in the period leading up to inspection and undue time spent upon them will only detract from important aspects that can be genuinely improved.

Stage 5

From these deliberations, make a detailed plan of action comprised of strategies, timescales, co-ordinating and management responsibilities, INSET and training needs, allocations of funding and resources. So, for example, as a result of the recommendations arising from an audit, a school may find itself committed to:

- an intensive two-term drive on reading provision and organization at Key Stage 2, involving all junior teachers, substantial INSET, additional allocation of resources and a large co-ordinating responsibility for a particular member of staff;
- radical readjustment of time management through the whole school;
- minor but important changes to communication processes with parents;
- the introduction of a range of strategies for the promotion of cultural development;
- increased provision for core subject co-ordinators to monitor pupils' progress through classroom visitation; and
- a whole school focus on formative assessment.

Decide how school INSET days can be used to promote particular features of the inspection preparation plan and organize these immediately. Valuable input to such training days can be provided by schools in similar circumstances who have already experienced inspection; by inspectors who are involved in the Offset process; by LEA advisers and teachers who are expert in particular aspects of school life and practice.

Constantly, from the outset, seek to reassure staff, help them realize that all that is being done in preparation is likely to enhance them professionally and enable them to show themselves at their best. Remind staff that for most of them inspection in one form or another is a familiar experience; through appraisal, and monitoring visitations from LEA staff, monitoring by heads of department, senior staff and subject co-ordinators, the moderation of their pupils' work, the provision of annual reports to parents, their accountability for public examination results and SATs. They are accustomed to dealing with it efficiently and systematically.

Involve the whole staff in making an inventory of what you regard as valuable in the life of the school; of achievement, progress, development, of initiatives and projects you have shared. If you do not do so already, begin making profiles of work of quality across all departments and subjects.

Consider how far you can provide evidence of 'value added' by the school to the whole development of pupils, cognitively, socially, culturally and physically.

Begin constructing, as part of the head teacher's statement (see page 72–73), but through the contributions and perspectives of all staff, a picture of where the school has come from, its journey in recent years to its present situation, its ethos and philosophy, what it hopes for and aspires to for its pupils. Perhaps even more importantly, start putting together from your development plan, and through the inspection preparation plan, a picture which is, ideally, both realistic and visionary about the future of the school.

Make sure that all staff know about, are familiar with, contribute to, understand and implement as far as possible, the critical documentation that underpins the life and work of the school: the development plan; policies about, for example, discipline, pupils' welfare, special educational needs, equal opportunities; schemes of work.

The issue of documentation often causes considerable anxiety to schools, possibly because it seems likely to be one of the first substantial pieces of evidence requested that will give clear indications of a school's preparedness, efficiency and good practices. The one thing apparently certain to cause general dismay is the realization that there will be gaps in the documentation required. During the course of the book, in, for example, the chapters on teaching, we shall deal with aspects of documentation in more detail – the provision of schemes of work, for example – but for the present will confine ourselves to broad general advice about the issue.

Inspectors will look for the following documentation:

- a completed head teacher's form and statement;
- school prospectus;
- school development plan or equivalent planning document;
- copy of last annual report to parents;
- minutes of governors' meetings for the last 12 months;
- staff handbook (if available);
- curriculum plans, policies and guidelines or schemes of work already in existence;
- other policy documents which are available in the school;
- a programme or timetable of the work of the school for the period of the inspection;
- other information the school wishes to be considered, including any documents about, and the outcomes of, any school self-evaluation activities;
- examination results;
- if the inspection takes place early in the year, samples of pupils' work from the previous year.

Schools often discover that they have more documentation already completed and in effective use than they initially realize: a school development plan, a prospectus, the last annual report to parents, governors' minutes and so on. The aspect of documentation likely to cause schools most concern and anxiety – and probably work during the period of preparation – is that of policies and schemes of work.

It is not uncommon for schools to find themselves with policies about which they are uncertain, which seem inadequate, dated or even redundant and, worse still, without any policies at all for important areas. Subject schemes of work are likely to be even more problematic. There is still considerable confusion about their nature and purpose and, even where schools are confident about what they should be, they often feel unable to provide for so wide a range in the relatively brief time before inspection.

In fact the development of relevant policies and schemes of work is more easily achieved than may seem immediately obvious. Guidance about policies will be given in relevant chapters and on subject schemes of work in Chapter 4.

What heads, senior staff and, indeed, all those responsible for the leadership and management of colleagues must avoid at all costs is cutting themselves off from the life of the school for prolonged periods in a frantic effort to complete a total set of documentation that, in the end, may be of limited value because it is created out of expediency and not the natural growth and development of the school. Plans or documentation, however elegant or imposing, will be regarded by inspectors as of little value if they are not perceived to be positively influencing the work and achievement of pupils or supporting the practice of teachers. Even more damagingly, such material may have been achieved at the cost of isolating senior staff from the work and concerns of colleagues and depriving them of vital guidance, support and encouragement.

Decide as a senior staff team, or inspection co-ordinating committee, or whatever body you set up to manage the inspection preparation, what is to be done about the documentation most likely to require attention: curriculum plans, policies and guidelines or schemes of work; document-ation about any school self-evaluation activities. Decide which policies appear to be essential, e.g. concerned with special statutory require-ments; educational needs; behaviour; spiritual, moral, social and cult-ural development; equal opportunities. Appoint relevant and informed teachers or groups to draft them for consideration and set dates for their completion.

Refer where necessary to any Ofsted criteria, to good exemplars from other schools and LEAs, to guidance from authoritative professional sources and educational literature.

Clarify what you mean by schemes of work (see Chapter 4). Identify where you need to make provision, decide what is most urgent (for example the core subjects, and possibly for primary schools the relatively 'new' areas of IT and design and technology) and feasible, establish a programme for development and use reputable exemplars. Remember, the purpose of subject schemes of work is not to satisfy inspectors but to support teaching and learning.

There is one other area of documentation that is vitally important: planning for teaching and learning. Few areas are more critically viewed by inspectors, and understandably so. Without systematic planning across a whole school there is little likelihood of coherence, continuity and progression in learning or of a systematically implemented curric-ulum. Such planning is now generally thought of in terms of long, medium and short term, that is, over a period of a year, a term or half a term and a week. Short-term planning is especially relevant to inspection since it is concerned with the work that teachers and pupils will do during the course of the crucial inspection week itself. We deal in detail with the matter of planning in Chapter 5.

Review arrangements for monitoring the implementation, and impact on teaching and learning of policies and schemes of work. What steps does the school take to ensure that policies are being carried out in classrooms and throughout the school? How does the school ascertain that schemes of work are being consistently implemented? How is the impact of schemes of work on teaching and learning in particular subjects measured?

Stage 6

One of the most important areas for schools to deal with from the very beginning of the preparation period is the issue of pupils' attainment and progress. There are two main reasons for this:

- Inspectors treat the matter as perhaps the most significant in the whole life of the school.
- For most schools the raising of attainment and the maintenance of progress to the fullest extent possible will be time-consuming in terms of analysis, action and monitoring. Literally every day counts, and delay means irretrievable time lost.

The difficult questions that need to be asked of curriculum co-ordinators and heads of department are:

'Are the standards of achievement in your subject high enough?'
'How do you know?'
'If not, what do you think are the reasons for this?'
'What needs to be done about it?'

These questions call for the implementation of certain strategies:

- regular moderation of work, especially in the core subjects, against National Curriculum levels;
- the comparison of examination results and SATs with national outcomes;
- the use of this information to contextualize pupils' achievement, to

determine what improvement is necessary and possible;

- the use of formative assessment and diagnostic testing to identify what steps are necessary to achieve progress and development;
- the maintenance of individual profiles of pupils' work to monitor improvement (see Chapter 6);
- regular monitoring of work and achievement by subject co-ordinators and heads of department;
- comprehensive termly reviews of attainment and progress;
- engaging the pupils in systematic supported self-review of the quality standards and progress of their work. Include a systematic interactive element in teachers' marking policy (see Chapter 6).

Stage 7

Now turn to the specific responsibilities that particular staff must undertake in connection with the preparation plan, together with the large concerns that are common to all, and decide how you will deal with them.

It is certain that the issues identified by your audit will be drawn from the following: assessment provision; special educational needs provision; the monitoring of teaching and learning; attainment and progression; the quality of teaching, including classroom management, use of time and resources, provision for differentiation and how these all impact on pupils' learning; planning; the roles of senior staff, co-ordinators, heads of department; leadership and general management; statutory requirements and coverage of the National Curriculum; financial management and value for money; behaviour, discipline and general ethos, spiritual, moral, social and cultural development; achievement in literacy and numeracy; the role of the governing body; relationships with parents and the wider community.

In many cases, of course, they will be linked and overlapping. The nature of planning and differentiation, for example, will affect attainment and progression; assessment will be closely related to teaching and learning.

You will have defined in the preparation plan your order of priorities in relation to these. Now allocate them for implementation to staff, both individually and, as often as possible, for the purpose of mutual support and comfort, to groups, however small. Decide with them what you hope to achieve, what is required and what seems feasible in relation to each issue; settle timescales, the support and resources needed for what has to be done, and evaluation measures.

Appoint, where possible, a co-ordinator for each major activity. Ensure that particular individuals are not required to carry unreasonable burdens and that groups do not create conflicting interests or demands. Remember, especially, that one of the greatest shortcomings of inspection is that it generates extraordinarily high levels of work intensity, piled on top of what is normally required. Such a situation cannot be maintained for long; you must 'pace' the demands upon staff by establishing and sticking to realistic expectations. Schools must avoid the danger of staff swamping each other with demands in their zeal to achieve designated responsibilities.

Senior staff need to have a comprehensive overview of the inspection process and what it will mean to the whole school. They must be absolutely clear about personal roles and their purpose, how they fit into and contribute to the whole school plan, how they relate to other areas of school activity, how they, as senior staff, relate to the head teacher and to other members of the senior management team.

They can inform themselves about the inspection process most effectively – and probably as a group – through prescribed reading, guidance and input from the LEA, possibly through INSET from reputable Ofsted inspectors, through reference to published inspection reports and by contact with schools that have already undergone the experience.

Senior staff will be expected to demonstrate to inspectors that they carry out their responsibility for the support and professional development of their colleagues. These will include the teachers with whom they are most immediately involved: members of phases, faculties and departmental teams, in some cases whole school staffs, temporary and supply teachers who, in certain instances, play an increasing part in the education of children, students in training, and a wide variety of support and ancillary staff. They will need to be able to give evidence of providing appropriate INSET, training, mentoring and monitoring and be able to quantify and justify the outcomes. Though it will not be confined to them exclusively, by any means, the monitoring of standards of learning, achievement and progress will be a particularly important responsibility for many senior staff. They will need to establish together a range of strategies common to the whole school, of the kind referred to earlier, for managing this.

They need to be aware that evaluation goes hand in hand with monitoring. There is little point in knowing that something is being done if one has no measure of the efficiency and quality of the performance.

Inspectors will pay particular attention to the work of staff with leadership and co-ordinating responsibility in relation to curriculum. Whether they be heads of large departments and faculties, or teachers in primary schools responsible for co-ordinating a number of subjects (sometimes without designated remuneration for the task), they are increasingly regarded as the crucial influence – in the case of heads of departments, the absolute one – on the quality of teaching, learning and attainment in their curriculum areas. The detailed discussion in which they will be engaged will range across the following issues:

- the perceived main elements of the role and how these are decided and acted upon;
- what is done by the co-ordinator in terms of training, research, study to keep abreast of developments on the subject;
- the state of the subject, its status, personnel and resources; place in the current school development plan; success in external examinations; degree of take-up; plans for future development; when last part of a development programme;
- the nature and modernity of the policy; the extent and quality of scheme of work and guidelines for staff;
- levels of attainment; how they compare with national norms; evidence of nature and quality of pupil progress;
- procedures for monitoring and evaluating teaching, learning and attainment: how much observation of teaching takes place; how this is used to promote staff development; how planning is organized; the nature of subject moderation;
- arrangements for INSET and staff development;
- how equal opportunities and special educational needs are provided for;
- how resources are allocated to the subject area – the control of the curriculum leader over the budget;
- cross-curricular elements in the subject; links with other departments and subject areas.

The major part of inspection, certainly in terms of time, will be devoted to classroom teachers. (This will impinge particularly heavily on individual primary teachers.) Much of the preparation must be concerned with them, with their preparation and support before and during inspection.

They need to have the following information about inspection and be aware of what it will mean for them:

- Inspectors will devote at least 60 per cent of their time to observation of lessons, and will make and record important judgements, numerically scored, about the quality of teaching throughout the school. These aggregated judgements will significantly influence the important section of the report, on teaching. Individual teachers will not be identified in the report but teachers judged to be demonstrating consistently high levels of performance or consistently poor teaching will be formally identified to the head teacher. Staff will almost certainly wish for opportunity to discuss the implications of this and schools will do well to put the matter in perspective as supportively and constructively as possible.

  Judgements about excellent and/or very good (graded 1 or 2) and poor and/or very poor (graded 6 or 7) performance have to be made over the *majority* of lessons observed. This obviously minimizes the possibility of mistakes being made in this extremely important matter. Indeed, where teachers consistently score at low levels then manifestly they are in need of urgent support and rehabilitation, both in their own interests and those of their pupils. Ironically, the difficulty for schools may arise in relation to judgements about excellence. Such accolades will obviously be welcomed by teachers who earn them – and they are unlikely to remain confidential for long. Consideration needs to be given, however, to the many committed and able teachers, some with years of service to their credit, who may narrowly fail to gain such recognition, whose performance may have fallen short of their normal level due to tension and anxiety. What schools need to avoid is the possibility of such teachers feeling less valued, of their professional confidence and self-esteem being diminished and of divisiveness being created between staff.

- Inspectors will observe timetabled lessons. The implications of this are important; it means that teachers can at least be secure in the knowledge that the lessons they plan are those that will be observed.

Theoretically, therefore, while inspiration may flag and things inevitably go wrong in some lessons, certain important elements can be well and consistently provided for: evidence of careful planning, objectives soundly related to the National Curriculum, relevant and engaging resources, differentiation, some formative assessment, appropriate teaching styles, sensible deployment of teacher time, good questioning and interactive engagement with the pupils, effective use of time, resources and any teacher support. In other words, teachers can be helped to realize that it is possible for them to exercise considerable control over the nature of the judgements that are passed.

- Should they wish for it, teachers will have an opportunity at some time during the inspection to discuss with inspectors the particular lessons observed, to clarify and elaborate on the particular approaches and forms of management and organization adopted by them.
- They can provide inspectors with further important evidence about the work observed through the provision of copies of lesson plans.

Some teachers, in primary schools particularly where it could mean extra preparation for an extensive range of lessons over the week, tend to balk at the notion of providing copies of individual lesson plans to inspectors. However, as we suggest in Chapter 5, a wide range of relevant information: objectives, links to programmes of study, provision for differentiation and formative assessment, use of teacher time, nature and duration of pupil task, employment of classroom assistance, can all be conveyed economically and yet clearly in less than a sheet of A4. Cumulatively, over a week, this certainly adds up to extra work for teachers, but provides vital evidence of important elements of good teaching to inspectors, all the more important if particular observed lessons do not work out in practice as well as teachers had hoped.

Teachers will need to manage assessment, particularly formative assessment, as a critical tool in pupils' learning. Equally, they must be supported by, and work within, a school policy that defines the information to be gathered, the purposes it will be put to and the strategies for gathering and recording it. But teachers will have to structure their own organization so that formative assessment, especially, is regularly gathered and systematically used to advance pupils' learning (see

Chapter 6 for discussion of this matter). Teachers need to treat pupils' achievement and progress as a matter of the greatest importance and work with colleagues from the outset to make it a central concern of their preparation. Its importance cannot be over-stated. The new Frameworks stress that the main priorities of inspection are to 'assess what pupils know, understand and can do' – that is to say their attainment; and 'to evaluate their progress'.

They go on to say that inspectors must report firstly on how the attainment of pupils at each stage of education compares with national averages in terms of results in key stage tests and assessments, or, where these are not available, expectations for the age group concerned. Expectations are based on inspectors' knowledge and expertise, informed by National Curriculum level descriptions. This, therefore, is an age-related judgement, which should not make allowance for pupils' perceived potential or ability.

The second judgement is concerned with whether, given their current levels of attainment, pupils are making – and have made – sufficient progress. This calls on inspectors to evaluate a complex set of evidence ranging over longer periods of time. Progress is defined as gains in knowledge, understanding and skill. Where pupils' attainment is concerned, the whole staff would be well advised to do the following, to make it a consistent feature of their work and to begin amassing information about it from the beginning of their preparation:

- If teachers are not already doing so, make immediately a collection representative of three levels of achievement from across the school and in all subjects. Some of these samples, from subjects such as art, will be maintained perhaps in display, others will be preserved through photography, recordings and video and filmed material. Continue to update the samples; date and annotate with relevant information that will provide a context for the work. This will be especially important in the case of pupils with learning or behavioural difficulty. Teachers may wish to consider the use of pupil profile books (see Chapter 6).
- Moderate the work on a regular basis against National Curriculum programmes of study and level descriptions. It would be reasonable to confine such moderation to a termly routine with the core curriculum, and perhaps twice annually with foundation subjects. Moderation may often be done initially in phase or year groups.

- Teachers need to develop their skills in recognizing the levels that pupils are performing at and especially the progress that is being made against previous achievement.
- Teachers must not be diffident about making demands upon pupils to attain at levels of which they seem capable; and they need to be constantly vigilant about the progress which pupils are making. This is particularly important where, often for reasons outside the control of the school, pupils are failing to match national norms.

Where schools can point to improvement and progress by pupils, where it is genuine, consistent and significant and where pupils can themselves recognize it, identify the reasons for it, and are encouraged by their achievement, shortcomings against national standards are put in context and possibly stand more chance of being rectified. From the point of view of inspection judgements, success by pupils in relation to previous achievement may well be a significant indicator of effective teaching, consistent assessment, good pupil response and positive attitudes to learning.

The quality of work, of course, is vital, but quantity matters as well. Inspectors will look for evidence of substantial effort by pupils in this respect. They will want to see mathematics that demonstrates ample opportunity not merely to practise important skills but to apply them to the solution of paper problems; they will seek evidence of increasingly 'extended' writing.

Collections of such work offering evidence of good teaching and learning are absolutely central to a successful inspection. Teachers may teach well, may rise splendidly to the challenge of being observed and judged, but it will be wasted effort to some extent unless it is backed by sufficient work of appropriate quality and in sufficient quantity on the part of the pupils.

Schools need to ensure that teachers are applying a common marking policy that promotes attainment and achievement.

From the beginning of the preparation phase teachers, in reviewing their classroom practice, need to pay particular attention to the matter of differentiation. In the intense scrutiny that inspectors bring to bear on the quality of teaching, few aspects receive more attention; it is central to effective teaching and vital for pupils' learning. Inspectors will be as concerned about how primary teachers ensure appropriate subject balance and how compatible it is with whole school practice.

Where, for example, a project-based approach is employed, then evidence of an appropriate balance of time for subjects will be looked for. This matter is dealt with in Chapter 4.

Many teachers at some time exercise responsibility for the work and varied contribution of classroom support staff. Teachers must be able to demonstrate that such a valuable and expensive resource is being properly employed to enhance pupils' learning. Additional staff must have the support and training that will develop their competence and skill, must be clear about the purpose of the work and their role in it. They need to know *why*, as well as *what* it is they are doing, and *how* it contributes to pupils' work and progress. They must be encouraged and helped to play a part in the planning process and not be expected merely to carry it out.

Stage 8

The pupils, the group least likely to be inhibited by the prospect of inspection, are, of course, the *raison d'être* of it all. Inspection has been put in place to ensure that the whole process of education is fulfilling their entitlement and appropriately serving their needs. Their response to teaching and to the work of the school in general will be one of the most decisive influences on the outcome of inspection.

Clearly the inspection will not be discussed with them in any detail until close to the time. Then they must be prepared for the role they have to play. Hopefully pupils will be accustomed to reflecting on and discussing their work, aware of the purpose of all they do, the progress they are making, the skills and knowledge they are acquiring and the things they can do. They will know and be enthusiastic about the whole range of extra-curricular provision available to them. They will understand and be able to respond to the arrangements for their welfare, they will know the people they can turn to for support in all circumstances. They will be able to talk with confidence about their work because such discussion with teachers is a regular feature of school life.

It will be for the school to judge when it is right to tell pupils about the inspection and to explain its purpose. With younger children this will probably be a week or two before the event; older pupils who are selected to provide samples of work may need to be informed about this and prepared some weeks in advance.

In preparing pupils for inspection, schools will probably need to do little more than make clear to them its main purposes, the important role they, the pupils, will play in it, the desirability of their being helpful, informative and co-operative with inspectors – as they are almost certainly accustomed to being with all visitors – and particular areas they may be asked about.

Inspectors will examine samples of pupils' work and will discuss them with the pupils responsible. The school will need to select the work of two above-average, two average and two below-average pupils from each year group across a wide range of the curriculum. In most cases they will comprise written work, with a particular focus on English and numeracy. Schools, of course, will be anxious that the writing presented ranges across subjects, and that the whole range of samples demonstrates major features of subjects and the skills, knowledge, ideas, and, indeed, attitudes regarded as central to them. Work in some subjects may be most appropriately presented through video, tapes and film, supplemented by photographic evidence.

Pupils whose work is sampled will be interviewed about it. It is advisable therefore to select those who, while genuinely representative of their groups, will be confident about discussing their work with strangers. It may not be advisable, for example, to select work of high calibre if the pupil responsible for it is likely to be over-anxious or nervous in the interview. Pupils will need to be assured that they are not being tested or inspected, merely being given an opportunity to talk about and describe their work. Before the inspection, establish a discussion routine with them, in the unlikely event that this is not already established school practice. Select a group of pupils to substitute in the case of illness on the part of your first choices and include them in the preparation process.

Remember, too, that inspectors will probably wish to discuss other issues with pupils – for example their perception of extra-curricular provision, or welfare arrangements. It will probably be most convenient if pupils whose work is being sampled are also nominated for such discussion.

Inspectors will wish to sample reading and numeracy from each year group. You will almost certainly decide to select different pupils for this purpose, though you will again be selecting on an above-average, average and below-average basis. Prepare pupils for this. As with their other work, they will almost certainly be accustomed to regular shared reading sessions with teachers, designed to help them develop skills, to achieve technical progression, to talk about content, plot, characters, style and so on in fiction and to relate the non-fiction they are engaged in to general learning activities. Prepare them for basic numeracy exercises so that they are not taken by surprise and put at a disadvantage. Remember, it may prove more truly representative if different groups are chosen to demonstrate reading and numeracy.

Inform the parents whose children have been selected, without, of course, going into the matter of levels of achievement. It will probably be necessary to go further in secondary schools, where you may have to enlist the co-operation of parents in encouraging their children to do as well as possible with course work, to maintain progress with it and to present it when required.

Finally, the way pupils behave during inspection is critically important. It will tellingly reflect the whole ethos and life of the school, the moral climate, the sense of communal concern, relationships and respect for others; in short, the quality of the school as a civilized community and an attractive and ordered environment.

Institutions of this nature are not created overnight. They can only be achieved by long, committed and caring labour. But schools can certainly take account of their current situation. This is an area where it is strongly recommended that schools obtain a detached, informed, external view at the very beginning of their preparation and take steps to rectify and enhance, over the months before the inspection, those aspects of behaviour that suggest any cause for concern.

Much can be achieved by attention to particular details. One of the first significant impressions inspectors may receive of the school in terms of ethos and behaviour is likely to be provided by the school assembly. It would be optimistic to expect pupils to respond enthusiastically, or very positively, if the occasion is treated casually or as of no particular importance, if music is not played, display and the general environment are poor and uninspired, if the content of the assembly itself is mediocre and ill-prepared.

Again, one may have impressive written policies on behaviour, on spiritual and moral development, but these will be called into question if pupils roam about the school in a noisy and disorderly fashion, showing scant regard for younger children and others, if mealtime arrangements are uninviting, noisy and conducted in unattractive surroundings. The way in which pupils behave towards each other in the playground and throughout the school, any incidents of uncouth, aggressive or violent behaviour, will have a very considerable impact on the tone of the report.

Schools are often genuinely surprised and disappointed to be adversely criticized about such areas. They may have fallen into a habit of complacency, of not reviewing or taking sufficient account of apparently routine matters. It is advisable therefore to examine carefully this part of the life of the school from the beginning of the preparation period. The school could invite a range of people to comment about particular aspects, perhaps enabling them to respond according to a five-point scale. Pupils could be canvassed for their views of meal times, of provision before school and during breaks, of the quality of the playground and other recreational areas, of the things that cause them unease, that they find unpalatable and unattractive. Representative groups of parents could give their opinions of the care devoted to their children's welfare, could suggest where the school might improve matters. Informed outsiders could be invited to evaluate the school as a total environment, the quality of corridors and the entrance areas, the provision for recreation, the use of the school grounds, opportunity for quiet study and reflection, and their impact on the pupils' learning. Parents and governors could be invited to sample the lunch times, both from the point of view of the quality of the food, but also as a social occasion. Consider how the school grounds and environment are used to enhance learning opportunity. Try to convey to inspectors a clear picture of the total educational experience of pupils, both within the formal curriculum and outside it.

Provision for pupils with special educational needs is particularly important, especially those who may have physical disability to cope with. Schools should pay the most careful attention to the needs of very young children. For many of them, as Ofsted points out, this may be their first prolonged separation from home. Both of these critical aspects are discussed in detail later.

Stage 9

There are two main groups, technically 'outside' the school, but a vital part of it, who must be involved in the preparation, and have a major contribution to make to the inspection process both before, during and afterwards. These are the governors and the parents.

Governing bodies, because of their status and responsibilities, have a leading role to play in inspection (that demonstrates remarkably the change of power from LEAs to governors), though the extent to which they choose to be involved varies from group to group. The governing body is the 'appropriate authority' (except in the case of maintained schools without a budget) to whom the inspection team presents its report. They are responsible for circulating a summary to the parents, for drawing up an action plan within 40 working days of receiving the report, showing what the school is going to do about the issues and for making this action plan available to all parents at the school.

The report must provide the governors with a clear picture of the school's strengths and weaknesses. In the case of a school requiring special measures, the governors are responsible for ensuring that stipulated action is carried out.

The role of governing bodies is to help schools provide the best possible education for their pupils. They answer to parents, the local community and in some cases the local education authority or church for the performance of the school.

It is well for schools to remember that inspectors will treat the work of the governing body as an important part of the inspection process. They will want to learn about the nature of their partnership with the school, and what the practical outcomes of that are, how they discharge their main roles – to provide a strategic view, to act as a critical friend and to ensure accountability – and their responsibilities in law, how they monitor the effectiveness of the school, the extent to which they are involved in policy setting and especially the implementation of the development plan.

It is suggested that the school should take the following steps to secure the positive involvement of the governing body in the inspection process. The majority of modern governing bodies need little urging to participate positively in inspection or to treat it as an experience likely to be useful to the school. However, as busy people with wide responsibilities elsewhere, they are likely to need sound briefing about the process and their role in it. You are advised to:

- inform the chairperson as soon as you receive official notification of the inspection;
- have a meeting as soon as possible afterwards where you discuss with the chair the possibility and value of a joint governor–staff team to oversee inspection preparation; an alternative may be the

involvement of individual governors in various working groups. The deciding criterion for action of this kind is that it should be of genuine value to the school in terms of the inspection – though many would argue that the mere presence of governors in such groups conveys important messages about governor–school relationships and the coherence of the school as an educational community in addition to strengthening teacher morale. However there is little point in adding to already heavy work loads and overladen diaries if such a group does not take preparation forward.

While you may decide with governors against that kind of formal involvement, there are certain aspects of your work and the preparation it will entail that significantly involves them because they are ultimately accountable to the community for its quality. They include the efficient management of the school, careful financial planning that ensures value for money, the provision of staff and resources.

Governors need to be informed, in broad terms at least, of the curriculum the school provides, how it is taught, how monitored and evaluated. Governors will best help the school by having at least a general understanding of:

- the development plan, the rationale, intentions, requirements and emphases that underpin it;
- the aims and objectives to which the school and they, its governors, are committed, about the community in which the school is located (they are likely to be particularly authoritative about this), something of current educational thinking, about the nature of the school curriculum and the ways in which teaching and learning are organized, about the school's educational outcomes and how they compare with national norms, about the school's monitoring and evaluation systems. They may well contribute to those themselves by 'pairing up' with curriculum co-ordinators, heads of department and other staff with designated responsibilities, and making themselves particularly informed about an aspect of curriculum or school business.

Governors, by virtue of their nature and experience, are likely to be particularly interested in and probably expert in the legal requirements of the school, in pupils' whole entitlement, in the provision of care and welfare. They will probably have considerable financial experience available to them within their own group; they will be aware of their responsibilities for the employment, discipline and welfare of the staff. Parent governors will be significantly concerned with and informed about parent interests. Their role is crucial, as is that of teacher governors, who can help to make an effective relationship between school and governing body.

Many governing bodies, especially in larger schools, both primary and secondary, will have established sub-groups to deal with major aspects of school life: staffing, curriculum, financial management, accommodation and so on. They can be encouraged and, where necessary, assisted in talking to the inspection team about their particular areas of interest and responsibility.

The inspection team will be anxious to have discussion with the chair and with the governor who oversees financial management during the course of the inspection and, indeed, within the constraints of a very busy week, with any governors who can enlarge their knowledge of the school.

It may be useful for the school to ascertain from the governors whether they would find useful the provision of brief aides-mémoire – often little more than collections of bullet points – about major areas of school life, management and business. So, for example, in connection with health and safety the aides-mémoire would refer to main inspection concerns in this respect: safe practice in play areas, classrooms and specialist areas; attention to health and safety in the preparation and conduct of expeditions out of school, together with information about the steps taken to ensure that requirements are being carried out.

School governors like to visit the school during the course of the inspection itself – in some cases to formally meet with inspectors. This can be cheering and supportive for staff and informative for inspectors, but care needs to be taken that it does not become oppressive, or an encumbrance for the staff especially, who will be preoccupied elsewhere.

Whatever part they play in the inspection preparation phase and during the process, governors are very actively involved as soon as the inspection is over. They have to prepare to receive the report. The RI *must offer* to meet them to discuss the inspection findings. This meeting is called by the governors and its composition is determined by them, but must include the head teacher. The governors of county and voluntary schools may, if they wish, involve representatives of the LEA. It may be worth noting here for heads that LEA officers need to be aware of their function at such meetings. It is to help governors and the RI, should it be necessary, to clarify any technical uncertainties. Concerned officers who use the occasion to contest inspection findings do not necessarily contribute to a more positive report.

The meeting with the governing body – which usually occurs within a week or so of the conclusion of the inspection – must take place before the written report is finalized. Ofsted suggests that governors will be better able to follow what is being reported if, for the purpose of the meeting only, they are provided with copies of the draft *Main findings* and *Key issues for action* and if the presentation draws on visual aids. Governors may need to be reminded that all information received by them in relation to the report is confidential until it is received in its final form by the chair.

During that meeting the governors may challenge items they suspect are not factually accurate, but cannot negotiate judgements of findings. However, the RI will be anxious to provide as helpful and informed clarifications as possible.

The governors must take particular action within 40 days of receiving the report. They must circulate the summary of the report to all parents at the school and produce within 40 working days an action plan showing how the school is going to deal with the key issues. This will obviously be done in conjunction with the school. It is not a mere formality of putting words on paper. Like the school development plan – which, of course, it may significantly modify – the report will call for decisions about how key issues are to be implemented, about time-scales, individual staff responsibilities, the possibility of corrective action in some respects, the allocation of resources, the establishment of evaluation systems.

The aftermath of inspection may make less immediately obvious but ultimately more far-reaching demands on governors than the preparation, or the inspection itself, did. Parents and the community may need clarification and assurances that an action plan will not always provide; the school staff will look for particular assurances, the quality of which may determine school–governor relationships long into the future. The governors' virtues of statesmanship, balance, insight and good judgement may be in demand in the best interests and future development of the school.

Stage 10

The parents are the second major 'outside' group which the school has to include in its preparation. Their views will be energetically canvassed by the inspectors by three main means:

- the official questionnaire;
- the parents' meeting (see page 132);
- informal chat with parents during the course of the inspection.

It is important that schools are fully aware of the importance attached to parents' viewpoints. This will be obvious both from the agenda for the meeting (see Appendix 3.2) and the nature of the questionnaire.

Schools tend to worry to some degree about this aspect of inspection. They are often concerned that a particular group of parents, for reasons peculiar to them, may undermine or diminish the work and achievement of the school through the stance they adopt at the meeting or the views they convey by means of the questionnaire. The fact is that there are always likely to be parents, individually or collectively, with an axe to grind. Some parents will express their views forcefully and persistently. Schools can take comfort from the fact that views appearing to represent obsessional or exaggerated concerns are usually put in a proper context by inspectors.

Where, however, a representative sample of parents express a concern, for example about provision in a particular area or a lack of attention to a specific aspect, then account will be taken of that. Such views will be conveyed to the head either immediately before the inspection (since parents' meetings invariably take place at a time close to the inspection) or during the inspection itself, affording opportunity for the school to respond to the inspectorate. Equally, account will be taken by the inspection team of the responses to the questionnaires. This is particularly important since it is likely to alert inspectors to any pronounced concerns of parents. Schools might do the following things to enable parents' response to the inspection and their part in it to be as constructive as possible and to gain from the process what they need to help them in relation to the enhancement of their children's education and their future partnership with the school:

- The school first needs to review existing provision for keeping parents informed about and involved as far as possible in the life of the school and the education of their children. This would mean examining the various means used to communicate with parents; schools will find it helpful, for example, to look at newsletters, brochures and various forms of messages used by other schools.
- From the outset of the preparation period, schools could gradually begin to discuss with parents the issues raised by Ofsted in the questionnaire and the meeting.
- Take findings about how informed parents feel about the school's work and achievement. Review the practical ways in which they are involved with their children's education: through opportunity for curriculum meetings, seminars and workshops, for discussion with teachers and shared consideration at reasonable intervals of their children's work and progress.
- Explore ways of supporting parents to contribute to their children's education out of school.
- Refer constantly to parent governors for their insights and views about parent concerns and needs.
- Schools can encourage parents to respond to the questionnaire and at the same time take the opportunity to remind them of the things the school has done in relation to the main areas of enquiry. Encourage parents to attend the meeting, to be forthright in their opinions, but to be as willing to recall and articulate the benefits and positive aspects of the school that persuade them to keep their children there as any shortcomings they feel they should raise.
- Suggest to parents who become more closely engaged in the life of the school or who support classroom teachers that they describe such experience and why they perceive it to be of value.

Inspectors will be anxious to talk, during the inspection week, with parents who work in classrooms. Again, schools may find it helpful to prepare parents for such encounters, especially those who may feel diffident about describing the help they provide.

In a sense, where parents are concerned, schools reap what they sow. It would be optimistic to expect a body of parents, resolutely kept at arms' length by a school, to respond enthusiastically to questions about partnership. In general, however, parents are anxious to be supportive of their schools. In the main they are afforded ample practical evidence of the concern of teachers for the educational success and welfare of their children and are usually eager to express their appreciation of it.

Stage 11

There are particular matters that need on-going review over the preparation period, simply because they are more liable to be subject to temporal change; they cannot be so securely bolted down like school policies or a budget or a developmental plan and safely left for an extended period. Among these are:

- the school environment, by which we mean the learning contexts and circumstances that schools provide for pupils, and the extent to which they promote their education;
- evidence of pupils' social and moral development and their behaviour generally as members of the school community;
- the nature and quality of extra-curricular provision;
- the implementation of equal opportunity;
- the quality of learning resources provided for all subjects;
- the consistency of pupils' progress;
- the extent to which pupils persevere and work hard;
- the quality of health and safety provision and the care for pupils' welfare;
- the quality of provision for special educational needs;
- the degree to which pupils read regularly in the school and the purposes to which they put reading;
- the appropriateness of the educational provision made for children under statutory school age who are placed in mainstream classes;
- the opportunity provided for pupils to use school resources, accommodation and facilities for assignments such as homework, especially where their personal circumstances might not provide for that;
- the consistent construction of profiles of pupil achievement.

Fix certain points throughout the preparation period – perhaps at the end of each half-term – for a review of progress. Don't try to take account of everything at once. Match the reviews to the order of priority and the timescales you have set yourself. Be patient about those elements that have protracted timescales allocated to them, and wait for them to come to fruition. Resist forcing premature delivery of objectives.

Ensure that project co-ordinators keep a careful record of development and feed back regularly – weekly or fortnightly – to the head or senior staff. Provide for respite periods throughout the preparation time, when inspection as a topic is accorded less prominence, if not banished completely from people's attention. Few things are more likely to help staff keep the matter in perspective. Maintain the normal life of the school as far as possible, the enriching activities, the experiences and events that make the school attractive and memorable.

Be vigilant about the welfare of staff. Ensure that senior staff, heads of department and co-ordinators are supporting colleagues as fully as possible and taking subtle care of particularly anxious or vulnerable staff. Consider whether an occasional input to INSET/staff development programmes by experts on stress management might be helpfully and naturally provided, without running the risk of exacerbating rather than diminishing tension. Strive to keep within reasonable bounds the intensity of effort and work inspection generates. Provide opportunity, where you think it would be welcome, for staff to enjoy social occasions together. Make staff aware, wherever they occur, of successful developments, of achievement and progress in all aspects of teaching and learning and school life generally. Secure regular support for the head and senior staff from external agents, such as the school adviser.

The inspection week

The most important thing to remember, perhaps, as the school approaches the critical week itself is that you have probably done as much as is humanly possible in terms of preparation and may have not been in a position before where you could so convincingly demonstrate the quality of the school. The following points may make a useful checklist for the week:

● ensure that staff have met the RI in as constructive and positive a way as possible *before* the inspection;
● take them through the range of issues their preparation has been concerned with, stress what has been accomplished and emphasize

for them the extent of their expertise, knowledge and experience;

- remind staff of the school achievements you have identified together;
- provide an opportunity, as far as possible, for individual staff to discuss daily the progress of the inspection from their point of view with a senior member of staff;
- encourage staff to meet briefly after school each day for review and reassurance purposes;
- provide staff with a 'letterbox' in which notes of any difficulties encountered by individuals can be left at the end of the day; the head will discuss these with the RI each morning;
- provide the inspection team with as attractive and comfortable a room as possible; ensure that they have requisite facilities and refreshment available to them. Provide as quickly as possible for them any additional information they require;
- ensure that inspectors are aware of extra-curricular activities they might attend;
- be prepared for inspectors to attend any staff meetings held during the week;
- the head teacher meets every morning with the RI before school in as civilized circumstances as possible to share dialogue about the progress of the inspection. The head uses the information received to bring to the attention of staff aspects of their work that may need more explicit demonstration or emphasis. A good example of this is formative assessment, often neglected by teachers in the anxiety of the inspection week. The head teacher draws to the attention of the RI any matters of concern that need resolving;
- the head, with the RI, ensures that dialogue between inspectors and individual staff is carried through;
- the head meets regularly each day with senior staff, heads of department and curriculum co-ordinators to gain their impressions of the progress of the inspection. The head receives feedback of meetings between staff with special responsibility and inspectors;
- the head gains each day from the RI initial impressions of inspection findings;
- pay particular attention to the health, morale and spirit of the staff during a week that will prove challenging however well prepared they are and however sympathetic the inspection team;
- ensure that capable supply teachers are available in case of need or emergency;

- pay particular attention to the behaviour of pupils around the school and outside during the day and before and after school;
- remember that while many staff understandably tend to wilt at the half-way stage of the inspection, this is usually counterbalanced by manifest success at various stages of the week and by a developing relationship and dialogue with inspectors.

After the inspection

The understandable instinct of many teachers, even those who have found inspection a positive and affirming experience, is to put it out of mind once the report is signed, sealed and delivered. The urge to do that is likely to be even more pronounced for teachers who have found inspection itself a mixed or unduly challenging experience. Many schools suggest that, no matter how well they have fared, the period after inspection is one of anticlimax, with teachers finding it difficult to renew customary enthusiasm for their work. Some heads claim that staff who have worked committedly to prepare for inspection become markedly more difficult to motivate in the aftermath, especially in connection with the management and implementation of the action plan. In some instances heads claim they have been obliged to deal with this aspect of the process almost unaided.

How can schools provide for the post-inspection period? Apart from the fact that the business of the management of the key issues has to be the concern of all staff and has to be dealt with vigorously and efficiently, it is obviously important that the school does not undergo a prolonged period of apathy. The pupils are still there, their entitlement, needs, interests and perennial enthusiasms still to be catered for.

The following measures are suggested:

- The follow-up to inspection has to be treated as part of the whole process of preparation. If schools separate the process into two, concentrating entirely on getting ready for and getting through the inspection, and leave what is to happen afterwards to fate, as a bridge to be crossed when the time comes, then inevitably teachers will feel they are facing a whole new range of challenges and difficulties when tired, psychologically drained and least ready for them. It's probably a bit like facing extra time after a demanding and rigorous game in the unyielding glare of public attention. In some cases schools may feel they have to come through a penalty shoot-out as well. Teams that do not prepare for extra time tend to fade from contention. The pressure on teachers unprepared for the additional post-inspection demands is probably little different. So schools need to make post-inspection requirements part of their overall planning, to accept that they mark the beginning of the most important part of the process. Schools need to bear in mind the importance attached by Ofsted to this aspect of the inspection process; in a sense it is the really significant part, where schools build on their achievements and tackle their weaknesses. All action plans have to be forwarded to Ofsted and sampled by them. In some cases schools are required to revise them; in others their implementation is monitored. The effectiveness with which they are managed will be a critical indicator for schools designated as requiring special measures of their capacity to remedy shortcomings.

Schools need to begin work on the action plan without delay to allow sufficient time for:

- analysis, evaluation and response to the findings;
- decision making on the form the action plan must take to secure the implementation of the key issues;
- building the action plan into the school development plan;
- deciding on and allocating responsibilities, timescales, resources, evaluation measures and success criteria to the process;
- maintaining the involvement of the governing body which is responsible for the production of the action plan within 40 days of the report coming into its possession.

The perception of inspection as a three-stage process that must be planned for and carried through as a unit is heavily dependent upon teachers maintaining their particular roles and responsibilities throughout. In this way a sense of continuity, of seeing things through, is likely to be more easily maintained. The sense of weariness and the difficulty of motivating people afresh may be more pronounced in smaller schools where fewer share the burdens. It is certainly more likely to be difficult to motivate where reports have not been as favourable as schools had anticipated or wished.

● In all cases, therefore, schools may find it helpful first to spend at least some time focusing on the positive findings of the report, recognizing, welcoming and celebrating them.

- Involve everyone as far as possible in translating the key issues into a practical action plan underpinning the implementation of the action plan by:
  - clarifying requirements in relation to each key issue for all staff;
  - identifying the staff already involved, defining their roles and responsibilities and providing the necessary support and resources for them;
  - providing essential and supportive documentation;
  - providing necessary training, consultancy and support for staff involved with different key issues;
  - deciding on and providing necessary resourcing;
  - setting timescales for completion;
  - deciding on monitoring procedures and evaluation measures;
  - establishing success criteria.
- Set a target for a speedy realization of at least one of the recommendations and mark it as a positive achievement that already takes the school beyond where it was previously.
- Make the timescales for the action plan as realistic and reasonable as possible. While schools will obviously want to deal with recommendations as quickly as possible, the implementation of some at least cannot be achieved overnight. Staff need to be assured that the demands made of them will be reasonable.
- Treat the achievement of all issues as something to be remarked and celebrated as indications of a developing and enhanced school.

Apart from the implementation of the plan there will be other issues that need to be attended to, and activities to be considered, some apparently trivial in themselves but important in the context of the staff's ability and readiness to respond.

- The head and senior staff need to talk with individual members of staff as soon as possible after the inspection. Some – a majority – need to be confirmed in their success, accredited for what they have achieved, made to realize its significance and to appreciate its importance as affirmation of their professional competence and quality. Some teachers, on the other hand – certainly a minority – will need sensitive support to cope with critical judgements, to retain their confidence and the will to continue with their professional development.

- Staff may feel that the inspection summary for parents would be illuminated by a written elaboration from the school, to clarify issues that might otherwise remain unclear. The school, almost certainly, will also wish to produce a press statement in conjunction with the LEA public relations department.
- The opportunity should be taken to cement the partnership with the governing body. One of the apparently trivial points, but almost certainly valued by teachers, is the growing tendency for governors to hold a reception for staff or arrange a joint social occasion to celebrate their shared work on inspection.
- Many heads attempt variations on the school INSET programme over the following couple of terms; to focus on topics less immediately related to the requirements of inspection, to pursue an interest of educational value but with a fresh and novel flavour, to find new and attractive locations.

A checklist for before, during and after the inspection

1 Be realistic about the targets for inspection you set yourself as a school. Remember, the handbook reflects an ideal state that schools may attain in places but not in entirety.
2 Be prepared for weaknesses to be identified. That is half the business of the inspection process. All schools will have such weaknesses. Inspection findings will enable you to act on them.
3 Staff need to be reminded of how much they know and what they can do. Reflect briefly on the curricular and pedagogical advances made by schools in the past decade.
4 Make an initial survey of where the school stands in relation to the main elements of the inspection schedule. Use your development plan and the evaluation of subjects as the basis for comparison.
5 Identify a range of priorities for attention.
6 Now carry out a 'mini-inspection' focusing especially on those areas your survey has identified as requiring particular attention. You may need to call on some external evaluation.
7 Out of this, construct an inspection preparation plan aimed at tackling your priorities. Decide as a staff how this will be done. Allocate responsibilities and resources; decide timescales, success criteria and review date.

8 As a staff make a list of the positive things in the school; match these against the schedule.

9 Make profiles of work of quality across all subjects and departments.

10 Work out where you can provide evidence of 'value added' to pupils' education.

11 Begin constructing the head teacher's statement.

12 Make sure staff are informed about and familiar with all school documentation, policies, schemes of work and statutory requirements.

13 Plan for new documentation only where it is absolutely necessary and likely to significantly improve teaching and learning in the school.

14 Begin – or continue – systematically monitoring the quality of pupils' work, attainment and progress.

15 Provide detailed advice and guidance to classroom teachers about the means by which their work will be evaluated and the ways in which they can effectively respond to this. Few areas of the school will affect the outcome of inspection more.

16 Encourage teachers to place particular emphasis on pupils' attainment and progress; make sure there is ample evidence to substantiate this.

17 Support teachers in providing systematically for differentiation and formative assessment.

18 Review and evaluate the ways in which post-holders, curriculum co-ordinators, heads of department and senior staff carry out their responsibilities. Pay particular attention to the means by which they monitor the quality of teachers and learning. Prepare them for inspection interviews.

19 Begin the process of putting samples of pupils' work together.

20 Prepare pupils for inspection.

21 Evaluate the ethos, tone, environmental quality of the school. If possible, involve 'outsiders' to obtain objective viewpoints.

22 Plan with the governing body their role in the inspection and the ways in which they can contribute positively to it.

23 Evaluate the school's whole relationship with parents. Work with parents who will play an active part in the inspection – e.g. parents who support teachers in the classroom or who lead official parent bodies in working for the school.

24 Identify routine but important issues and aspects of school life so that they can be lightly but consistently monitored (see page 114).
25 Set dates through the preparation period for review of progress.
26 Monitor staff health and welfare.
27 Establish 'respite' periods during preparation.
28 Make a schedule of what needs to be done during the inspection week (see page 115–117).
29 Constantly make post-inspection business part of your preparation.
30 Establish procedures for implementing the action plan.
31 Affirm and support staff after the inspection.

The following questions to the TES column 'An Inspector Writes' highlight some of the aspects of preparation that schools have expressed concern about.

Q We have now been preparing for inspection by quietly trying to get our house in order and to continue to do our best for the children. Colleagues at a neighbouring school had a very stressful inspection week. This seems to be worst for the conscientious older teachers, one of whom was reduced to tears by it all (despite being one of the best teachers we know). How are we to prepare ourselves so that this does not happen to us?

A This question reflects the ordeal that inspection is proving for many. The essence of the answer may be inherent in the question: methodical review and preparation, recourse to professional experience, successful practice and instincts about what is educationally good for children, and a determination that whatever is done will be accomplished as a team.

If there is one thing that inspection has brought home, it is that isolationism and unilateral behaviour erode the capacity of a staff to provide what is best for pupils and for each other. Where a staff does not prepare together for inspection – or for anything else of importance – then it is likely that individuals will be vulnerable.

There is no mystical formula to avert trauma, I fear, unless you count a humane and cultivated but professionally invigorating school regimen as such. I can suggest only initiatives essentially related to the business of teaching, since I believe that personal confidence and security are most likely to flourish where there are degrees of professional certainty.

- Arrange for a head and teachers who have been inspected to share their experiences with you. Take from their accounts only what will be relevant to you. Treat with scepticism the occasional lurid anecdotes already beginning to cluster about inspection – good for making the flesh creep, but unlikely to be a reality. (I was recently enthralled by a vivid story of how I had conducted an inspection at a school, the whole effect eventually ruined only by the fact that I had never been near the place in my life.)
- Invite a reliable and qualified person – an LEA adviser or perhaps another head – to carry out a mini-inspection/audit for you. Establish a realistic action plan based on the findings. Reference to the school judgement recording form in the Office for Standards in Education handbook will help you do this. Decide what is essential, what additionally can be managed, and what has to be put aside for another time. Identify what is good in the school, share it with the staff and emphasize their contributions to it. Decide with them how the action plan will be managed and their individual roles. When the time comes, share with the inspectors how the priorities were arrived at, and let them know what has had to be delayed for more opportune times.
- Read, as a staff, some recent inspection reports.
- Keep inspection in perspective; be realistic in what you seek to do, especially in a limited period of time. Hasty cosmetic changes will not produce enduring development. Treat the handbook as a valuable guide, but not something that mortals are likely to achieve in its entirety.
- Become accustomed as individuals to evaluating the pupils' levels of achievement, at least in the core subjects, in relation to national standards and their own abilities, the quality of their learning and the quality of your own teaching, using the inspection observation sheets from your handbook. Use the handbook to help identify characteristics of good learning and teaching. If possible, have pairs of teachers support each other in this process, and perhaps even observe each other teach.
- Share and analyse each other's long- and short-term planning and individual lesson plans.

- Seek advice from other schools about subjects of which you are uncertain, but be realistic about what you can implement in a limited time. Take courage from the fact that the subject lessons you timetable and prepare for will be what are inspected. Inspectors will respond to your timetables.
- Share ideas for differentiation, the management of assessment, and the effective use of information technology in the classroom.
- Keep and be encouraged by a record that charts your progress and achievements. When the inspection finally arrives, be cheered by what you have accomplished and be aware that things will always remain to be done, no matter how hard you try. Teachers who have done their best have little to fear from inspection.
- During the inspection, meet early each morning with the RI to identify possible concerns, try to be particularly supportive of staff on the second and third days when they are most likely to wilt, encourage them to meet together briefly at the beginning of each day for a few minutes' mutual cheer.
- Finally, as head, establish as soon as possible where and to whom you can turn for your own moral and professional support, apart from what you will undoubtedly receive from a staff you are helping to grow through the inspection process.

Q Our problem is a simple but alarming one. It is highly unlikely that we shall be able to provide all the documentation required by Ofsted. For example, we have no policies or schemes of work for some subjects. Will Ofsted inspectors compromise on this, or does it mean we have already made a bad start?

A Schools, with their respect for the written word, tend to attach exaggerated importance to documentation. Relevant documentation is vital to the effectiveness of the school and the realization of its aims, but it is important not to become obsessive about it to the detriment of more important issues.

You may find it helpful to bear the following in mind:

- There is probably more material available to you than you suspect: probably at least some form of school prospectus, staff job/role descriptions, some records of governor meetings.

- Some information that is not formally documented can be quickly assembled, based on a collection of your present practice – a marking policy, a record of extra-curricular activities, for example.
- Resist desperate preparation of policies and schemes of work, too hastily thrown together to be of any relevance or value to teaching or learning. Continue to work steadily with the schemes and policies you are engaged on. Inspectors, aware that many schools are reviewing documentation in the light of Dearing and the Special Needs Code, will treat what already exists on its merits and as evidence of intention about what remains to be done. Just ensure that in the absence of subject documentation you have, at least, broad outlines that guarantee general continuity and progression across the key stages.
- Make sure that your documentation is as faithful a blueprint as possible of the life and work of the school. The most lyrical written plans for spiritual education, for example, are unlikely to impress if the reality is a school bereft of music, the creative arts, carefully conceived religious education and harmonious relationships.
- Most important of all, as a head teacher, do not allow the preparation of documentation to become a substitute for more urgently required action, or to distance you from the work, concerns and needs of classroom teachers. Appropriate support for teachers will yield more benefits than the most sumptuous documentation.

Q   We are not sure that our school can teach the full National Curriculum at Key Stage 2. What does this mean in relation to our forthcoming inspection?

A   Many primary teachers may be anxious not just about their knowledge and skills across ten subjects, but about the emphasis on subjects, rather than the 'whole curriculum' in the Office for Standards in Education's framework for inspection.

- This focus upon subjects raises important issues about the nature and form of inspection reports. It may well be that the real tension lies not so much between Ofsted and schools as between the expectation of the School Curriculum and Assessment Authority and the obligations of Ofsted.

- The Dearing 'solution' insists that all nine subjects and RE should be taught across all key stages, albeit in a slimmed-down form. Initial inspection evidence suggests that Ofsted will find itself identifying many schools, at primary level anyway, as failing to meet National Curriculum requirements in perhaps two, or even more subjects.

- To what extent are initially positive judgements about, say, the leadership, management and efficiency of a school modified when inspectors realize that curriculum requirements in technology, geography and IT are not being met? What picture emerges of teachers in a key stage who are seen to demonstrate 'shortcomings' in, say, three out of ten subjects? Indeed, can judgements made about teachers' competence, often by inspectors with exclusively secondary experience and on the basis of isolated subjects, really encompass teaching quality? And how will parents react to schools that are perceived as being inadequate in some subjects?

- It is now clear that Ofsted is aware of the 'subjects' dilemma. In its recent guidance on interpretation of the inspection framework, it advised inspectors that where 'a subject' was not being taught at the time of the inspection, standards could be evaluated by reference to a 'sufficient sample' of pupils' work together with other available evidence. It suggests that 'inspectors will expect to see teaching in the core subjects and whatever else the school does as part of its normal programme'.

- Such 'concessions' could have implications reaching far beyond this. Is Ofsted merely accepting that primary schools, as distinct from secondaries, are occasionally unlikely to teach all ten subjects in any single week, or is it tacitly accepting that many primary schools cannot, in fact, deliver what has been legally defined as children's educational entitlement?

- Can inspectors really make valid judgements about the quality of learning on the basis of work alone, without direct acquaintance with the children responsible for it and the circumstances in which they achieved it? Will schools be tempted to 'hide' subjects where they feel most fallible, thereby marginalizing them further?

- Might we reach a stage where schools can offer a 'best seven out of ten subjects', and risk primaries being labelled as less likely than secondaries to provide a full curriculum? Is there a possibility that the inspection process, in the end, might contribute to the negotiating away of the National Curriculum?

Note: Reading this question again, I feel it is too fanciful and speculative, and begs too many questions to be of practical value to schools who must do all they can to provide all subjects for their pupils. Nevertheless, I am going now to add to the conjectural nature of the piece and wonder how I would react as RI to the primary school that told me it was putting some subjects of the National Curriculum 'on hold', with the permission of governors, until all children in the school could read adequately – that is, for the sake of argument, read at Level 3 by the end of year 3. The full National Curriculum would then become available again at some time during year 4. I am increasingly convinced that such a step is necessary in some schools, and that we should be prepared to accept it where evidence is forthcoming that the reading emphasis is proving successful. I believe it to be more likely that the National Curriculum will be mastered in its entirety where children can cope competently and confidently with texts. It would certainly extend their autonomy and control as learners.

Q I am discovering as head teacher that the aftermath of inspection is as difficult in its way as what went before. Our report has been very sound; the problem is that the staff's enthusiasm has vanished and their teaching has gone off the boil. How do I deal with this malaise?

A I suspect that many people still facing inspection would gladly exchange places with you and your present problem, for the joy of a good report and the trial over and done with; rather like a patient awaiting surgery envies the convalescent, whatever the temporary discomfort.

But the post-inspection trauma you are facing is a serious matter, common to a number of schools.

It is likely that teachers will feel drained by the cumulative effect of the inspection process and your staff are probably behaving as most people do when they have survived an ordeal, whatever its scale. Anxiety may have caused many of them to do things by the book during the inspection and avoid the adventurous, the risky or the unpredictable. If this tendency persists in a general mood of anti-climax, then it is hardly surprising if teaching remains cautious and apparently uninspired.

There is, of course, urgent business to be attended to before you set about helping staff recover the enthusiasm of old. A main function of inspection is to provide schools with a useful basis for action in building on strengths and eradicating weaknesses.

You and your governors are responsible for drawing up an action plan in response to the key issues, complete with realistic timescales, resource provision and staff responsibilities. That plan has to be supplied to all parents.

A staff in the weary aftermath of inspection may wish for oblivion for a while, but there is a world watching and waiting for action.

Allocate responsibility for particular aspects to individuals or small groups of staff; ensure that this is an affirmation of your confidence and an opportunity for regeneration for those for whom the inspection has not been auspicious, and an accolade for the successful. Set targets and arrangements for review.

No head should be attempting to cope alone with such vital business. You have a right to expect the full involvement of senior staff and, where necessary, appropriate use of available finances to secure expert advice and support from outside.

In relation to the wider question of staff renewal you may wish to consider some of the following:

- It is not too late to celebrate formally your fine report (some governing bodies acknowledge the work of staff with a party or dinner).
- Try for the next couple of terms to make your INSET programme as varied, enjoyable and memorable as possible; consider an interesting location, and avoid, for this time, basing many of the themes on inspection issues.
- Put particular emphasis for half a term on the creative arts; give pupils and staff an opportunity to have as wide and practical experience as possible of music, drama, dance, painting and sculpture. Bring in, where you can, performers and artists.
- Consider a temporary suspension of at least part of the normal timetable to allow groups of staff and pupils to engage in a pursuit, project or activity of their own choosing.
- Explore the possibility of an initiative that benefits the wider community, ranging from older pupils supporting the literacy pro-

grammes of primary schools, to a range of small-scale environmental enrichment projects.

- The inspection process will have added significantly to your professional awareness and honed your skills. Take advantage of this; consider whether, as a staff, you might devise INSET, guidance and advice for other schools.
- Do a whole school project that taps the creativity, inventiveness and talents of staff and pupils – perhaps a video devised, written, acted and produced together.
- In the end, however, the real solution will be found in teachers' irrepressible urge to respond to pupils' constant interests, needs, demands and enthusiasms.

In the meantime, for schools yet to be inspected, it may be sensible to make provision for the implementation of the action plan an essential part of pre-inspection planning with, where possible, particular responsibilities assigned in advance.

Q   When we are inspected it is inevitable that our children fall below national standards in most subjects. No matter how hard we try, we cannot really make up the difference. How do we explain that to parents without adding insult to injury by suggesting that the blame lies mainly outside the school?

A   I assume you work in an area of social and economic deprivation, where parents' personal experience makes them sceptical of the value of education and they lack the resources and assurance to play a role in their children's schooling.

Many educationists would argue that under-achievement and deprivation are not synonymous and point to substantial evidence suggesting that even the most disadvantaged contexts, especially where they win the support of parents, can be transforming influences in terms of children's achievement.

Equally, there is ground for believing that a majority of children who achieve below national standards live in adverse and impoverished circumstances. It is almost inevitable that most such children will fall below national standards.

Inspection summaries, describing such achievement, will make for dispiriting reading that might drive many parents to one of two chilly conclusions: the school is failing their children, or the children are less able than many of their contemporaries.

I suggest you consider the following:

- As a staff, make an account of the wide range of experiences that you provide, not tellingly reported by inspection, that illuminate children's lives, extend horizons, nurture interests, enthusiasms and pursuits; the expeditions, ventures and projects unique to different classes, the myriad of out-of-school activities. Such things may be most memorable and formative for children. Certainly many parents will value them as much as the achievement that inspection emphasizes.
- Try to define for parents the academic progress the children have made since their first days in school. Such a process of assessment will illustrate the often significant gains that children make in their first years of formal education.
- Use inspection findings as the basis for an ordered, practical programme to improve achievement in targeted subjects. Establish whether children are being intellectually challenged, precisely what pedagogical strategies in relation to differentiation are used throughout the school and how effective they seem to be; whether reading competence, especially, can be extended. Let the parents know about this, at least, and involve them as far as possible.
- Consider ways in which a new generation of parents and children can be supported in terms of pre-school literacy and numeracy.
- Consider using the inspection report as an opportunity for a constructive debate with parents about their children's education. There are always some parents ready for a fresh beginning, especially if encouraged to become involved with the affairs of their children's class, as distinct from the needs of an entire school. Help parents to accept your joint responsibility and vital interdependence in terms of the children's education. Try, hard though it may be, to get children to own books from an early age through sponsorship and book clubs.

Finally, if the report emerges as you anticipate, consider accompanying the summary with brief but clear written comments, highlighting any subjects where you have matched or nearly matched national standards, and those areas where children's efforts have led to positive comments.

Appendix 3.1: The parents' meeting

The RI will begin the meeting by explaining the purpose of inspection and the way in which it will be conducted in the school and the form the report will take. The purpose of the meeting will be described as a chance for the inspection team to hear the parents' views on the school – a statutory requirement. The RI will make it clear that the views expressed by parents will be taken into account as part of the inspection, but the validity of opinions and views will not be commented on by inspectors at the meeting. Parents will be encouraged to state questions and express views in general terms to minimize the possibility of naming or identifying individuals.

Discussion will focus on the following agenda of issues:

- the attainment and progress made by pupils;
- the nature and quality of information, including reports on pupils, provided by the school for parents;
- the quality of help and guidance available to pupils from the school;
- the standards of pupil behaviour and their attendance and punctuality;
- the role that parents play in the life of the school and the contribution they are enabled to make;
- the school's response and attention to suggestions, complaints and concerns expressed by parents;
- the attitudes and values that the school cultivates and develops;
- the quality and appropriateness of homework and the contribution it makes to pupils' education and development.

Appendix 3.2: The order of inspection

- School notified of the inspection date.
- RI contacts the school to discuss the information and documentation required.
- Preliminary visit by the RI to the school.
- Governing body organize the parents' meeting.
- Inspection team inspect the school for the appropriate number of days.
- Feedback to senior managers.
- Feedback to governing body.
- Report of the inspection and summary is provided for the relevant persons.
- All parents receive a copy of the summary of the report.
- The report and summary must be available for inspection by any member of the public.
- Action plan devised, setting out action in the light of the inspector's report.

The following outlines will help to clarify for schools the chronology of events and the form of discussion and interchange between the inspection team, and the head teacher, the governing body and the parents.

The RI, the head teacher and staff

- Initial telephone discussion to confirm inspection dates, to fix date(s) of preliminary visit(s), to explain their purpose and to prepare the school for the process that must be followed when the visits take place.
- To discuss arrangements for the parents' meeting, the arrangement of which will be the governors' responsibility.
- To inform head about documentation required from the school and arrangements for its provision.
- To fix a meeting with staff – should they wish it – on the occasion of the first visit, and to offer opportunity for meeting with the chair of governors on the same occasion.
- Talk about head's form and let the head know that it will arrive before preliminary meeting.
- All these matters will be confirmed in writing by the RI, together

with letter and questionnaire for parents, Ofsted forms for completion by head and copies of 'Keeping your balance', and health and safety proforma.

Preliminary visit to school

At the meeting with the head teacher the RI:

- explains purpose and function of inspection; draws head's and staff's attention to framework;
- describes the entire inspection process up to the publication of the report and the action the school must take afterwards. This account includes:
  - reference to the various ways in which evidence will be collected – classroom observations; discussions with staff, parents, governors; examination of documentation; examination of pupils' work, records of assessment and records of pupils' achievement and attainment;
  - discussions with head, senior staff, heads of departments, co-ordinators;
  - the nature of feedback to staff;
  - the nature, timing, publication and distribution of report;
- discusses the head's form with the head and offers any necessary advice;
- finalizes the details and form of meeting with parents; advises, where necessary, need for letters in other languages; gives details about those permitted to be present, i.e. the parents only of pupils registered at the school at the time of the inspection;
- finalizes arrangements for interviews with senior staff, heads of departments, year and phase leaders, subject co-ordinators;
- arranges dates, times, form of feedback to staff: class teachers, heads of departments, year and phase leaders; finally arranges time and date of oral feedback about whole report to head/senior management team and governors and describes the form it will take;
- arranges for samples of pupils' work to be available to team by first day of inspection; enquires about any 'additional' or unusual activities taking place during the week that the school would wish inspectors to know of; these would include all extra-curricular activities;
- holds a meeting with staff to explain purpose and form of inspection, and to answer any queries they may have;

- makes arrangements for matters such as accommodation of team during inspection, the provision of refreshments, lunches and car parking;
- meets the chair of governors; explains purpose of inspection and the form it will take; provides information about composition of inspection team and responsibilities; describes how report is produced; gives dates of feedback to head/senior staff and governors;
- arranges to meet with chair and, where possible, chairs of sub-groups and especially finance group during the inspection;
- informs chair that information will be sought about the extent of the governors' role in relation to school policies and management for finance and budget; staffing; curriculum, especially RE, SEN and sex education; behaviour and discipline; management and administration, including the annual parents' meeting.

The RI will then make a brief preliminary tour of the school.

On the second visit the RI will:

- collect documentation, Ofsted forms and class timetables;
- discuss the PICSI with the head;
- collect any completed parent questionnaires;
- confirm all arrangements previously made, including dates and times of all interviews, and provision for scrutiny of work samples;
- have extended discussion with head and possibly some discussion with senior staff;
- begin to put together some evidence about main aspects of school for the Record of Inspection Evidence.

On this occasion the RI, accompanied by a colleague as note taker, will hold the parents' meeting.

Following the visits to the school the RI will:

- provide the inspection team with an initial commentary and pinpoint issues for inspection focus;
- require team members to scrutinize all documentation relevant to them and identify issues for inspection focus;
- provide all team members with completed lists of issues for focus;
- complete all routine arrangements for comprehensive coverage by inspection team.

Appendix 3.3: Presentation of oral report to governing body

1 The meeting is the governors' meeting to which RI and others are invited.

2 The chair will normally open the meeting and introduce the RI and companion (normally a member of the inspection team, present to take minutes and help in response to GB questions).

3 RI will explain that one of his/her colleagues will take notes of the meeting for recording purposes but that these will not be circulated or published. Governors may make their own notes, but the report, at this stage, is confidential (this is to be stressed).

4 RI will explain that, when completed, copies of the report and the summary will be sent to the 'appropriate authority for the school' and HMCI.

5 A brief synopsis of the inspection procedure will then be outlined, including the meeting with parents, any special features, numbers of lessons seen, etc.

6 The RI will explain that inspectors' judgements cannot be changed, but that factual inaccuracies and matters arising from those inaccuracies may be corrected. The GB will be given the inspection findings during the meeting so that the published report will contain no surprises.

7 RI will present the inspection findings couched in language that helps the GB understand the message. The exposition is unlikely to last for much longer than 60 minutes. Visual aids, e.g. OHP and transparencies, are sometimes used.

Appendix 3.4: Characteristics of effective schools

1 Professional leadership

Firm and purposeful
A participative approach
The leading professional

2 Shared vision and goals

Unity of purpose
Consistency of practice
Collegiality and collaboration

3 A learning environment

An orderly atmosphere
An attractive working environment

4 Concentration on teaching and learning

Maximization of learning time
Academic emphasis
Focus on achievement

5 Purposeful teaching

Efficient organization
Clarity of purpose
Structured lessons
Adaptive practice

6 High expectations

High expectations all round
Communicating expectations
Providing intellectual challenge

7 Positive reinforcement

Clear and fair discipline
Feedback

8 Monitoring progress

Monitoring pupil performance
Evaluating school performance

9 Pupil rights and responsibilities

Raising pupil self-esteem
Positions of responsibility
Control of work

10 Home–school partnership

Parental involvement in their
children's learning

11 A learning organization

School-based staff development

4
Teaching: Part I

The inspection will treat teaching as the major factor contributing to pupils' attainment, progress and response. Assessment is integral to the teaching process.

There are few elements more important than teaching in the whole of the inspection process or likely to influence more decisively the eventual judgement of the school. The new Framework views teaching in a radically different light from the way in which it was perceived at the beginning of the cycle. Then there were suggestions that teachers need not regard themselves as 'being inspected'; the process, it was implied, was essentially concerned with what the pupils were doing and learning. The new Framework marks a sea change. Ofsted states that their analysis of inspection reports, evidence and grades demonstrate that good teaching is the key to achieving high standards. They were clearly concerned that teaching was 'tucked away' in the first Framework; inspection reports 'often said surprisingly little about it', and it was 'often underplayed' by comparison with 'management systems and other aspects of provision, which were accorded extensive critiques'.

It is important to bear in mind that teaching, like the other elements in the quality of education section, is defined as 'contributing' to the educational standards achieved by pupils at the school, and is judged according to the impact it has on pupils' achievement. However, it is treated by Ofsted as the major factor contributing to attainment, progress and response. Evidence of this is provided by the insistence that inspectors spend at least 60 per cent of their time in classrooms and devote a significant part of that to observing teachers and making judgements on the quality of their work and performance. The balance of these accumulated judgements is likely to have enormous consequences for the final nature of the report, where a commentary on teaching occupies a prominent part; additionally, teaching judged as accomplished is likely to imply positive developments elsewhere. Certainly wherever a school is seen to fall short, and however much teachers may regret that, they are likely to regard as even more important the judgements on teaching, like actors or sports performers analysing their critical notices, and treat favourable comment as powerful vindication of their work.

The current Framework introduces significant new dimensions to the judgements of teaching. First of all, the grading system has been extended to achieve more finely tuned judgements and a more elaborate hierarchy of quality. More worrying, possibly, for teachers is the provision and requirements that those whose teaching is judged to be poor are formally brought to the attention of the governing body. This would obviously have serious consequences for teachers identified as 'failing'. Those who argue that such action is unnecessary, since heads would be well aware of inadequate staff, misunderstand its significance; in fact it formalizes opinions, gives them a kind of imprimatur. In the case of such judgement a head would clearly be expected to take decisive action to guarantee marked improvement and adequate teaching on the part of the person involved. Furthermore, it is possible that management that had permitted such a situation to continue without effective intervention in the first place could itself be called into question.

Whatever the assurances that such instances would be rare, they are unlikely to ease the anxiety of teachers about being inspected. Many believe that inspection is a fallible process and are not convinced that observation of an arbitrary collection of lessons, over a brief period of time, can give a true evaluation of their work. For, conscious that lessons can fail and things go wrong unaccountably, they fear misjudgements for reasons and causes beyond their control.

There is, as we have said elsewhere, a further side to the identification process that might yet become a cause of concern and anxiety. This is the provision for naming teachers whose practice is judged to be very good or outstanding by inspectors. The purpose of this seems clear. It is intended by Ofsted to be part of fresh attempts to make the inspection process more constructive and developmental; such judgements, it is felt, would boost schools, enhance teachers' sense of professional worth and identify valuable models of practice. It might well be a step towards something the profession has often proposed: the notion of a master teacher.

But inherent in this measure are worrying possibilities. Thought needs to be given to the impact on many teachers, capable, conscientious, often long serving, well regarded by parents, whose teaching is judged to fall short of the 'excellent' or 'very good' category. The blow to their professional self-esteem could be considerable. A move designed to raise teachers' morale and enhance their performance could well have the opposite effect for many and, at worst, lead to divisiveness and resentment among colleagues. In Chapter 3 we referred to the sense of deflation and anti-climax that many schools, even those judged to be successful, experience after inspection. It seems likely that the identification process could well exacerbate that.

What can schools and teachers do to ensure that as far as possible their teaching is seen in the best light and that inspectors gain a proper appreciation and understanding of the quality of their work? Teachers will have clear perceptions of what good teaching is about, but for the purpose of inspection it is essential that they take full account of the criteria set out by Ofsted and relate their preparation to that.

The first requirement for inspectors judging the quality of teaching is that they report on the extent to which it promotes the learning of all pupils. It is important therefore for teachers to reflect upon their work in the light of how it affects and influences the learners. Pupils learn in a variety of ways. They learn through play, from a variety of experience, through being given information, being taught and shown how to acquire skills and do things by being instructed; they learn by trial and error, deduction and analogy, by problem-solving of a practical and intellectual kind, by imaginative and exploratory work. If learners were to be treated merely as passive recipients, then their learning would be severely circumscribed. Pupils bring their personal experience, their interests, habits and particular learning strategies, their culture and heritage to the process. Learning takes place across the earliest stages with an emphasis on first-hand sensory experience – play, talk, story, supported discovery, creative activities and carefully timed adult intervention – to a time when the learner can operate in an abstract dimension, capable of sustained rational inference, logical hypothesis, the ability to move successfully from the general to the specific, increasingly autonomous in her/his learning.

A characteristic feature of effective learning, at whichever stage it occurs, is that it is active. Active learning is not to be confused with simply having practical things to do, with lots of activity. It is much more complex than that; it is intellectual engagement with a task or a problem, whatever the age of the learner, that takes her/him eventually to Vygotsky's 'zone of proximal development' where the next step is likely to require supportive and informed intervention. Active learning can apply to a practical task, to a conversation, to simply sitting still and thinking about things. The activity itself may be mental or physical. By contrast, a pupil might be engaged in busy activity which involved little or no active intellectual engagement: passively following through a routine with structural apparatus, concluding a limited literal comprehension exercise, filling in an outline, going through the motions of a science 'experiment', the outcome of which is already known.

Good teaching takes careful account of how pupils learn, provides for it, responds to it and interacts with it. Effective learning takes place where there is concentrated and purposeful exchange between the teacher and the learner.

There is a sense in the profession of a growing emphasis by influential sources on the didactic and transmissional aspects of teaching. But that can only be part, albeit a very important one, of the teaching and learning process.

Teachers' first responsibility is to teach the National Curriculum which is, in effect, an extraordinarily complex mixture of knowledge, skills, ideas and concepts. These can only be mastered through the application of that wide range of learning strategies referred to, and through opportunity for active learning.

Learning of the kind demanded by the National Curriculum is a most intricate matter. Providing for it, as effective teaching does, is equally complicated and challenging, with enormous implications for classroom management, organization and pedagogy. It is in this context that we can consider the various criteria for good teaching that Ofsted suggests and consider how schools can provide for them.

Inspectors will base their judgements of teaching on the following criteria, the extent to which teachers:

1 Have a secure knowledge and understanding of the subjects or areas they teach.
2 Set high expectations so as to challenge pupils and deepen their knowledge and understanding.
3 Plan effectively.
4 Employ methods and organizational strategies which match curricular objectives and the needs of all pupils.
5 Manage pupils well and achieve high standards of discipline; use time and resources effectively.
6 Assess pupils' work thoroughly and constructively, and use assessments to inform teaching.
7 Use homework effectively to reinforce and/or extend what is learned in school.

Let us examine these facets of effective teaching, as defined by Ofsted, and consider how the school may take account of them in preparing for inspection. Items 1 and 2 are dealt with in this chapter, items 3–7 in Chapter 5.

A secure knowledge of the subjects or areas they teach

The teacher needs to know the subject or area thoroughly in terms of the National Curriculum and programmes of study. For the secondary specialist this should present little difficulty in most important respects, and is an area where secondary schools can expect teachers to be at their best. Whatever their skill, their capacity as classroom managers or organizers of learning activities, one can hopefully assume that teachers have retained the enthusiasm and concern for a subject that first attracted them to it. It is the quality that makes many teachers enduringly memorable: their absorption in and passion for a subject and their capacity to infect pupils with it, to reveal further horizons to them, offer new insights, open windows on to other worlds.

Thorough knowledge of a subject will be reflected in teachers' ability to interest pupils, to support the less able and extend and challenge the talented. It will enable them to deal more confidently with the practical demands of teaching: the formation of objectives, the organization of differentiation, the presentation of ideas and information in comprehensible form, the use of effective questioning, supportive feedback, and engaging presentation. Heads of departments and senior teachers have a critical role to play in developing teachers' subject knowledge. In practical terms, they need to do the following:

- provide INSET that analyses and reviews subjects according to National Curriculum requirements so that all teachers feel familiar with and confident about every element. In some cases this will mean new learning for teachers following the Dearing review, particularly in some subjects;
- provide authoritative support through appropriate literature and subject guidelines;
- use textbooks that will constructively supplement teachers' expertise;
- regularly observe, monitor and feed back in relation to the quality of subject teaching;
- systematically discuss the subject as a department or a phase, with teachers contributing, especially about those aspects in which they have a particular interest or specific expertise;
- give teachers the opportunity to observe each other in practice and, where possible, to plan, work and teach together;
- systematically provide brief and relevant aides-mémoire about elements of subjects (see Appendix 4.3);
- provide a personal lead and model in terms of subject knowledge, commitment and interest.

The matter of subject knowledge is infinitely more complicated for primary teachers, responsible, as they generally are, for teaching the whole curriculum to a class. The breadth and complexity of the National Curriculum makes this extraordinarily challenging, even for teachers of young children, as is evident from a glance at just one item, chosen at random from the extensive agenda of skills, information and knowledge that must be taught in any subject at Key Stage 1.

Information Technology	Music	English (Reading)	Science
Pupils should be taught to: recognize that control is integral to many everyday devices.	*Pupils should be taught to:* record their compositions using symbols where appropriate.	*Pupils should be taught to:* identify and use a comprehensive range of letters and sounds, including combinations of letters, vowels and diagraphs and paying specific attention to their use in the formation of words.	*Pupils should be taught to:* construct simple circuits involving batteries, wires, bells and buzzers.

Obviously these are not items of great intellectual substance, but cumulatively, over nine or ten subjects at Key Stage 1, they represent a large repertoire of skills, a considerable body of knowledge and concepts for teachers to acquire and be thoroughly informed and confident about.

Where children at Key Stage 2 are concerned, especially those in the upper half, some of them operating at Levels 4 and 5, a few even flirting with Level 6, then the demands upon their teachers in terms of knowledge are formidable. What can primary schools do to help teachers meet this Ofsted expectation? It is not helpful to pretend that such expertise can be easily acquired; people cannot become expert overnight in so wide a range of subjects. It will be, inevitably, a gradual process.

School leaders need to remember that confidence is a crucial element where subject knowledge is concerned. Competence, for example in a subject such as design and technology, gained from specific training, formal qualification, practical experience or merely deep personal interest, affords a teacher not merely a sense of professional expertise and control, but the reassurance to master other and, especially, related subjects. The wide expertise that all teachers command in at least one subject – and often in more than that – their insight into the relationship of vital skills, knowledge and ideas, and how these can be effectively taught, is a basis for mastering subjects about which they are less confident.

It is widely accepted, of course, that subject knowledge on its own does not make a good teacher. Equally, the more one knows, understands and, indeed, cherishes a subject, the more likely one is to teach it well.

Schools can help teachers to acquire and extend knowledge of subjects by encouraging them to:

- Enhance personal expertise in their specialist subject – or subjects – through INSET and regular reading, and by collaborating with teachers – their immediate colleagues and those in other schools – who share similar interests and expertise.
- Lead on the subject in school or at least take opportunity to provide informal support for colleagues.
- Search for and inform themselves about the connections between their specialisms and other subjects – the natural links between geography, science and maths, for example; the role that IT can play in most subjects and the ways in which their particular subject can promote reading, writing and numeracy.
- Continue to extend their awareness and competence in the core subjects, especially English and mathematics. Despite the undeniable complexity of mathematics at the upper end of Key Stage 2, its generally regular and logical sequential nature, evident in good commercial schemes of work, makes it easier to come to terms with than some other subjects.

Most teachers feel they can approach the teaching of English with some confidence. Several things are particularly important in relation to this central area of the curriculum:

- A thorough knowledge of the teaching of reading so that one commands a range of strategies that can be appropriately applied at any stage of children's development. This, as we shall later see, has important organizational implications for the class teacher as well.
- The ability to help pupils write competently and, especially, with confidence. This, together with competence in reading, does more than most things to give pupils control of and autonomy in their

learning and, as we shall again consider later, provides the teacher with a vital organizational tool.

- Teachers should refer constantly in their planning and preparation to the National Curriculum programmes of study.
- A personal agenda can be made over a period of time for developing teachers' subject expertise; teachers should accept, and be happy to justify, that some areas will not be provided for in the immediate future or cater for children to the same extent that their 'strong' subjects do.
- Teachers should seek the support, advice and expertise of curriculum co-ordinators, especially, and of other colleagues to help with areas about which they are less confident; try their successful ideas and strategies, the things that work effectively for them; ask guidance about materials and professional literature they have found helpful.
- Professional literature, including the old National Curriculum non-statutory guidance, should be used to provide ideas and suggestions. A notion still persists in some quarters that it is mildly improper for teachers to use learning material in this way: that it should all be invented and designed for their particular groups of pupils alone. The truth is, of course, that apart from the fact that the curriculum is just too vast to allow for such constant creativity, it would be quite unrealistic for teachers not to take advantage of the high quality of work across all subjects being achieved by colleagues, often in the same school.

The role of subject co-ordinators is crucial in helping colleagues to develop subject expertise. Ideally they provide the lead through good systematic INSET, the creation of a scheme of work and assessment guidelines, the acquisition, maintenance and up-dating of appropriate and essential resources, the establishment of banks of useful materials, literature and artefacts, the systematic monitoring and evaluation of teaching and learning, and giving practical support to colleagues in their classrooms. The school has to establish a clear programme for such development. Quite obviously it would be quite impracticable for every co-ordinator to be monitoring standards of achievement and working alongside colleagues in classrooms; primary school timetables do not allow for that, apart from which teachers would soon be over-whelmed by competing co-ordinator demands, intervention and input. Schools need to make feasible plans, to devise rolling programmes, whereby a subject or two is accorded main emphasis over a period of time, with the particular co-ordinators receiving priority in the allocation of non-contact time available, to enable them to carry out at least part of their work, especially that which requires their presence in colleagues' classrooms. All co-ordinators can continue to be steadily engaged in particular aspects of their role – the compilation of materials banks, the acquisition of resources, the construction of schemes of work, developments that will support colleagues by being on offer but not mandatory at particular times.

The school will find it helpful to:

- encourage curriculum co-ordinators to put particular emphasis upon establishing valid links between small groups of subjects, by identifying common areas of knowledge, understanding, concepts, skills and ideas;
- build up subject banks of guidelines about strategies, collections of ideas and suggestions, good supportive literature, artefacts, materials, tapes, film and video;
- make collections of effective and successful lessons and especially sequences of lessons in particular subjects. These obviously would not be adopted in an uncritical sense, but could be referred to for inspiration and be adapted where appropriate.

Above all, primary schools especially – and, indeed, secondary schools as well – must provide schemes of work if teachers are to teach effectively those subjects where they lack confidence and expertise.

This is an issue that continues to create anxiety for many schools. Some object to schemes of work on ideological grounds, seeing them as restrictive of teachers' capacity to be creative and spontaneous, to seize upon and exploit the unexpected for learning purposes, to capitalize on pupils' particular learning needs; in some cases there is uncertainty about what is meant by schemes. Most schools now accept, however, that the inspection process has made their use in schools obligatory. As we said in Chapter 3, it is the aspect of documentation about which most schools feel least well prepared.

There are some important points to make about schemes of work:

- They are almost certainly, at their best, one of the most effective and supportive ways of extending teachers' subject knowledge and enhancing the manner in which they teach the subject in the classroom.

- It is likely that not all schools will have complete sets of schemes of work related to all the National Curriculum subjects at the time of inspection; there are all kinds of good reasons for this, to which inspectors will give a sympathetic hearing: the sheer weight of work required to produce schemes; the fact that most schools will be systematically working their way through a programme of development in this respect, beginning with the core curriculum; that many schools reviewed existing schemes, or delayed beginning work on them until after the Dearing review.

- There is no reason why schools cannot adopt schemes of work from other sources: schools and LEAs, for example. There is resistance to this idea in some quarters on the grounds that teachers must have 'ownership' of schemes, must have directly contributed to their creation to ensure that they are meaningful to their practice. In an ideal world, of course, there would be no argument about this. The fact is, however, that making schemes for all the National Curriculum subjects is a massive task for which not all schools have the time, resources, necessary expertise or even energy. Nor do they have the time to allow for delay; while such detailed guidance is unavailable, certain subjects are unlikely to be effectively taught.

Skilled and perceptive teachers can make creative use of reputable schemes from elsewhere, by adapting and adding to them, by selecting the elements they require and discarding what they do not perceive to be useful. Teachers, accustomed to making sense of the changing requirements of the National Curriculum, will not find it difficult to turn other people's schemes to their best advantage. But schemes of work have other important benefits apart from the support they offer in terms of subject knowledge. They make the complicated task of whole school planning much easier and help to provide for differentiation and formative assessment in the classroom. Schemes of work are dealt with in more detail in Appendix 4.1.

The inspection schedule breaks down the criteria against which inspectors evaluate effective teaching into a range of competencies and skills. In relation to the criterion of subject knowledge inspectors will assess teachers':

- competence in planning activities and carrying them out;
- skill in asking relevant questions and providing explanations;
- perceptiveness in marking and responding to pupils' work;
- ability to draw on a range of contexts and resources to make subject knowledge comprehensive to pupils;
- success in providing demanding work for the more able pupils.

Let us consider these in more detail and explore practical ways of helping teachers to acquire, develop and practise them.

Competence in planning activities and carrying them out

This is an area to which inspectors will pay the most rigorous and searching attention. Efficient planning is regarded as one of the essential elements of an effective school. It provides for the systematic teaching and balanced coverage of the vast National Curriculum, ensures coherence, continuity and progression in teaching and learning across a whole school and promotes achievement. Planning is contributed to and underpinned by teachers' subject knowledge.

We deal in detail with planning further on in the chapter when we consider the third main Ofsted criterion for effective teaching.

However, it will be useful for teachers to bear in mind the range of learning activities that may need to be planned for and implemented to meet the diverse requirements of the National Curriculum. They are broadly these:

Problem solving activities

The child will have a clear idea of what s/he wishes to achieve, but may not have an equally clear conception or command of the strategies that are necessary. S/he may, for example, want to make a bed for a doll or a scale model of a motor car. The teacher's intervention here will be concerned with encouraging the child to define the strategies that are necessary, helping her/him to translate these into practice and providing the necessary tools.

Exploratory activities

These will be more open in that the outcomes are less predictable. Because they put the pupils in situations where they do not know what will happen, they are rich in terms of learning potential. Play, science and drama all offer many tasks of this nature.

Practice activities

These demand the rapid application of familiar knowledge and skills to familiar settings and problems. The pupil is familiar with both the content and context of the problem: the demand is not to acquire a fact or a skill, but to speed up and make automatic processes already in the pupil's repertoire. For example, a child who was totally familiar with the process of subtraction might be asked to do as many 'take-away' calculations as s/he could in three minutes.

Enrichment activities

These demand the use of familiar knowledge, concepts and skills in unfamiliar contexts. They extend the range of application of concepts and skills. However, what is being added is not new knowledge as such, but ways of applying that knowledge. For example, children very often know how to multiply, but do not know when to multiply when they see a problem. Sometimes they do not see, for instance, that the problem 'If a metre of ribbon costs 20p, what do 5 metres cost?' demands multiplication. They need to learn when to call on particular skills and knowledge. Typically such tasks take the form of problem solving in mathematics or comprehension in language.

Restructuring activities

These have the pupil working with familiar materials, but s/he is required to discover, invent or construct a new way of working at problems. For example, the task might be directed to lead her/him to invent multiplication as a short cut to repeated addition or to discover a spelling rule. The learner may be given hints, tips or clues to provoke such inventions.

From these examples it is clear that teachers are likely to struggle in providing learning activities of appropriate variety and substance where their subject knowledge is limited. To provide, for example, reading activities and materials that would enable pupils to 'analyse and discuss alternative interpretations, unfamiliar vocabulary, ambiguity and hidden meanings' would require a particular knowledge of literature and an informed understanding of writers' intentions.

As Ofsted points out, planning is obviously an indicator of the degree of subject knowledge possessed by the teacher, but it can also go a long way towards identifying areas where further support is required by her/him if the pupils' learning needs are to be successfully met.

In planning the various learning activities, the teacher needs to keep in mind:

- What learning purposes the activity is intended to achieve, and how well it is matched to the learning needs of a class, group or individual. There is little point, for example, in providing practice tasks for pupils in a process they have already securely mastered.
- The extent to which the activity seems likely to promote a relevant area of a programme of study.

Skill in asking relevant questions and providing explanations

Inspectors will expect informed questioning to achieve the following:

- identify what pupils know and understand about a subject or aspect of it without diminishing their confidence or enthusiasm;
- provide pupils with a secure basis from which to venture further by drawing out what they know;
- help pupils understand that reflective questioning can lead one out of an impasse; suggest possible solutions to problems;
- stimulate enquiry and excite curiosity;
- convey a sense in pupils that they have worthwhile suggestions to make;
- encourage divergent thinking, speculation and hypothesis.

Skilled and subtle questioning of this nature is heavily dependent, of course, on the confidence and awareness that subject knowledge brings. But all teachers, however uncertain they may be about subject elements, can pay particular attention in the planning of lessons to the structuring of a range of questions that seem most relevant to the objectives being taught and most likely to meet at least some of the purposes referred to above.

Perceptiveness in marking and responding to pupils' work

As with questioning, effective marking is considerably dependent on subject knowledge. Some of the functions of marking suggested here may not be fully realized without a thorough knowledge of the subject on the part of the teacher and the capacity such awareness brings with it for analysis, diagnosis and constructive suggestion to the pupil for further development. Skilled marking can play a decisive role in enhancing pupils' learning by:

- displaying concern, interest in and sympathy for their work. This will include rigour, challenge and correction where appropriate;
- acknowledging pupils' efforts and by finding in the most unprom-ising material at least some element on which future development can be constructed;
- encouraging further engagement, study, research and exploration of aspects of work that suggest and indicate particular interest on the part of the pupil;
- illuminating and enlarging what has been presented with the occasional 'This is very interesting; did you know that...?';
- intervening constructively to deal with conceptual errors or misunderstandings that could inhibit progress;
- constantly highlighting the progress being made.

Ability to draw on a range of contexts and resources to make subject knowledge comprehensible to pupils

Here we have a further reminder that effective teaching is something far more complex, subtle and multi-faceted than a transmissional model alone could be, however well presented, organized and argued. Contexts and resources will include that wide range of events, materials, expeditions, artefacts, reference material, multi-media that add to the learners' perceptions and understanding, that illuminate things for them and allow them opportunity for genuine study and engagement. The following are some examples:

- a local study or field visit;
- the use of video material to illustrate modes of living in other cultures;
- the use of computer simulations to construct images of the past;
- artefacts and primary historical evidence;
- maps, atlases and photographs;
- drama to explore issues and problems;
- paired and group work for speaking and listening;
- the use of play areas and activities to stimulate 'writing';
- the provision of multiple copies of texts to encourage group study of a subject, or exploration of a novel.

These things, of course, are second nature to teachers. They need little reminding of their importance for teaching and learning. However, in the heat and flurry of inspections they may often fail to employ them or, more commonly, decide not to, in order to 'play safe' and avoid risky or adventurous activities. It would certainly be understandable for a teacher delivering an 'observed' science lesson on the water cycle to opt for a less demanding and potentially less hazardous demonstration or talk supported by visual aids, in preference to small group experiments requiring a wide range of resources, extensive preparation, increased organizational and control demands and the greater opportunity for something to go conspicuously wrong. But the chances lost will be obvious to a trained observer. Safe, restricted lessons, limited in the range of contexts and resources employed, may ensure sound un-exceptional judgements but, equally, they set bounds to learning opportunity and diminish the possibility of high quality teaching of pupils, and the likelihood of inspectors encountering the best that teachers can offer.

Teachers need to make consideration of contexts and resources an essential part of their planning. They merely need to ask themselves what resource, context or particular opportunity or experience is likely to capture pupils' interest and broaden their understanding.

It is a matter that should be relatively straightforward for subject specialists. One would be justified in expecting the teaching of scient-ists, linguists, mathematicians or geographers to be characterized by regular and effective reference to contexts and resources. Primary teachers, working across a range of subjects, are obviously likely to be less certain in devising appropriate opportunities and identifying – and, indeed, having access to – relevant artefacts and resources. Schools can help in the following ways:

- by providing, in all schemes of work, suggestions for learning con-texts and guidance on resources;
- by setting up easily accessible guidelines to subject resources;
- by the systematic building up of banks of essential subject resources and materials. This would be a co-ordinator's function;
- by having teachers regularly sharing each other's planning;
- by systematic reference to professional literature such as the weekly Primary and Early Years section of the *Times Educational Supplement*.

Providing demanding work for the more able pupils

Very few of the components of effective teaching can be considered in isolation from each other. This is evident here. Setting work that challenges more able pupils has implications for continuity and progression, achievement and differentiation. These in turn are inextricably linked to assessment. Inspection judgements about provision for more able pupils may well condition their perceptions of other aspects of curriculum and practice. It is commonly asserted that schools generally are not particularly successful in providing for the very able. Key Stage 2 provision is particularly vulnerable to such criticism; Ofsted evidence and SATs outcomes seem to suggest that able children are underperforming, particularly in aspects of the core curriculum. Blame for this is often attributed to a lack of subject expertise on the part of teachers.

Schools can expect inspectors to pay particular attention to the issue. It is suggested that schools use formative and summative assessment systematically to provide consistent evidence of pupils' capacity. Without such information, teachers' frequently expressed concern 'to start from where the children are' is likely to prove little more than a pious hope.

What kind of criteria and measures can teachers employ to do this?

There are now clearly defined national 'desirable outcomes' in relation to young children's learning. These can support the use of entry, baseline and development profiles. The National Curriculum provides a consistent range of achievement levels related to national norms. SATs provide standardized test outcomes matched against national norms. Many primary schools are employing standardized testing in addition to the SATs; for example at year 4 to determine levels of pupils' progress and development and to bridge the long interval between the Key Stage 1 and Key Stage 2 SATs. Many secondary schools set children standardized tests in reading and numeracy soon after entry. A majority of primary schools are now emulating what has been common practice with older secondary pupils by moderating work and maintaining examples of levels of achievement. Many schools are also taking account of the relationship between SATs and teachers' formative assessment.

It is difficult, obviously, to challenge more able pupils when there is uncertainty on the teacher's part about the meaning of levels of achievement and, even more critically, how they can be achieved. There is bound to be significantly less chance of a pupil achieving at Level 5 in aspects of a subject where a teacher is not quite certain about what that implies. This difficulty applies particularly to primary teachers responsible for a wide range of subjects. They need to be supported by schemes of work that define progression in practical ways, by banks of support materials and possibly by documented exemplar lessons. Schools need to consider the value of various forms of ability grouping and setting.

The dilemma for secondary teachers in relation to more able pupils is likely to be different. They may be very familiar with subject structures, but may be less in a position to exploit such insight than primary colleagues simply because of the constraints imposed by mixed ability classes working to timetables that do not always provide for prolonged work. Nevertheless, they may find that the following measures encourage more able pupils to give their best:

- Plan learning tasks for three levels of ability.
- Find an opportunity to 'publish' completed work in various ways – photograph or copy it for records, display it in the classroom or elsewhere, make carefully presented compilations, tape the pupils' accounts and descriptions of how they went about the work, send photocopied extracts home to parents.
- Set, where possible, problems that are seen to have a practical application.
- Encourage pupils occasionally to engage in a project for younger pupils: write a book, make a model, construct a game.
- Make marking interactive on occasions, to praise and, at the same time, to encourage pupils to further effort; for example: 'Your description of Lindbergh's great feat is quite splendid. It struck me that it would make a wonderful film. Would you be interested in writing an opening scene so we could see what it sounded like? You'd need to think about characters, setting, how to start it off, perhaps Lindbergh explaining his plans, showing a model of the plane and the way his wife and friends react...'.
- Create an expectation of 'extended' writing from more able pupils.
- Judiciously mix writing tasks with other forms of presentation.
- Provide an opportunity for pupils to word process their work.

This brings us back in both primary and secondary sectors to issues of organization. Once teachers have planned material for, say, three broad groups of ability – with the extremes of ability in much smaller groupings – they then have to consider implementation strategies. They need to decide, for example, whether additional time is allocated to pupils who are likely to enjoy, and are capable of, exploring subjects in depth; decide how this time can be provided for so that pupils do not drift too far from the mainstream curriculum and are helped to maintain a balanced course of study.

Teachers must be careful of their own time management in this respect. It is an understandable temptation to allow pupils capable of independent or small group learning activity to go on too long without intervention.

Teachers need to consider their response to questions likely to be raised by their organization of the learning of more able pupils.

- Who do you mean by more able pupils and how do you identify them?
- Do you base identification on the programmes of study?
- Do you restrict special provision to particular subjects?
- Are there profiles of levels of achievement in the school linked to the National Curriculum that you can refer to?
- Where can you turn for guidance and practical advice and support in creating the tasks that will challenge more able pupils?
- What resources are going to be required?
- How will able pupils be organized to work – in groups or individually?
- What proportion of the total time available can you justifiably and productively devote to more able pupils?
- How do you monitor their work and evaluate the outcomes?

Attention may now be turned to the second facet/criterion of effective teaching defined by Ofsted.

Set high expectations so as to challenge pupils and deepen their knowledge and understanding

This is obviously a critical prerequisite of effective teaching and successful learning. The possibility of a pupil achieving a high level in a particular subject is seriously diminished if the teacher is not certain as to what that implies or requires in terms of teaching, support and essential resources. Failure on the part of teachers to set high expectations is frequently quoted by critics of the education system as a main cause of failure and under-achievement on the part of pupils. Certainly schools will be anxious to avoid in their report any suggestion of low or undemanding levels of expectation. But what exactly is meant by high expectations?

First of all, this is really about match, a concept regarded as central to good teaching and effective learning; in other words, whether a teacher is suitably matching the substance of lessons and learning tasks to pupils' levels of ability and stages of development. High expectations are not simply about what we expect and require of able pupils, but about appropriately challenging and having rigorous expectations of all pupils, whatever their ability. (Though as we shall see elsewhere, when discussing differentiation, the teacher working within the constraints of the average class size will generally have to set expectations for about three broad groupings, rather than smaller groups or individuals.)

Realistically, high expectations are most likely to be arrived at where there is necessary subject knowledge and an informed awareness of the learner's understanding. So teachers need to constantly consider the purposes of learning activities and tasks, which aspects of subjects they are likely to help pupils master and whether they justify, in terms of the outcomes, the time and effort spent on them. They need to be especially careful that learning activities do not become largely occupational, an organizational device to free the teacher to engage for longer periods with particular groups or individuals.

This common practice is understandable in the light of multiple demands on teachers' time. It is likely to benefit only those pupils who receive a favourable share of the time available. But 'occupational' activities – limited comprehension tasks, trivial problems that call for extensive reading, the compiling of maps and graphs that convey little in the way of information – all these betray limited expectations and result inevitably in routine and unremarkable work.

Pupils too are capable of subtly negotiating a reduction in the demands made upon them, so that teachers can almost unwittingly begin to accept routine, 'satisfactory' but increasingly minimal performance. This is not uncommon, for example, with mathematics and writing in primary schools. Teachers can counteract this to some extent by defining time limits for tasks, by giving pupils opportunity to work on 'one-off' mathematics problems in separate and 'special project' books, by frequent variation of writing tasks, from the brief commentary, the informative note, the carefully crafted paragraph about a personal experience, the set of instructions that will facilitate the work of others, the story designed for younger children, to more extended pieces of factual description and imaginative fiction.

Expectations will be realistic where they take account of pupils' ability and stages of learning. This can only be managed through systematic reference to assessment outcomes. We shall refer in detail to this in Chapter 6, The curriculum and assessment.

Teachers' marking can consistently convey high expectations by encouraging pupils to venture further, through a judicious mixture of praise and challenge.

There is a significant link between pupils' presentation of work and their perceptions of teacher expectations. A wide range of presentation is evident across schools and classes, much of it attributable to what teachers require and expect. It is important to remember that the quality of pupils' presentation of work is sometimes accorded a disproportionate degree of significance in inspectors' evaluation of teaching expectations and, indeed, pupils' progress. This is possibly due to the fact that the limited time available to inspectors for detailed study of pupils' work may well lead to undue value being attached to appearance. It would be quite misleading to imply that presentation will be considered by inspectors as important and significant as the content and substance of work, but teachers would do well to reflect on the fact that both pupils and outside observers may come to particular conclusions about teacher expectations from their response to pupils' presentation of work.

Teaching: a checklist for action

- Remember that teaching is judged on the basis of its contribution and nature of its impact on the educational standards achieved by pupils. Review it, evaluate it and work at it in this context.
- Take account of the new grading system (see page 75).
- Consider the ways in which pupils learn (see Chapter 4) and evaluate as heads of departments, subject co-ordinators and class teachers how teaching is providing for these.
- As a whole staff make yourselves familiar with the criteria that inspectors use to evaluate teaching. Apply them yourselves from your particular perspectives.
- Review the ways in which teachers' subject knowledge is enhanced and supported in the school.
- Encourage teachers to adopt appropriate strategies to improve their subject knowledge.
- Review and evaluate the role of subject co-ordinators and the ways in which they work.
- Provide comprehensive schemes of work for core and foundation subjects.
- Ensure that all teachers are familiar with the teaching competencies described in the handbook.
- Provide a marking policy.
- Implement strategies for teaching more able pupils.

These answers in response to questions raised by teachers in the TES column 'An Inspector Writes' touch upon aspects of teaching.

Q How can an inspector recognize a good teacher who is having a 'bad' day?

A This question may be particularly pertinent in the light of the added emphasis on teaching in the new inspection Framework. The possibility of good teachers having the kind of off-days that belie their true ability is serious enough for some HMIs to caution against the use of the inspection process to identify failing teachers. Conversely, it is suggested that incompetent teachers could perform, albeit temporarily, in a way that creates an impression of moderate or even greater ability.

I believe that all this implies a simplistic view of the nature of teaching and the way in which inspection is intended to work.

There is little doubt that teachers of high quality do experience days when lessons go wrong and work falls below their best. Indeed, even within the same day, for the most consistent of teachers some lessons will be conspicuously more successful than others.

Various individual factors, or a combination of them, will be responsible for this: attempts to implement over-ambitious teaching and learning objectives, the adventurous or unorthodox learning opportunity carefully planned but ineffectual in practice, the difficulties of exploring challenging concepts or teaching complex skills, working in a relatively unfamiliar curriculum area, difficult personal or health circumstances on the part of the teacher, an exuberant or fractious class, the reactions of disruptive or exhibitionistic pupils. Add to these the fact that many teachers are genuinely unnerved and adversely affected by the presence of observers, especially those inspecting professional competence. This may apply with particular force to primary teachers, who face the formidable prospect of being evaluated in multiple lessons over a wide range of subjects.

But lessons are not auditions. Of course, good teachers often call upon the performer's arts: energy, vitality and projection in presentation, sharp timing, flexibility and a capacity for improvisation, sensitivity to an audience and the skills to engage, stimulate and exhilarate them, a gift for the memorable effect and the arresting phrase. Such qualities may well be the ones most likely to falter under the strain of inspection.

But good teaching is infinitely deeper, more subtle and complex than such a repertoire of skills alone represents, however valuable they may be to the teacher. It seeks to take the learner beyond mere captivation to intellectual fascination, to an appreciation of myriad ideas and possibilities, the acquisition of competences and skills, and through all of it to a realization of undreamt of personal potential.

Such teaching calls for equally subtle and perceptive inspection that takes account, in its judgements, of a whole range of contributory matters that lie outside the immediate execution of the lesson itself. The new framework reminds us that inspectors will look for evidence of:

● detailed and consistent planning, together with evaluative strategies, not merely for individual lessons, but for sequences designed to achieve continuity, progression and achievement in learning over periods of time;

- the nature and quality of work previously achieved by pupils and the indications it provides of progress made;
- systematic, formative assessment used to plan and inform teaching;
- the way in which teachers interact with individuals and groups of pupils, and the treatment and marking of work, conveys high expectations, supportive and encouraging attitudes and a concern for improvement and achievement;
- illuminating and challenging environments and opportunities provided over time rather than overnight to provide for on-going learning;
- the teacher's personal enthusiasm and subject expertise, her persistent concern to stimulate and promote learning;
- positive and supportive relationships with pupils that flourish only with gradual nurturing, and reflect the mutual regard and enthusiasm of teacher and learner.

It is the capacity to provide for these that makes good teachers and teaching and it will most surely endure and shine through whatever off-days or bad days may befall.

Q   We are beginning to get an impression from other schools of the way inspectors observe individual lessons. It looks as though it would be best for us to prepare a series of one-off 'secondary-type' lessons for the inspection week with the teacher 'up-front', teaching the whole class. We are quite serious about this because we want to show our teaching in the best light. But it is not a primary way of working, where many lessons have the teacher in a low-key role and the children may be carrying on with work from before. What do you think?

A   Certain factors are prerequisites of effective teaching, whatever style and form that takes, and will be evident in the work of good teachers, be they charismatic and high-profile or low-key and unobtrusive. Indeed, many teachers will adopt a range of styles and approaches, depending upon circumstances and the needs of pupils at a particular time.

The characteristics of effective teaching have been consistently documented by Ofsted. They include knowledge and understanding of the subjects and curriculum areas taught and certainly enthusiasm for them as well. The ability to plan well, to assess and build on what pupils know and can do, to make the best use of time and resources, to support, inspire and challenge the learner in terms of involvement, achievement and progress would also be expected. All this certainly implies an ability to convey things clearly, to gain and hold attention, to arouse curiosity and spark enthusiasm.

There is another quality that brings us to your particular dilemma. That is what the Ofsted handbook describes as the ability to 'employ methods and organizational strategies which match curricular objectives and the needs of all pupils'. It is largely that, together with the complexities of managing the curriculum, that make it inevitable that teaching and learning, whether primary or secondary, are not a series of fits and starts, of clearly defined beginnings and endings, of clear, convenient breaks at the ends of lessons.

Inspectors will usually come to observe at the beginning of sessions, though they may leave before the end, especially where the lesson extends into a second period. They will be reluctant to come where sessions are well underway, since it would be distracting for both teacher and pupils. At the beginning of the period, even where work may be largely progressing from a previous lesson, it is likely that the teacher will draw the class together for review, advice or some change of emphasis.

It is probable, too, that long before the lesson ends there will be an opportunity to observe the teacher, displaying at least with a group, her ability to instruct, clarify, question, demonstrate or encourage.

But inspectors will also look for evidence of learning that is built on what has gone before, that it is characterized by continuity and progression, matched to pupils' development and needs and engages them in a protracted way and not just intermittently. They will hope to see pupils with a clear understanding of the purpose of their study, able to organize their work, to secure and use the necessary resources, to know when they need help and to learn collaboratively.

Inspectors understand that effective teaching, whether primary or secondary, is complex and not comprised merely of disparate skills or demonstrated in individual lessons. Just remember to make clear from your general planning that individual lessons are almost certainly part of a larger sequence or whole, whether they be those where the teacher is playing a prominent 'up-front' role or where the children's active involvement and work constitute most of what is on view.

Q We don't seem to hear much about the inspection of under-fives' education, and would welcome advice on the matter.

A Though it is no longer part of the inspection handbook, the technical paper 'The Inspection of Education for Under-fives' in the original handbook is a lucid, down-to-earth and helpful document to begin with.

I don't think one should venture practical advice about probably the most complex, esoteric and important of all educational domains, without some brief 'theoretical' preface, however homespun.

Young children between birth and five, differentiated by personality, experience and background, developing physically and intellectually at a never-to-be-repeated rate, are united by common characteristics as learners. Their learning is achieved out of active engagement with the world around them, through making sense of objects, materials, experience and encounters, through observation, listening and talking, through play, trial and error and experimentation.

It is through this active process that young children acquire, at a personal rate of development, vital skills, a network of concepts that allow them to plan and organize and make sense of experience and, at best, perceptions and attitudes that incline them to be positive, adventurous, responsive, self-reliant and perennially curious.

How might teachers provide for this in practical terms? I think inspectors would hope to see at least something of the following:

- An ordered social context, with secure routines that guarantee children's safety and welfare in what, for many, is their first prolonged separation from home; provision and experiences that reflect and extend the home and maintain partnership with it; organization, teaching and care, informed by a shared staff philosophy, that nurture in the learners a sense of self-esteem and personal worth, and hold high expectations of their potential.
- A rich learning environment that provides, through a broad, differentiated and balanced curriculum, the opportunity for children

to make choices and decisions; to hypothesize and conjecture; to experiment and take chances; to devise and execute plans; to reflect on outcomes; to ask questions, to develop essential physical and manipulative skills; to communicate, collaborate and form relationships; to learn through trial and error and to concentrate and persevere.

- The curriculum will be organized in broad areas of experience; will make appropriate connections, at the relevant stage, with the National Curriculum; will draw together, through integrated activities, various areas of learning. These areas of experience – generally described as aesthetic and creative, human and social, language and literacy, mathematics and physical science, technology, and spiritual and moral – will afford provision and opportunity in at least some of the following aspects of learning experience: paint and 'workshop', sand and water play, cooking, investigation and science, woodwork, music and sound, construction, graphics, books, computers, role play, games and puzzles, visits and outdoor play.

Providing for content and organization of this curriculum will be the main business for under-fives' educators.

- Provision through such a curriculum and environment for language development, and particularly talk, will enable children to question and enquire, to reflect and reason, to make assumptions and draw conclusions, to communicate and form relationships.
- Most vitally, the provision of play enables children to explore the properties and nature of things, to understand how people behave, to represent personal experiences in many ways, to develop skills, to manage objects and artefacts, to be imaginative and inventive.
- Thorough and effective observation, assessment and recording arrangements twill enable teachers to provide most appropriately for children's learning.

Note: Since this was first written very detailed advice on the Early Years Curriculum has been provided by the OFEE document 'Nursery Education: The next steps. Desirable outcomes for children's learning on entering compulsory education'.

Q   We realize that inspectors, when judging the quality of teaching, pay particular attention to differentiation. We think we provide for it. But we find it a complicated matter; we are not confident that what we are doing is adequate and cannot agree about it as a staff. Can you clarify the issue for us?

A   I share your confidence that you are providing for differentiation. Teachers have tried to do so down the ages through some of the following approaches:

- ordering the complexity of learning tasks to match different levels of ability;
- devoting additional time to pupils experiencing difficulty;
- ability grouping;
- the provision of support materials;
- an acceptance of varying levels of achievement, modes of presentation and timescales for completion of work.

Differentiation has often been provided for in random ways, as a spontaneous reaction to pupils' responses and difficulties.

There can be little argument that the diversity of ability and development in any class makes differentiation essential to effective teaching. But differentiation is inevitably affected by the cognitive development of pupils and the peculiar circumstances of key stages.

In the early years phase, for example, there is a constant emphasis on carefully organized environments, the promotion of learning and language acquisition through play, investigation, exploration and experimentation. Differentiation is provided for through the ways in which teachers, guided by observation of children's behaviour and responses, engage them in planned learning experiences.

On the other hand, a group of older secondary pupils will have differentiated needs provided for through carefully ordered questioning, suggestion, constructive criticism and reference to previous academic experience rather than environmental structuring and enrichment.

Primary teachers, often less fortunate than secondary colleagues in the matter of class size, may find differentiation easier to provide for because of more permanent teaching locations and extended contact with the same class and, as a consequence, opportunity to be more flexible in the use of time.

In responding to your question, therefore, it may be helpful to offer a definition of differentiation: the need to match what is taught, and how it is taught, to pupils' abilities and aptitudes. As the Warnock Report put it: 'The purpose of education for all children is the same, the goals are the same. But the help that individual children need in progressing towards them will be different.'

What strategies and methods will provide for such differentiation? The following examples represent some common approaches:

- general learning tasks and assignments are structured at varying and escalating levels of difficulty;
- pupils are organized in different ability groups;
- pupils in the same unit or class work at different stages or strands of a subject;
- teachers base pupils' subsequent learning assignments on current performance; able pupils are given opportunity to study at a more challenging intellectual level;
- pupils are encouraged to pursue areas of particular interest through investigation and research;
- classroom assistants are employed to support pupils with special educational needs or to work with some groups;
- for extra support teachers may call on designated classroom assistants, senior teachers and co-ordinators who may have restricted teaching commitments; Section 11 and special educational needs staff, college of education students, older pupils and parents.

Q   We are Section 11 teachers, employed by a local education authority on a project concerned with teaching English as a second language to bilingual pupils. What expectations will the Office for Standards in Education inspectors have of our work and what will they want to know?

A   You will find the Ofsted publication 'Educational Support for Minority Ethnic Communities' helpful in your work, and in relation to your particular question.

Under Home Office regulations arising from the 1990 review of

Section 11 posts, all bids for new projects had to specify the particular needs of a focus group (such as under-achieving children of a particular ethnic minority group) and give details of the targets the projects were expected to achieve. Projects concerned with teaching English as a second language to bilingual pupils form the largest group of S11 education projects.

Inspectors will probably wish to be informed about the following:

- the precise nature of your project;
- the number of schools and pupils involved;
- the aims, objectives and specific targets;
- how these are to be achieved and evaluated;
- the division of your time between direct teaching and consultative, advisory and support functions to schools and staff;
- the number of stages of English language development to which you work;
- how the stages are defined;
- whether the stages can be related in any sense to National Curriculum levels;
- how you decide when children are competent to progress from one stage to the next;
- how you identify the precise needs of ESL learners in English and the extent to which you take the following factors into account: previous educational experience, including literacy in the first language; experience of schooling; disrupted patterns of education; familiarity with the Roman alphabet; experience of spoken English at home; age, in the case especially of late arrivals; the learning environment, including the amount and type of indirect support available, for example access to peer group support; opportunities for interactive learning; classroom organization; opportunities for use of the first language in learning;
- the assessment, recording and reporting processes used;
- how effectively these evaluate pupils' progress and achievement and enable schools to adapt their teaching approaches, and match the work to pupils' needs;
- how you monitor the impact of the project on teaching and learning and children's achievement;
- how it is helping ethnic minority pupils 'to achieve standards commensurate with pupils of similar age and ability';
- how you operate in schools;

- how you decide on a balance of direct teaching and advisory support and monitoring work;
- how you make an impact on the quality and orientation of mainstream teaching and raise awareness of the needs of ethnic minority pupils throughout a school;
- how you disseminate good practice.

The degree of expectation implied in these questions may help to explain why many LEAs took the opportunity afforded by the new regulations to give Section 11 teachers a better career structure by upgrading posts.

Appendix 4.1: Schemes of work

It is becoming clear that in order to teach the National Curriculum, comprised as it is of a wide and mandatory range of subjects, each one representing a hierarchy of complex skills, knowledge and concepts, detailed schemes of work are necessary for all subjects.

These need to contain watertight plans for progression and continuity in both teaching and learning and also to reflect an informed understanding of the curriculum pupils have already experienced and what they should progress to in the future. They should also enable teachers to translate the programmes of study into effective, practical classroom activities.

What exactly are schemes of work and why are they so important?

- They are detailed guidelines to ways of providing the knowledge, skills, concepts and understanding that pupils must acquire in all subjects.
- They suggest relevant teaching and learning activities, which are linked to the programmes of study, and are designed to achieve such objectives.
- They help to maintain the critical balance between practice and reinforcement of skills and the acquisition of new learning.
- They provide advice about resources, equipment and materials.
- They support progression and achievement.
- They provide suggestions for the *differentiation,* upon which match, progression and continuity are so dependent.
- They indicate elements for assessment.
- They suggest ways of making cross-curricular links and integrating subjects.
- They can offer guidance on the development of particular complex skills and processes such as drafting.
- They suggest ways of promoting genuine collaborative group work.
- Most vitally, they provide the way to detailed planning. Because they provide detailed suggestions for continuity and progression, schemes of work simplify the vital and difficult business of whole-school planning and help to ensure coherence across the school.

Schemes of work are clearly of great potential value, but in many quarters there is continuing resistance to their use.

What are the drawbacks and disadvantages?

It is suggested that:

(a) *Schemes of work restrict the teacher's capacity to be creative and spontaneous, to seize upon the unexpected, to capitalize on children's particular interests.*

On the other hand, it could be argued that good schemes, prolific in terms of ideas and suggestions, provide secure frameworks supportive of flair and inspiration within which teachers can afford to be creative.

(b) *The emphasis schemes place upon individual subjects artificially fragments pupils' experience and is incompatible with the way they learn.*

Of course there is a real danger here. However, the fact that the National Curriculum is defined in subject terms does not mean that teachers cannot venture outside the subject boundaries to make cross-curricular connections. It is impossible to engage with any subject, for example, without English being massively involved. But, most important of all, many subjects can be built on as the lead elements in projects, referring to and drawing upon other subjects.

(c) *Subject-based schemes are so overloaded with detail that cumulatively they create an impossible management problem for teachers.*

Of course the curriculum is overloaded. Managing it is one of the largest problems facing primary schools. Schemes, however, can lighten that burden rather than add to it because they clarify the critical elements that have to be taught, and provide learning programmes that select judiciously.

If you decide to make schemes on your own – and not become involved with other schools in the process – then be quite single-minded about selecting a small group of subjects to begin with and complete them one at a time. Unless you are a very large staff, anything else is likely to prove quite impracticable. It might be advisable to begin with the core curriculum subjects, if only because you are liable to find a considerable amount of useful relevant curriculum material already in existence that you can draw on.

How to put schemes of work together

- Decide who is going to be responsible for leading on the subject – in many cases this will be the subject co-ordinator – which members of staff may be called upon for support; and how much time, including non-contact time, will be available to them.
- Consider whether the co-ordinator, or even the working group, will have an opportunity to visit other schools and LEA subject or resource centres, to see relevant materials and literature that may be already available there.
- Investigate whether you might link up with other schools or other co-ordinators engaged in a similar process. It may be possible to exchange and share ideas, materials and experience.
- Make the closest possible link between your scheme of work and the National Curriculum programme of study.
- Don't forget to refer to the valuable advice and ideas contained in the old non-statutory guidance if this is still available to you.
- Remember that you will certainly have in the school a great deal of valuable material, indeed the basis of powerful schemes, collected and put together by teachers over the years. Among them will be collections of ideas and suggestions that can enrich anything you do.
- Don't hesitate to use reputable schemes of work now being developed by growing numbers of LEAs and schools and study them thoroughly. Once purchased, adapt them, amend them, add to them and turn them to your particular purpose.
- Involve, if possible, as part of your working group, a secondary subject specialist, or a skilled advisory teacher.
- Don't forget to build in formative assessment opportunities.
- Try to provide for three broad levels of differentiation, with the main bulk of the work directed at the 'average' pupils.
- Invite your fellow co-ordinators to evaluate the draft scheme. Offer it to good specialists for comment and advice.
- Pilot parts of it with Key Stage 1 and 2 children, and perhaps with year 7 in a secondary school.

Appendix 4.2: A summary of desirable outcomes for children's learning on entering compulsory education

The DFEE in conjunction with SCAA has published 'Desirable Outcomes for Children's Learning on Entering Compulsory Education'. These are categorized in six areas of learning:

1 Personal and social development
These outcomes are about children's ability to interact and co-operate with groups and individuals other than the family; linked to personal, social, moral and spiritual development, they are concerned with children's personal development, sense of self and relationships with others.

In practical terms, children will:

- have positive perceptions of themselves, be outward-looking and confident about trying things and seeking and responding to experience;
- relate well to others and work co-operatively in groups;
- be capable of working on their own, getting on with and completing tasks, seeking and using the support of others;
- be interested in finding solutions to problems and answers to questions; they will express and try out their ideas;
- be mastering a wide range of practical skills, developing awareness of the resources they need for tasks and how to use them;
- be developing an understanding of appropriate behaviour; showing concern for the feelings of others and being able to respect their will and intentions. They will allow others their share and opportunity to lead, use things, be in charge and take control;
- be demonstrating a growing understanding of the difference between right and wrong and the desirability of the former in terms of behaviour, response and treatment of others;
- begin to appreciate the environment and living things and understand that they have a responsibility to care for them;
- begin to show themselves capable of a range of feelings and emotions, of wonder, awe, pleasure, joy and sorrow.

2 Language and literacy

These outcomes are about the growth of language and competence in literacy, about children's developing capacity in speaking and listening, reading and writing.

In practical terms, children will:

- talk about and describe their own experiences and listen to the experiences of others. They are interested in stories, songs and nursery rhymes. Their vocabulary and command of language structures are developing; they use them effectively and appropriately to describe, question, express their feelings and concerns, to share ideas, to give accounts and tell stories;
- begin to develop critical early reading skills: understanding what books are about, how they are put together, how they work and how they should be managed. They know how books are read. They begin to recognize and name letters; to know how they sound. They recognize certain words: their own names, words from TV, the names of shops, food, characters in books, street names, the names of animals and pets;
- begin to understand what writing is for and write in various ways themselves – inventing letters, using shapes, symbols, letters, words they know to convey messages.

3 Mathematics

These outcomes are about the initial stages of mathematical awareness. In practical terms, children will:

- use certain mathematical language about shapes, the position of objects, whether things are bigger or smaller, the names of numbers;
- recognize and be able to make patterns;
- recognize, name and use numbers - usually up to ten – but be able to talk about larger numbers;
- count, put things in order and sequence, match things on a one-to-one basis;
- record numbers and solve simple mathematical problems.

4 Knowledge and understanding of the world

These outcomes are about the earliest stages of children's understanding of issues in geography, history, science and technology, their developing awareness of the larger world, and the immediate environment, its natural and constructed features. They begin to take account of the place and role of other people in the environment.

In practical terms, children will:

- demonstrate interest in and knowledge of the environment and an ability to describe and discuss it;
- demonstrate awareness of the features that make up the environment, constructed, manufactured, natural and living;
- be aware of how the environment changes and develops;
- use materials in the environment for a variety of purposes;
- begin to develop a range of technical skills and the ability to select and use appropriate instruments and materials to make, build, join things, and construct.

5 Physical development

These outcomes are about children's growing physical competence, their acquisition and mastery of physical skills, their capacity to be co-ordinated, to control their physical movements, to use space safely and constructively, to manage various environments.

In practical terms, children will:

- show themselves capable of managing space safely and effectively, both alone and when sharing with others;
- manage effectively a range of materials and equipment;
- climb and balance safely;
- manage tools and equipment for their proper purpose;
- control balls;
- work effectively with a variety of apparatus.

6 Creative development

These outcomes are about the development of the imagination, creative capacities, of the ability to communicate in a variety of ways and through a range of materials.

In practical terms, children will:

- respond in various ways to sensory experience;
- respond to story, music and dance;
- turn increasingly to materials, tools, equipment and instruments to convey their feelings and ideas;

- demonstrate ability to listen, observe and be involved in activities for prolonged periods;
- respond imaginatively to experience.

Appendix 4.3: Examples of aides-mémoires for aspects of a subject suggested by curriculum co-ordinators. This kind of material will valuably supplement schemes of work

Discussion of novels with experienced readers might take the following form:

- What is there about the book, either in terms of character or events, which make it worth telling as a story?
- What makes it different from ordinary routine life?
- Are there events or characters that are not strictly necessary to the story?
- Can you think of a change to a single character or event that would alter the whole course of the story?
- What do you learn about the nature of the characters from the dialogue?
- What does the author do to make you understand what his or her characters are like?
- Does the writer tell you what they are like, do other people in the story give you information about them, or is it through their own language and behaviour that you know?
- Is the ending predictable?
- Does this detract from the enjoyment of the story?
- In what types of stories should the endings be difficult to predict?
- Are there events and characters in your life that could be developed to make a story, play or film? If so, say why you think they are suitable and how you would go about making a story or a play based on them.

Writing themes

Some general points should be made before themes are introduced:

- With some themes and on some occasions, give the children a set period of time; 20 minutes for children at Keystage 2, 10 to 15 for younger ones.
- Give them support before they begin by discussing the piece, by putting words and phrases on the board or on a sheet of paper given

to them, by helping them to decide a simple structure and then first getting them to put their thoughts on paper.

- Encourage them to have a go, to put down what they want to say. While they are working, look at as many as you can and make a few suggestions for improvement.
- The pieces could be written in a drafting notebook/writers' journal kept specially for that purpose and then re-drafted in their regular writing book. You would need to vary this with younger children, for whom in many cases the first effort would be the only one.
- In all cases discourage any idea that the drafted first attempt can be written in any old way. This leads to slovenly writing, which children find very difficult to turn off.
- Be cautious about children being required to re-draft whole pieces by writing them out again. Consider re-drafting one or two pieces that can be written out on different pages, or even done in some cases on a scissors and paste basis. More capable children manage this well and enjoy it. By showing the process at different stages in the notebooks, children build up very impressive-looking evidence of how the writing is developing.
- By helping them with the structure of pieces nothing more ambitious is meant than something along the lines of:
  - for younger children:
      ...the audience for whom it is written and who the narrator is;
      ...a beginning, middle and conclusion;
  - for older children:
      ...a location, a time line or sequence of events;
      ...whether action moves backwards or forwards in time;
      ...whether dialogue could be used;
      ...the nature of the characters.
- Encourage children to *read over* completed pieces and to read them to a partner.
- Some children can be encouraged to offer comments to each other.

Themes
- Physical descriptions and character.
- 'Snapshots' – a few paragraphs – of people they know.
- 'Snapshots' – of specific objects: toys, kitchen utensils, etc.
- Encourage arresting openings:
    'It stands on the table like...'

- 'You would never think/imagine...'
- 'The first time I ever saw one...'.
- For young children, writing letters, complete with envelopes.
- Making books about creatures, objects, artefacts, toys, bicycles, etc., along the lines of 'looking at tiny creatures'.
- For young children, making lists:
  - 'likes and hates' list;
  - 'things I can do' list;
  - 'things I am learning to do' list;
  - 'people I know' list;
  - 'things to take with you' list for holidays, visits to grandparents, days out.
- Making their own alphabet book.
- Making up dialogues or 'thought' bubbles for characters in a book.
- For older children:
  - their greatest dread or phobia;
  - what they anticipate about secondary school;
  - what they regard as the four/five most memorable things in their primary school life, starting with their time in nursery/infant school.
- If teachers have time to make up and provide wallets, cases, boxes, with different materials, possessions, artefacts and documents, children could be encouraged to write detective reports or speculations about the owner of the wallet, the person who owned the case (business, occupation, personality, etc.), or the place where the box came from. Writing could be accompanied by labelled drawings of the artefact.
- For less able children, photocopy printed versions – perhaps written out by the teacher – of stories read and told, cut up the versions, leave out the occasional word or phrase, put in an envelope and get the children to re-assemble and paste neatly in their books. Put a brief note with such stories to indicate for visitors how the process was managed and what the purpose was.
- Write descriptions/instructions for tasks and jobs: how to use a camera; a video recorder; a tape recorder; a calculator; a word processor; a mariner's compass.
- Write about how to: toast bread; feed a baby with a bottle; make a phone call; shampoo hair; ride a bicycle (including safety pre-cautions); use a tin opener; iron a handkerchief; make a cheese salad sandwich.

- Ask children to give reasons why they could not do the following jobs: dentist; pilot; sailor; mountaineer.
- Devise three tests for an alien who can disguise him/herself as an earthling, but does not yet know all our conventions.
- Snapshot biographies of themselves, friends and people in school:
  - 'I wonder if you know my friend...'
  - 'The first time I was sent to the head's room...'
  - 'I wasn't that keen on him at first...'
  - 'Let me just tell you about our baby...'
  - 'The funniest person I know...'.
- A lifeline, i.e. children select five most important items in their lives, do cartoon-type illustrations and write captions, paragraphs, about each one.
- Write a brief guide to the school. (This could be done on a more ambitious group basis and presented to visitors, including inspectors.)
- A guide to the immediate outside environment.
- A description of their journey to school.
- Biographies of school staff to go into a book.
- Brief speculation about what might happen or be done in certain emergencies: a dog runs into the playground while the children are at play; a tarantula spider climbs out of a box delivered to the school kitchen; the school is cut off from the surrounding neighbourhood by a sudden flood; a rare bird from abroad settles exhausted in the school courtyard.
- Create a context for certain statements: 'That'll teach him not to do that again'; 'All we know is that it was quite tiny when it was washed down the drain'; 'At first we thought it was just a strange light in the sky'; 'Don't touch it whatever you do!'.
- Describe how particular jobs are done: mending a puncture; building a sandcastle; making a puppet; making a boat that will sail from scraps and how it can be steered.
- Create scenes/stage sets for 'small world' figures and describe them, e.g. a collection of small ducks sailing on a 'glass' pond with a castle in the background.
- Re-telling big book stories, 'We're going on a Bear Hunt'. This can be done as a whole class lesson with the teacher writing the drafted contributions on the board; then the children can write it from memory or with their own amendments. A variation would be to

give the children a copy of the original, or part of it, to paste in their books to contrast with their version on the opposite page.

- Ask children to write up science experiments as a description of what they actually did, why they did it (to prove hypothesis), how they tested it, and what they think they found out.
- Do a garden/patch of ground observation book on the school court-yard, with drawings, between now and April.
- Write about three/four things most precious in their lives after their family: material possessions, songs, stories, clothes, places; and why; the things they would take to a desert island.
- Encourage children to make applications for classroom/school jobs and positions of responsibility.

This aide-mémoire offers advice to newly qualified teachers from mentors.

- Ensure that your practice is in line with school policies.
- Compare the quality of samples of the work your pupils do – for example in writing and mathematics – with similar work in parallel classes or in a year group below or above yours. Check for consist-ency of marking style.
- Work out strategies to provide for differentiation, that is, the different levels of ability and development in the class; think about three broad bands of ability and plan lessons and pupils' work in relation to these.
- Develop strategies, materials and activities for developing the pupils' autonomy and independence as learners – word banks, number tracks, taped stories, a wide range of reading materials, group tasks such as diaries, logs, handwriting cards, personal projects and pieces of research, science, history, geography and mathematical puzzles and games.
- Identify curriculum elements for weekly assessment with particular groups of pupils.
- Regularly evaluate the balance of pupils' activities between 'prob-lem solving' and 'practice'.
- Briefly evaluate the effectiveness of your work at the end of each week. Identify some of the things you have taught the pupils.
- Make yourself as informed and expert as possible about the initial stages of reading.

- Think about your reading policy. How often and in what way do you hear pupils read? What other reading experiences do they have outside their 'reading book'? Do they have opportunities to talk about their reading books to an adult or another pupil or pupils? How do you help less able readers? How do you challenge competent readers?

- Make yourself familiar with a range of good fiction and stories for telling in relation to your particular subject or subjects.

- Monitor the balance of subject provision in your class, especially if you are working through projects/topics/themes.

- Observe the 'pace' at which pupils work; talk about it with colleagues. Decide whether you are satisfied with it.

- Focus on a part of your classroom each half-term for developing, enhancing, improving.

- Regularly collect and file ideas and suggestions from educational magazines such as *The Times Educational Supplement*.

- Set yourself a regular programme of about an hour or so each week of educational reading. Keep abreast of topical events by reading the TES; subscribe to at least one educational journal.

- Create as rich a language environment as possible in your classroom with samples of pupils' writing, quizzes and puzzles related to displays, interactive labels and captions that pupils can be responsible for maintaining.

- Begin to make yourself expert in an area of the curriculum, or of pupils' learning, other than your own subject.

- Regularly review and discuss with pupils displays and centres of interest in class.

- Take every opportunity to watch other colleagues' teaching; take particular notice of things like pace of lessons, teacher expectation of achievement, provision for differentiation, style of questioning and interchange between pupils and teachers.

- Find a colleague with whom you can regularly share and discuss your work.

- Draw on your own particular interests, experience, special knowledge and areas of expertise in any fields – whether these be gardening, music, mechanical toys, sailing, mountaineering, photography, knitting, mini beasts, astronomy, local history, stained glass, cooking or whatever – to enrich the life of your classroom and the learning of your pupils.

- Plan ways that will ensure regular and efficient collection of pupils' work, especially where this extends over protracted periods of time.
- Plan for productive and harmonious beginnings and ends to days; ask pupils at the end of the day to briefly review and recount what they feel they have learned and found memorable.
- Introduce an interactive element into your marking that regularly, but not on every occasion, sets a question or a challenge that will encourage pupils to study or pursue a particular matter further.
- Keep a regular check on individual pupils' progress; involve pupils in this by discussing selected pieces of work with them, however briefly.
- Identify, on a regular basis, aspects of your own teaching and work that you feel are developing and being successful.

5

Teaching : Part II

Schools will find that few aspects of teaching receive more stringent attention from inspectors than planning in its various forms: whether it be that of whole school, phase, year group or the individual teacher. This reflects the more pronounced emphasis in recent years on the importance of whole-school curriculum coherence on continuity and progression in pupils' learning, on matching content to pupils' ability and development and on raising levels of attainment. It is generally accepted now that without effective planning such educational objectives stand little real chance of being achieved. Most obviously a complex National Curriculum is dependent for its implementation on detailed planning throughout the school.

What we are considering here is the planning required of the individual teacher. Clearly unless teachers plan within a whole school context it will be almost impossible to guarantee curriculum coherence, continuity, progression and satisfactory attainment. Therefore individual teachers' planning will have to take account of the aims and intentions of the school development plan, and, in more detail, of phase, departmental and year group planning, and the development plans that curriculum co-ordinators have laid down for individual subjects. For this reason we stress again that good subject schemes of work are essential to effective planning. They provide a picture of what is happening in subjects at different stages throughout the school and a map of the learning terrain that pupils will be travelling across. Theoretically a good maths scheme should chart pupils' mathematical experience through the whole of their school life. The schemes themselves have to be translated, of course, into meaningful classroom activities timed, differentiated, resourced and carefully managed.

Effective planning calls for more than references to schemes of work, however detailed and constructive these may be. Clearly there are other factors to take into account, not least where individual pupils are located in terms of their personal learning. Planning is significantly dependent on efficient assessment and informative records.

The Ofsted criteria define the following as being characteristic of good teacher planning:

- teaching in a lesson, session or sequence of lessons has clear objectives for what pupils are to learn and a clear idea of how these objectives will be achieved;
- the differing needs of pupils are taken into account;
- there is evidence of teaching intentions and how they will be met;
- there is coverage of the areas of learning for under-fives;
- the National Curriculum programmes of study are incorporated;
- there is a statement of clear objectives;
- there is a summary of what pupils will do and the resources they will need;
- there is clarification of how knowledge and understanding can be extended and the work adapted to suit pupils.

Inspectors pay particular attention to structure and progression in the planning of topics which involve a number of subjects. The planning should indicate very clearly the learning objectives and how teaching will be organized to challenge pupils, and provide evidence that continuity and progression in each subject has been considered.

Where possible, inspectors should also discuss with teachers the context of the session or lessons, how the lesson fits into a longer-term plan and why, for example, particular methods are used.

In nursery and some primary classrooms and in particular secondary departments, inspectors will be required to consider how support staff are used, how they are informed about teaching and learning objectives, and the extent to which they are involved in planning.

Let us consider first planning in relation to the teaching and learning of children under five.

Planning to cover the areas of learning for under-fives

Teachers of young children under five, whether they are located in nursery settings or mainstream classes, will find it helpful to relate their planning to the DFEE's 'Desirable Outcomes for Children's Learning on Entering Compulsory Education'. The objectives they describe give teachers clear targets to plan and aim for. For example, in language and literacy it is stated quite explicitly that children begin 'to associate sounds with pattern in rhyme, with syllables and with words and letters. They recognize their own names and some familiar words. They recognize letters of the alphabet by shape and sound. In their writing they use pictures, symbols, familiar words and letters to communicate meaning, showing awareness of some of the different purposes of writing. They write their names with appropriate use of upper and lower case letters.'

There is a similar degree of specificity in relation to mathematics. Children are expected 'to be able to use language to describe shape, position, size and quantity, to be familiar with number rhymes, songs, stories, counting games and activities. They should be able to compare, sort, match, order, sequence and count everyday objects. They should be able to recognize and use numbers to 10 and be familiar with large numbers from their everyday lives.'

Such detail about learning objectives makes it easier for inspectors to evaluate both the quality of young children's learning and the effectiveness with which teachers plan for it.

At the beginning of Chapter 4 we talked about the various ways in which pupils learn. Young children, especially, learn through play, practical first-hand experience, through opportunity for talk and, especially, in response to careful adult intervention through questions, suggestions and explanation. Young children require extended periods of time that allow for sustained involvement in particular activities.

They need opportunity for observation and reflection, for investigation, exploration and experimentation, for discovery through trial and error and guided experience. Their whole development, cognitive, physical, social and emotional, will take place most effectively within flexible timescales that allow for wide variations between children and fluctuating growth within children themselves. At the same time there will be a clear recognition of the significant experience and wide-ranging skills they bring to the business of learning, at this stage perhaps the most significant of their entire lives.

Planning for this most complex area of children's learning will require teachers to focus on:

- the learning environment and particularly appropriate resources;
- the structuring of a wide range of particular learning activities;
- the maintenance and extension of learning activities in the home;
- the use of all learning activities to promote the outcomes identified in the six main areas of learning;
- the promotion of linguistic and literacy competence;
- the effective use of time;
- the provision for detailed observation, assessment and evaluation by the teacher and other involved adults.

So, for example, a teacher planning for learning in the area of language and literacy would be likely to place particular emphasis on resource provision and organization as an essential starting point. Out of children's interaction with carefully selected materials and a subtly structured environment will come developments in language and literacy: a wide range of talk and modes of conversation, enriched vocabulary and developing fluency, the capacity to 'express thoughts and convey meaning to the listener, to respond to story, songs, nursery rhymes and poems, to make up stories and confidently take part in role play, to enjoy and begin to understand books; to make marks, patterns and emergent writing that represent and convey messages, notices, instructions, accounts and descriptions'.

Planning for the other main areas of learning and development will place a similar emphasis upon appropriate resources and on carefully organized and ordered learning environments, all designed to promote the learning objectives identified in the main curriculum areas.

Teachers, however, recognize that such objectives or outcomes –

linguistic, mathematical, scientific, physical, creative, the development of personal social, spiritual and moral qualities – are not achieved merely through resourcing and environment, however appropriate, effective and specifically organized they may be.

So activities, inspired in the first instance in many cases by the challenge and stimulus of resources and environment, are in turn enriched and extended as learning opportunities to achieve particular objectives by subtle and well-timed teacher intervention, question and suggestion. Activities will vary in length and time depending on the degree to which children become involved, the demands and distractions from other sources, the need for specific time-demarcated sessions with adults. It is accepted that there will be a variation on the amount of effort children put into tasks, dependent on individual interest and development, the particular demands and intrigue inherent in the activity, the timing and effectiveness of adult intervention.

There will be greater flexibility in the use of time in pre-school settings. The length of children's engagement in particular tasks is as likely to be determined by their degree of interest and involvement as it is by a timetable. That is not to imply that time is wasted or casually organized or managed. One of the characteristics of good pre-school education is the degree of absorption and involvement in a whole range of activities achieved by children.

Learning activities will be planned round a variety of contexts, as suggested below.

- through individual subject areas, e.g. science

	Suggested topic heading
Living things	
Planting/growing (vary conditions for growing)	● Food
Group plants according to particular characteristics, e.g. flowers/no flowers; colour of plants; shape of leaves	● Minibeasts ● Pets
Make collections of plants from the local environment	● Growth and change
Explore the differences between plants and animals	● Babies

Suggested topic heading

Living things

Observations from walks in the local area • Ourselves

Caring for animals in the classroom • Plants

Observe similarities/differences in hair • Keeping warm and
  colour, height, eye colours, etc.   keeping cool

Collection of photographs, families, babies

Explore ways of keeping clean and healthy

Environment

Change focus in the imaginative play area • Materials in the
  (e.g. shop; travel agents)   environment

Looking at the local area and identifying • Our school
  particular features   • Buildings

Collections of waste products to be used for • Weather/seasons
  junk modelling/interest tables, etc.   • Looking at holes

Bury a small range of materials in soil.   • Animal homes and
  Check after a week – what has   habitats
  happened?   • Change in the weather

• through topics and centres of interest

A group of children observed a nearby building site over a period of time. They drew pictures, used outdoor play equipment to simulate scaffolding, made junk models of lorries, diggers, bulldozers and cement mixers, adopted and played out various roles, built 'brick' walls with shoe boxes, wore goggles, wellington boots and hard hats for 'tarmac spreading'. They made simple pulleys and rubbish chutes. They discussed jobs with some of the workmen; they made a book as a record of development.

• arising from a resource, in this case a series of books about the sea and the seashore

Teachers planned an outing to the 'sea side', that took place entirely within the confines/context of school and grounds. Children discussed what they knew and had learned of the sea from experience and their books; they decided what they would do when they arrived there. They made lists of what they would need to take and packed bags and cases for the trip. Towels, bathing costumes, sunglasses, hats, buckets and spades, nets and binoculars were made ready. A picnic was prepared. They travelled by train comprised of chairs and tables in the hall, managed and organized by a group of the children. They disembarked at the seaside (in the playground), played in the sand and 'rock pools' set out there, swam and rested in deck chairs under large umbrellas, explored caves, climbed cliffs, visited the lighthouse, went for boat trips round the bay, played on the fairground activities, viewed the horizon through telescopes and binoculars. They dipped in the rock pools and played beach games. They watched a Punch and Judy show. Finally they had sandwiches, cakes and ice-cream before returning home on the train.

● through a particular classroom area, e.g. sand and water provision

---

Sand
Exploring dry sand with fingers and magnifying glasses
Looking at the way sand goes through sieves and funnels
Sand flowing through a variety of sizes of holes
Making sand cones
Finding hidden objects in sand
Pouring water through channels in sand
Exploring wet sand with hands
Comparing wet, dry and damp sand
Comparing different containers of sand – full/empty/heavy/light

Water
Water play – plastic bottles with several holes same/different sizes/
  positions
Using a plastic water pump
Capacity of containers
Siphons
Making a water clock, e.g. dripping paper cup
Making a bottle 'xylophone'
Water as a magnifier – looking through drops of water and containers
Water pressure – balloons under water, hand in a plastic bag under
  water
Dyes in water
Mopping up spills – cloths, sponges, paper towels
Ice and water – melting ice in cold water, hot water, etc., and timing

Surface tension – floating pins on water, then adding soap solution
Observing drops of water from a variety of sources, e.g. pencils, lollies
falling onto various surfaces. Listening to splashes
Ripples of water
Blowing soap bubbles
Dissolving kitchen 'chemicals', e.g. salt, flour, washing powder, in
water (**care** – see Association for Science 'Be Safe')
Floating and sinking
Making boats – powered and unpowered
Weight of things in water
Cooking

But such activities will not be arbitrary or unrelated. Teachers will
plan carefully to achieve through such contexts the skills, attitudes,
competence and understanding prescribed in the 'desirable outcomes'.
For example, the activities described will have provided opportunity
for:

- Different kinds of talk; for logical sequenced explanation and
  description; for giving instructions and conveying information; for
  questioning and obtaining advice; for making up stories and playing
  roles; for referring to books and gaining information and ideas from
  them; for using various devices, pictures, symbols, familiar letters
  and words to communicate experiences and ideas in 'writing'.
- Mathematical experience, including number recognition, counting,
  comparing, sorting, matching, ordering and sequencing; for using
  mathematical understanding and skills to solve problems; for recording numbers.
- Developing knowledge and understanding of the world, of the purposes of features and aspects of their environment, of living things,
  objects and events in the natural and made world, of similarities,
  differences, pattern and change.

Teachers' planning for children's learning in the early years of education
is based on consistent and detailed observation, conducted in a variety
of contexts, and supplemented by information and insights obtained
through discussion with parents. Great emphasis is placed upon observation of the 'whole child' from a variety of perspectives – social, cognitive, emotional, physical. Note is taken of children's physical capacity

and health, their attitude and approaches to learning, their strengths and weaknesses, their ability to collaborate, the degree of confidence they exhibit. On the basis of such information, recorded in profiles of development, much of the planning for subsequent work takes place. Much planning is set down very successfully and adequately.

But what teachers will be seeking to convey to inspectors through discussion and explanation, through any supplementary lesson notes, through children's work and recorded outcomes, through documented observations, are the learning intentions and curricular objectives inherent in the activities. Such elaboration to inspectors may be necessary to establish the extent of the learning opportunity and potential planned into diverse, fluid, often apparently unrelated and ostensibly incidental and random experiences, with less tangible evidence of 'work' than will be available at later stages.

It has been said, somewhat cynically, that judgements of early years education are sometimes made by inspectors, inexperienced in that field, on the basis of children's obvious happiness and involvement. Teachers therefore may need to convey a sense of the profound learning often taking place in the context of ostensibly unproductive activities and the extensive and subtle planning that has provided for it.

To meet the requirements for planning set out in the Ofsted criteria, schools are finding it helpful to plan on a long-, medium- and short-term basis.

Long-term planning
Long-term planning is concerned with subject planning for each year group, over a period of a year. Such planning is obviously a first stage and will be broad in nature. It will set out:

- the subject content that is to be taught;
- how that content will be organized into units of work designed to achieve a progression of learning objectives;
- the broad amount of time needed to teach and assess the work;
- how the content will be allocated over three terms. The following is an example of long-term planning in science for a year 2 class.

Of course, such a programme might well prove overly optimistic; not all of it might be experienced, mastered or concluded by the children.

Year: 2	Focus: Grouping and changing materials. **Key question:** How do we group materials? What materials change?	Suggested topics: Our clothes, Building, Food (Cooking)	AT: Materials and their properties

Programme of study (National Curriculum)	Suggested activities	Resources
Grouping materials a) to use their senses to explore and recognize the similarities and differences between materials; b) to sort materials into groups on the basis of simple properties, including texture, appearance, transparency and whether they are magnetic or non-magnetic; c) to recognize and name common types of material, e.g. metal, plastic, wood, paper, rock, and to know that some of these materials are found naturally; d) that many materials, e.g. glass, wood, wool, have a variety of uses. **Changing materials** a) that objects made from some materials can be changed in shape by processes including squashing, bending, twisting and stretching; b) to describe the way some everyday materials, e.g. water, chocolate, bread, clay, change when they are heated or cooled.	• **Explore and compare** a variety of materials (in a 'feely' box). • To sort and group materials according to their properties, i.e. a set of wooden/shiny objects. • To recognize and classify natural and man-made materials, i.e. to look at a selection of spoons **and to explore a variety of uses.** • Looking at clothes – why are wellingtons made of rubber? • Why do we wear cotton clothes in the summer? **Make predictions of the materials and their properties. Compare findings – make tables and charts to show results.** • **Investigate bread making.** Do you think this piece of bread has always looked like this? Can you change the shape of the dough before cooking? How does the dough change when it is cooked?	Collins Primary Science KS1 Set 1: Houses and Homes, Wet and Dry KS1 Set 2: Clothing Story references: *The Three Little Pigs, The Great Jam Sandwich* Nuffield Primary Science: Materials **Equipment** A selection of materials Magnifying glasses **Visits** Kew Gardens, 'Threads of Life' Exhibition Victoria and Albert Museum **Level description references** Can pupils … 1.2 Describe and group materials according to their properties. Describe how some materials are changed, i.e. by heating/cooling processes. 1.3 Describe ways of sorting materials, explain why some are particularly suitable for certain purposes, use metal for making electrical cables.

Medium-term planning

Medium-term planning would then translate the year plans into more detailed units of work. Planning in relation to these units would provide for explicit sets of objectives, the ways in which the units were going to be taught to the pupils, and how differentiated, assessed and recorded.

Short-term planning

Finally, short-term or weekly and daily planning would incorporate the medium-term planning into detailed teaching and learning activities.

Short-term planning will usually be the work of individual teachers, or teachers working within a year or phase group, informed by curriculum guidelines, by reputable textual material, by aides-mémoire and banks of lessons, by guidance provided by the subject co-ordinator. There will now be considerable detail because this is the stage of planning individual lessons and sequences of lessons. Teachers have to decide:

- how the work in the lesson or sequence of lessons relates to the children's previous learning experience;
- how much time will be devoted to the particular theme; whether the sequence of lessons will comprise an uninterrupted block activity;
- whether the particular activity will involve the whole class at the same time; if so, how groups will be organized;
- whether differentiation will be planned into the activity, whether it will arise through outcomes or whether it will be achieved through ability grouping;
- whether there will be planned cross-curricular elements;
- how the theme or learning activity will be introduced – how much time will be given to this and how it will be managed through demonstration, exposition, question and answer and so on;
- exactly what the pupils will be required to do; the materials and resources they will need;
- how they will present their findings;
- how the teacher will divide her time: working with particular children, marking the children's work while they are engaged in the process, supporting less able pupils;
- how additional classroom help will be managed and most effectively involved;

- whether any time will be allocated during the lesson to formative assessment;
- how children who complete set work before others will be catered for: by additional work on the theme in hand, through more challenging 'extension' activities, by opportunities to turn to on-going work that is being completed over extended periods of time, to practise a particular skill or to engage in private reading.

Inspectors will obviously wish to know what is planned for each lesson they observe. Without such information they can only guess at the teacher's rationale, aims and objectives, the reasons for particular organization, the way in which individual lessons fit into longer-term plans for the class, the phase and the school. Careful and detailed planning of each lesson during the inspection week is vital therefore; copies of planning for each lesson need to be provided for inspectors. Many teachers quail at the demands this is likely to make on their time. The measure is recommended, however, for the reasons given below.

One thing teachers can be certain of is that the lessons inspectors observe are clearly timetabled for them. Inspectors cannot visit a class and request to see a subject or curriculum area different from the one planned by the teacher and notified to them. Theoretically, therefore, it would be possible for a teacher to plan the lessons for the inspection week in such detail that all eventualities would be provided for, nothing would be left to chance and little could go wrong. Of course, as anyone with knowledge of teaching will immediately recognize, such thinking would be wildly optimistic. All kinds of things go wrong with teaching; at times the planning itself might be ill-conceived or fail to take off in practice; one or two vital elements might have been overlooked or not prepared for in sufficient detail; resources might prove unsuitable or inadequate; the time allowed for a process might be insufficient; pupils may not respond for no perceptible reason, or, worse still, prove fractious. Such misadventures haunt the work of all teachers; they are just as likely to occur as the flash of sudden inspiration or the memorable improvisations that illuminate so many lessons. The best of teachers will deliver some lessons every day that disappoint them and fall short of their expectations. Nevertheless, planning to provide for the crucial elements in every lesson – the introduction, the target setting for pupils, group organization, the management of time and resources, the teacher's role throughout, provision for differentiation – will pay off in very important ways.

It will, of course, reduce considerably the chances of things going wrong. But even where a teacher may fail to live up to consistently high standards and fall short of what he/she knows he/she is capable of, the evidence from detailed planning will convey significant messages to inspectors. They will be able to see that:

- content is related to the National Curriculum and to programmes of study;
- that it arises from pupils' previous learning experience and leads on to the next;
- that there are precise aims and objectives that relate to particular forms of learning;
- that the lesson has a clear structure;
- pupils are organized for the work they have to do;
- the teacher has allocated a clear role for herself;
- differentiation is provided for;
- some formative assessment may take place;
- resources are adequate, relevant and accessible to the pupils;
- the work of any classroom assistant is carefully defined; she is informed about the total planning and understands her role in the teaching and learning process;
- provision for special educational needs is detailed and adequate.

However far a lesson falls short of a teacher's best expectations, such planning provides incontrovertible evidence of his/her thorough understanding of his/her role, of the teaching and learning process, of the pupils' educational needs and how these are best served and of his/her command of important pedagogy and management.

But however much they might be prepared to accept the value of this, teachers will be understandably concerned about the amount of work such planning would involve. Primary teachers who are likely to be visited about six times in the course of an inspection week, and secondary teachers less frequently than that, may well wonder whether it is either necessary or realistic to suggest that they should prepare in detail all the lessons for that period to ensure that they are well prepared for the times when an inspector is in the room.

Clearly teachers do not go into exhaustive detail in their normal short-term/weekly planning, but they do know – or they certainly need to if their teaching is to be effective – how they intend to deal with and provide for the issues already referred to; to be sure – however briefly and with whatever personal shorthand they use to document it – why they are teaching something, where it fits into long-term planning, how it links to the National Curriculum, what the pupils will be required to do and so on.

What is being suggested here is that teachers need to exercise that degree of planning for all lessons in the inspection week and document the planning so that it serves as a clear guideline to inspectors about what they are observing. Of course, the degree of documentation required will vary according to the nature of certain lessons. Where, for example, a particular issue, aspect or element is being introduced, where the lesson constitutes the beginning of work that will spread across more than one lesson or a sequence, then the documentation will need to make that clear. If, for example, a series of lessons designed to help pupils use a map and compass to follow a route and set figure grid references to locate features on an OS map is going to incorporate orienteering activities round the school and subsequently some field work, then the written plan for the initial lesson may necessarily be more extensive because it has to include some information about that. There is some similarity here to early years planning, where the evidence of a single 'lesson' is likely to give little idea of the cumulative richness and complexity of what is a fluid process, rather than a series of discrete links. There will be other occasions – probably more frequent – when the substance of a lesson is a continuation from what pupils have engaged in immediately before and where a major part of the period may consist of the class engaged in work, while the teacher focuses on groups. After all, not all lessons can be one-offs, with the content neatly parcelled up, the teacher making a substantial introduction, the pupils working for the main part of the session and everything satisfactorily concluded, skills mastered, understanding total, concepts assimilated, by the end. Many lessons must 'run on' from what has happened before. It is all the more important in such cases, where teachers will be little seen 'teaching/performing' in the conventional sense, to be able to offer inspectors written information that will provide a full insight into what is taking place in teaching and learning terms.

It is not uncommon for primary children to be engaged on more than one subject in a single session – a variation of the integrated day. Some might be writing a story, some working on a science experiment, some reading while a mathematics group is taught by the teacher. In cases such as these the inspector may make it clear in advance that one subject (probably the 'taught' one) is being observed – though he is likely to take account of and possibly formally evaluate a second one. Whatever, the planning evidence provided, while focusing on the taught element – or whichever one has been identified for evaluation – should also make reference to the objectives of the other subject activities and how these are being provided for.

It is also common in primary schools for subjects to be taught through topics or projects, with a number of subjects incorporated within a particular theme. The handbook states firmly that 'Inspectors should pay particular attention to structure and progression in the planning of topics which involve a number of subjects. The planning should indicate very clearly the learning objectives and how teaching will be organized to challenge pupils and evidences that continuity and progression in each subject has been considered.' For example, if a project on 'change' is in fact used to involve pupils in learning particular aspects of history and geography and science, with a bit of design and technology thrown in for good measure, then the planning must indicate, for each separate subject, objectives that incorporate skills, knowledge and concepts, and which must link to the whole year or school curriculum. Planning must indicate the proportion of the whole project that particular subjects will occupy and the part that constitutes the total time available for each subject. In other words, planning will be required to demonstrate that the integrity and needs of individual subjects are being preserved inside the topic.

Project or thematic approaches to subjects are necessarily complex. They are still greatly favoured in primary schools, especially with younger children, because:

- they are seen to be particularly compatible with the ways in which children view and learn about the world and acquire knowledge and understanding, and
- because separate subject approaches are seen to be both uneconomical in terms of time and unwieldy and difficult for teachers to manage within the constraints of the timetable.

Teachers need to remember, however, that the planning for project lessons needs to be particularly explicit and clear. As the handbook says: 'A set of activities arranged in a topic web is not enough'. What inspectors will be concerned to establish are:

- why the teacher has chosen a topic approach and in what ways he or she thinks this is more likely to enhance the children's learning than discrete subject teaching
- the status of each subject in the project: whether individual subjects are planned for with all the same attention to detail they would receive were they being treated individually;
- whether particular objectives are clearly identified and related to the National Curriculum programmes of study; whether the concepts, skill and knowledge that constitute a subject are comprehensively treated.

What format should teachers use for planning? This will obviously vary considerably from school to school and even from teacher to teacher within the same school. However, a particular format is beginning to emerge that sets out economically the main issues for each lesson. In many cases individual lessons may be described adequately in less than a sheet of A4.

Key features in planning include:

- clear objectives;
- the work is linked to the National Curriculum programmes of study;
- differentiation is provided for through the nature of the tasks;
- there is a clearly established plan for the organization of the work and the way in which the pupils will be grouped;
- resources are provided for;
- the lesson is part of the long-term planning framework;
- pupil's work and achievement are systematically evaluated against the main objectives in the long-term plan.

However, teachers will have their own modes of planning, which are equally valid.

Methods and organizational strategies which match curriculum objectives and the needs of all children

Methods and organizational strategies are the most overt elements of teaching. They are in many respects what shape and determine a teacher's 'style', the means by which observers most conveniently and immediately categorize him or her. They are also among the most contentious of educational issues. For years argument has polarized along unhelpful lines of 'traditional' versus 'progressive' and 'formal' versus 'informal' in debate about method and organization, with teachers being all too easily and casually allocated to one camp or another on the basis of the most scanty evidence.

Terms have seldom been clearly defined. Many teachers' anxieties about inspection arise from a belief that judgements may be made on the basis of inspectors' personal adherence to particular forms of methodology and their antipathy to others. The handbooks stress, however, that 'the choice of teaching methods and organizational strategies is a matter for the school and the teacher's discretion'. But it emphasizes that judgement about this will depend on whether the methods chosen 'are fit for the purpose of achieving high standards of work and behaviour'. In other words, methods and organizational strategies are means to an end and not ends in themselves. This insistence on methodology and organizational strategies being selected on the grounds that they fit particular purposes – in other words, matching tools to the job in hand – endorses the practice of many, if not a majority, of teachers. They have little to fear if they can justify in a rational way and where possible, by reference to outcomes, the organizational strategies they have opted for.

Schools need to establish a policy about effective teaching and the methodology and strategies most likely to make it so. This, remarkably, seems to receive far less attention and discussion in many schools than issues and policies of a less urgent kind. Certainly, so far as inspection is concerned, schools need to take account of what the handbooks say about methodology and organizational strategies. Teaching methods are seen as including exposition, explanation, demonstration, discussion, practical activity, investigation, testing and problem-solving. Ofsted reminds us that the 'test of their effectiveness is the extent to which they extend or deepen pupils' knowledge and understanding and develop their skills. They are likely to do this when they are selected and handled with careful regard to:

- the nature of the curricular objectives being pursued; and
- what pupils know, understand and can do and what they need to learn next.'

Staff would be helped where schools:

- suggested an explicit definition of such teaching methods;
- provided guidelines about their mastery and implementation;
- backed this with constructive observation of teachers' practice;
- gave opportunities arising from such observation for shared evaluation of teachers' work;
- followed this with informed, supportive and practical advice about development.

There are few more sensitive areas in education than the matter of analysis of teachers' practice. It is one of the reasons for the prevailing hostility to inspections. For long it has been a taboo area. However, school-based INSET, appraisal, monitoring procedures carried out by senior staff, heads of departments and curriculum co-ordinators, the moderation of pupils' work have all contributed to teachers' gradual acceptance of such provision as an entitlement with potential to enhance their professional expertise and status. The process is made easier where there is broad agreement in a school about what constitutes effective methodology and organizational strategies.

For inspection it may be helpful for teachers to consider the following in relation to the elements identified by Ofsted:

Exposition and explanation

This is one of the most important features of a teacher's stock in trade. However sophisticated the teaching and learning approaches in vogue, there will always be important matters that simply have to be described and explained. Whole areas of learning largely dependent on exploration, reflection, investigation and practical experience on the part of the pupils, still demand expertise and instruction as an essential part of the process. (Very often such exposition may be given on a whole-class basis as the most economical way of conveying important information.) For example, if children are to learn about place value in number they will need a great deal of practical experience and practice; but that would not be sufficient without sensitive, skilled, oral explanation. The proper use of complicated equipment and tools, the political contexts of Shakespeare's plays, the skills of map reading and orienteering, the management of musical instruments, writing conventions and grammatical skills, all have to be explained and described. Ofsted says such explanation should be informative, lively and well structured.

It is an element of teaching that inspectors are bound to observe and make judgements about. In preparing lessons it is important that teachers identify elements and features that will have to be explained, important information that has to be conveyed, how this can be most thoroughly and effectively done, whether it needs to be supplemented by demonstration and visual aids, how much time it will demand, the ways in which the explanation can clarify matters, excite enthusiasm, interest and curiosity.

Effective questioning will be an important part not merely of explanation and exposition but a powerful way of extending pupils' understanding and thinking, of gaining and sustaining their interest, encouraging them to reflect, analyse, express their views and perceptions, to listen to and take account of the views of others, to appreciate the extent of their own knowledge.

The subtle skill of questioning is, in important respects, spontaneous, nurtured in teachers by constant practice. But it can be prepared for as other elements of a lesson can. Teachers should decide:

- what questions will supplement their explanation and exposition;
- to whom they should be addressed;
- how they can be used to draw out what pupils know, just as much as their areas of uncertainty;
- how they can be used to encourage less assured or less capable pupils;
- how they can be most clearly presented;
- how they can ensure discussion by being open-ended;
- how the pupils themselves can be encouraged to question constructively.

Practical activities

Explanation and questioning are essentially 'teaching' activities; practical activity, investigation and problem-solving are learning activities. The major part of all lessons observed by inspectors will be concerned with what the pupils are doing. A significant part of this, especially with young children, will be of a practical and active nature. It will range across play, handwriting practice, sand and water investigation, painting, clay and junk modelling, making and playing percussion instruments, to the use of sophisticated scientific and technological equipment, designing and making, intensive practice on musical instruments, biological dissection, geography field work, word processing and the wider use of information technology. Because they are in many ways the least predictable and therefore the most likely to go wrong, practical learning activities need detailed preparation. Teachers need to be very clear what it is they want the pupils to learn and whether the particular activity chosen is the most effective and economical way of doing that. A routine unglamorous handwriting exercise, where children are practising carefully demonstrated letter shapes, may well be more effective in achieving particular literacy objectives than an exciting and more immediately attractive treasure hunt for words and letters. But the particular approach will be selected because it is likely to be more effective, not because of a commitment to 'formal' or 'progressive' theories. What teachers need to keep asking, in planning pupils' learning activities is:

- whether the activities will usefully extend pupils' knowledge and competence;
- whether what the pupils are to learn is likely to be most efficiently achieved through a particular form of activity, problem-solving, or investigation;
- whether problems and investigation are always what they purport to be: for example the mathematics 'problem' which turns out to be a simple, brief calculation after the lengthy written language in which it is expressed is unravelled;
- what resources will be required and what time is to be allocated;
- what the size and composition of the groups involved are to be and how the participation of all the members of a group can be guaranteed;

- whether pupils will be encouraged to reflect on and record what they have learned.

Group work

This brings us to the organization of pupils, whether as individuals, groups or a whole class. There will be times, of course, when it is most appropriate and natural for pupils to work as individuals; much of their work will be done in this way: writing for a range of purposes, painting or reading a novel. Sometimes it will be most productive for them to work in pairs or small groups – composing a piece of music, solving a mathematical problem, setting up and conducting a science experiment, interpreting data, reading a map. There will be times when a whole class is engaged in the same practical activity: making a model, working on a piece of inferential comprehension, planning a large-scale project, constructing a piece of drama.

Grouping, comprised of four or six pupils, has always been a common form of organization in primary schools. It is often used as a hidden form of streaming or setting. If anything, there is an increasing emphasis on group work because it is seen as one of the most effective ways of using a teacher's time economically and of securing protracted interaction with pupils. There is equally, however, an insistence that group work can only be effective where pupils are trained to work collaboratively, as distinct from individuals working separately within the framework of a group.

Teachers may find it helpful to bear these things in mind when planning the organization of classes:

- Group work, properly organized, offers the best opportunity in normal sized classrooms for extended interaction with pupils.
- Such extended interaction contributes powerfully to pupils' learning.
- Some subjects and areas of learning will call for groups based on common ability levels.
- The need to vary the composition of groups for different subjects; whether, for example, it would be most productive in primary classes to have the same groups for English, mathematics and technology.
- The need to teach groups to work effectively as a unit. This is not an easy matter; effective group working calls for sophisticated skills on the part of the participants. It will be necessary to teach pupils to

work to agreed ground rules: the importance of listening to and taking account of other people's viewpoints; readiness to express personal opinions clearly and objectively; willingness to acquiesce in group decisions; effective use of time; a need for clear objectives and targets; readiness to respond to and support group leadership; the need for systematic review of on-going work and evaluation of outcomes; willingness to seek outside support, consultancy and advice when needed; readiness to communicate outcomes clearly to others.

● Group tasks will often be open-ended: making a book, finding as many ways as possible to constitute a number, planning the administration and organization of an educational visit, composing a puppet play to be presented to younger children or building a working model. It may be necessary for teachers to make clear to inspectors why group approaches have been adopted, to point up benefits, to amplify complexities of organization and subtleties of working, to demonstrate that extended teacher–pupil interaction has been facilitated.

Effective management of pupils, high standards of discipline, the effective use of time and resources

The following points are important in a consideration of the effective management of pupils and high standards of discipline as a component of good teaching.

The pupils should be working at least as hard as the teacher; it is not uncommon to see a teacher work energetically and enthusiastically to introduce a learning activity only for pupils to drift through it in a desultory way. It is too easy to attribute such a response to unpalatable or irrelevant tasks. Of course, the more enticing, relevant and rewarding a task is, the more likely pupils are to work hard at it. But pupils' readiness to respond positively is often only achieved through consistent and clear expectation on the part of teachers and, in turn, by positive acknowledgement of pupil effort.

Obviously the way in which learning activities and tasks are structured and prepared is very important. Pupils need to see a clear purpose, to know why they are being required to work in a particular way, to be interested in the outcome, to be anxious to learn the skill, the ideas or the information on offer. They need to have a clear view of the time the task will take, to have indicated, during the process, the progress they are making. The completion of a task, the achievement of objectives, need to be marked and recognized and acknowledged appropriately. Pupils need to be kept aware, both at the end of single sessions and over extended periods of time, what they have learned and achieved, the progress they have made, the things they know now, and the skills acquired, that they did not possess, say, a term before. Pupils need to be helped to evaluate their own success, to be critical but not frustrated about where they have fallen short, to decide maturely whether they are satisfied with what they have achieved. It is particularly important for them to consider the pace of work and to judge whether the volume and quality of what they achieve in particular periods is adequate. This is a matter about which teachers need to be insistent.

Inspectors will pay keen attention to the ways in which resources are employed to support, extend and enhance pupils' learning. This most important matter does not always seem to receive the attention it requires from teachers. For example, younger children engaged with mathematical problems do not always have available to them concrete materials that may help to bring complicated concepts within their grasp. Place value in number seems to be a classic case of this. Again, pupils engaged in writing tasks do not always have access to the dictionaries, thesauruses and word books that will not only support their writing but generally extend their learning autonomy.

Teachers need to do the following in relation to resources:

- decide what materials and resources need to be consistently available to pupils;
- label and organize them so that they are readily accessible;
- keep in reserve those resources unlikely to be immediately required in order to avoid confusing clutter;
- train pupils to recognize the purpose and value of specific resources and how to use them effectively;
- ensure, no matter what the maturity and competence of pupils, that literacy and numeracy aids are constantly available;
- train pupils to research information;
- train pupils to use IT equipment to support their learning;
- decide upon the resources necessary for particular lessons, make sure they are easily available to pupils and that their purpose is understood by them;

- teach pupils to share resources and equipment in a mature and sensible way;
- keep as informed as possible, especially as a primary teacher with a wide curriculum brief, about current developments in resources and materials. This is essential information that needs to be systematically provided by heads of departments and curriculum co-ordinators.

Assess pupils' work thoroughly and use assessment to inform teaching

We deal with assessment in detail in Chapter 6 on curriculum and assessment. In this particular section we shall focus briefly on formative assessment, which is increasingly recognized as a critical characteristic of effective teaching. Pupils will only learn effectively, and teachers teach well, if learning tasks are based upon an informed understanding of what the learner already knows and where, in their learning, they should move next.

Teachers need to bear these things in mind about formative assessment:

- There is nothing new or mystical about formative assessment; good teachers have always ascertained what pupils know and can do before planning the next part of their learning. So formative assessment is a continuous process in a classroom; much of what a teacher learns by observation of a pupil's learning behaviour, by astute questioning, by analyses of completed work, may be mentally filed as part of an accumulating bank of knowledge about a pupil, to be consistently referred to when planning learning programmes. Increasingly, however, teachers are regularly putting time aside for formative assessment and conducting this in relation to systematic schedules of criteria and objectives. In practical terms, this may be confined to a couple of subjects a week, involve small groups of pupils, the information economically recorded according to an agreed school system.
- Assessment is done to identify and measure pupils' achievement and progress and to inform teachers' planning. It will, of necessity, be diagnostic in nature. But it can be done in a manner that motivates pupils' learning, through questioning that enables a pupil to

contribute to the process, by identifying and acknowledging progress and achievement and the areas where they need to acquire new skills and develop particular competencies, through interactive marking that stimulates further study, through shared analysis of problems, through the rapid correction of mistaken ideas, through the prevention of prolonged floundering by pupils, through judicious praise and encouragement.

The use of homework

The notion of homework as a formal, regular feature of pupils' education is a relatively recent phenomenon in primary schools. It needs to be tackled with particular sensitivity in the case of very young children especially. Inspectors will look for evidence that:

- Schools have established a clear purpose for homework; that it seems likely to contribute to and extend pupils' learning; that pupils see the purpose of it.
- It is not a strategy to complete work that should have been dealt with in school time.
- There is a clear understanding on the part of parents about the purpose of homework, its likely duration and the expectations that teachers have of it.
- It is not seen in any way by parents as an abrogation of teachers' responsibilities.
- It does not make unrealistic demands upon the resources and facilities available to less advantaged pupils.
- Provision is made for pupils who may not be able to deal with homework at home to do so comfortably in school.
- Pupils' general learning is not critically impeded because they cannot, for one reason or another, consistently attend to homework. This is a difficult matter; clearly homework that is properly planned will extend pupils' learning. That is its purpose. Equally, teachers must remember that the opportunity to take advantage of that is not always available to pupils, especially those for whom the need may be greatest.
- Where possible, parents should be given opportunity to contribute to pupils' homework and their learning outside school, through their particular interests, knowledge and access to particular environments.

- In the case of homework for younger children, and in particular aspects of literacy and numeracy, succinct and helpful guidelines will be welcomed by many parents.
- For the parents of older pupils, where homework becomes increasingly esoteric, then at least brief but helpful information regularly available to them about the nature and purpose of the work will be reassuring and may enable them to offer encouragement.
- Work is regularly and immediately responded to. Nothing is more destructive of pupils' attitudes to learning than casual, negligent or irregular response to what may have demanded a considerable expenditure of time, energy and effort on their part. Neither does it encourage and sustain parents' confidence in a school.

A checklist for action

Inspectors will use the following as the main sources of their evidence.

Before the inspection
- The head teacher's form will give a preliminary view of staff experience, expertise, qualifications and training.
- The staff handbook may include a policy for professional development.
- Schemes of work and teachers' planning documents should provide insights into teaching methods and organizational strategies deployed in the school, and their relationship to the sequence of work and curricular objectives.
- The assessment policy should indicate how day-to-day formative assessment is intended to help provide pupils with appropriate and challenging work.
- Pre-inspection meetings with the head teacher, governors and parents are likely to provide a range of perspectives on the overall quality of teaching at the school.

During the inspection
A view on how plans translate into practice will be arrived at through:

- observation of lessons;
- a scrutiny of pupils' work and how it is marked;

- discussion with teachers and support staff, exploring the extent to which the teaching sets high expectations and promotes the learning of all pupils.

Schools are recommended to consider a review of the following kind where feasible:

- Teachers must plan within a whole-school context. Their planning must take account of phase, year and departmental plans.
- Good schemes of work are essential to the process.
- Planning needs to take account of assessment information, especially in relation to planning for differentiation.
- Take careful account of Ofsted's detailed criteria about planning.
- Ensure that all the areas of learning are provided for in relation to children under five.
- Consider the advantages of offering inspectors copies of lesson plans for the lessons they observe.
- Schools might consider the advantages of offering inspectors a cross-section of planning done by teachers even for those lessons they have not observed.
- Where lessons are incorporating more than one subject with pupils working in groups, teachers need to ensure that their planning refers to all the subjects in addition to the subject timetabled for observation.
- Ensure that subjects within topics receive the same degree of planning that they would if they were being taught discretely.
- There are advantages to a common format for planning throughout the school (see example on page Chapter 5).
- Review as a staff the teaching skills defined by Ofsted in the handbook.
- Pay particular attention in lesson planning to the practical work that pupils will be doing.
- Plan carefully for the ways in which pupils will be organized during the practical work of the lesson.
- Ensure that planning takes account of the resources that will be required and how they will be made available and used.
- Build formative assessment into lessons on a regular and systematic basis.
- Consider very carefully the purposes of homework and ensure that time is allowed for a response to it. Consider making provision for

pupils who may find it more convenient to complete homework in school.

The following questions to the TES column 'An Inspector Writes' highlight some of the aspects of planning that schools have expressed concern about.

Q   Every class teacher in this school writes detailed termly plans for every area of the curriculum. What other levels and kinds of planning will be acceptable to inspectors as good practice – weekly, half-termly or any others?

A   In order to illuminate their teaching and the pupils' learning, teachers will want to make their planning available to inspectors. However, the essential purpose of planning is, of course, to ensure that the lessons taught enable pupils to learn successfully.

Planning will bear a teacher's personal stamp and be done in ways that suit individuals, but, increasingly, schools are adopting common formats and styles – a good example of collegial practice.

In view of the extensive range of subjects that individual primary teachers have to teach, planning has to be economical and purposeful, free of superfluous detail and description.

The Office for Standards in Education has provided detailed advice on planning in its publication 'Well Managed Classes in Primary Schools', and the vital features of effective planning are set out in 'Curriculum Organization and Classroom Practice in Primary Schools' (the 'Three Wise Men's Report'). Particularly important for primary schools is the SCAA publication 'Planning the curriculum at key stages 1 and 2'.

Planning should take place over a range of timescales: long-, medium- and short-term, or, more precisely, yearly, termly, half-termly, weekly and daily, all complementary to each other. Schools may be selective, choosing between the termly and half-termly, for example. Nevertheless, the yearly concept as the starting point for planning is a vital one; it will be part of a school-wide system, designed to ensure coherence, continuity and progression across the key stages and to cover the National Curriculum.

Where there are other classes in the year group, planning will benefit from being done in collaboration with colleagues.

Planning will obviously be based on whatever curriculum model is followed by the school: topic, theme or subject basis, and will reflect that. Planning will establish the subjects incorporated within the theme or topic, their order of priority and emphasis, and the balance of time devoted to them.

Termly or half-termly planning will obviously translate broad annual programmes into more detailed practical plans. Teachers then wishing to plan individual lessons based on such a termly programme would need to consider the following:

- the purpose and duration of the lesson; what it is intended the pupils should learn, in what way this would be related to the National Curriculum, to previous work and how it would be developed thereafter;
- the practical part the teacher would play and where the focus of her main effort would be – the whole class, groups or individuals;
- what the pupils would be expected to do, how differentiation would be provided for, the resources needed to support the learning, and whether formal assessment would take place.

Such lesson components would be carefully planned to ensure effective practical outcomes, but in fact each would require little more than a few lines of written description.

On occasions when individual lessons or small clusters of lessons exist apart from the National Curriculum programmes of study or from large topics, teachers' planning notes are likely to be minimal.

I am sure the termly planning you refer to takes account of what has been described here and is likely to make for successful teaching and to be informative for inspectors.

Q In any discussion of inspection people always seem to talk knowingly about the importance of planning, but never say just what they mean by it. What exactly will Ofsted look for in terms of planning?

A I think Ofsted would regard a development plan as essential to an effective school: such a plan, usually based on an analysis of existing curriculum provision, would set out the school's main educational objectives in an order of priority. It would include detailed information for the year ahead and broad objectives for the following two years. The school development plan (SDP) will derive partly from individual plans drawn up by subject co-ordinators.

The detailed information about current intentions and plans – sometimes amplified in separate action plans – would define specific targets and related tasks, the allocation of responsibilities, timescales, costings, resource implications (both in terms of personnel and of materials and equipment), and procedures for monitoring progress and evaluating the effectiveness of outcomes.

The essential thrust of any SDP is educational – that is, the achievement of the most effective teaching and learning possible. But if that is to be managed then a school has to be concerned with other issues: institutional efficiency, the management and professional development of staff, the effective use of finance and resources, the assessment of learning, the monitoring of objectives, initiatives and achievement, all in turn calling for planning in their own right.

Curricular elements

In order to manage the National Curriculum, schools are increasingly organizing their curriculum planning at three levels.

- Long-term planning seeks to set up a broad framework of provision for each year of each key stage. In effect, this provides schools with a map of the experiences pupils will encounter in all the main areas of the curriculum across their entire primary life. In an undertaking as ambitious as this, some schools' planning may still be at a stage where subject time allocations, and broad frameworks of concepts, skills, knowledge and content, are still being worked out.

- Medium-term planning, related to termly or half-termly provision, aims to translate the broad subject maps into more detailed units of work and learning for each year.

- Short-term planning is about teachers' weekly and daily planning, designed to achieve day-to-day learning for the pupils. Of necessity, it will be succinct, will indicate the work the pupils are daily engaged in, how that links to the National Curriculum, the resources required, the role played by the teacher in specific lessons, how teaching support is utilized, the provision for differentiation and special needs, and what assessment might take place. It is desirable, as far as possible, to make short-term planning for the inspection week available to inspectors.

Schools will also provide evidence of planning to cater for pupils with special needs.

Financial planning

This needs to demonstrate good housekeeping in the best sense, not merely that the budget balances, but that money has been well spent, and, where possible and necessary, judiciously saved. Financial planning should show, as far as possible:

- costings for all activities, with allocations of responsibilities for delivery, management and monitoring;
- how the procedures for efficient financial control set out in Ofsted's document 'Keeping your Balance' will be kept in relation to projects;
- how a school aims to determine whether value for money has been achieved: how it will establish whether particular decisions have proved worthwhile and profitable in the context of total-school needs.

School management and development

Planning for the management, deployment and professional development of staff will ideally give some indication of:

- how teaching and non-teaching staff are deployed in a way which makes the best use of expertise and experience;
- how the staffing structure and allocation of responsibilities reflect the school's overall aims and objectives and curriculum priorities;
- whether teachers have adequate non-teaching time to carry out identified responsibilities;
- how arrangements for staff development are meeting the needs of individuals and the school as a whole.

Assessment and recording

Planning for assessment and recording will be concerned with arrangements for providing:

- 'summative' assessment that measures and records children's achievement;
- 'formative', on-going assessment to underpin future planning;
- diagnostic assessment to identify and analyse learning difficulties.

6

The curriculum and assessment

In this area the inspection focuses on the extent to which the content and organization of the curriculum and its assessment provide access to the full range of learning experiences and promote the attainment, progress and personal development of the pupils. The curriculum comprises all the planned activities within and beyond the timetable. Inspectors must evaluate and report on the extent to which the curriculum:

- is balanced and broadly based, promotes pupils' intellectual, physical and personal development and prepares pupils for the next stage of education;
- meets statutory requirements to teach the subjects of the National Curriculum, religious education and sex education, where these apply;
- provides equality of access and opportunity for pupils to make progress;
- meets the curricular requirements of all pupils on the school's code of practice special educational needs register;
- is planned effectively, providing continuity and progression of learning;
- is enriched by extra-curricular provision, including sport.

In relation to assessment, inspectors must evaluate the extent to which:

● there are effective systems for assessing pupils' attainment;
● assessment information is used to inform curricular planning.

Therefore, in accordance with the Education Act, primary schools have to ensure that the curriculum:

● is balanced and broadly based;
● promotes the spiritual, moral, cultural, mental and physical development of pupils;
● prepares pupils for the opportunities, responsibilities and experiences of adult life;
● provides for religious education;
● includes the subjects of the National Curriculum as prescribed in regulations.

Secondary schools have to ensure in addition that the curriculum:

● provides for sex education in accordance with the school's policy.

They should also provide careers education and guidance and health education, including education about drug misuse.

Primary schools' practice on assessment needs to be seen in relation to:

● records of progress for under-fives;
● the assessment requirements of the National Curriculum at the end of Key Stage 1 and 2;
● the requirements covering pupil records and reports, including annual reports to parents;
● the additional requirements which apply to pupils with statements of special educational need and those at Stage 2 or above in the code of practice.

The secondary school's practice on assessment needs to be seen in relation to:

● the assessment requirements of the National Curriculum at the end of Key Stage 2 (for middle schools) and Key Stage 3;
● public examination requirements at Key Stage 4 and post-16;

- the requirements covering pupil records and reports, including annual reports to parents and reports to school leavers;
- the additional requirements which apply to pupils with statements of special educational needs and those at Stage 2 or above in the code of practice.

Under-fives

Ofsted states that the curriculum in nursery schools and for under-fives should provide teaching in the following areas of learning: linguistic and literacy; mathematical; scientific and technological; human and social; aesthetic and creative; physical; moral and spiritual. The curriculum should take account of children's developing intellectual, physical, emotional and social abilities; make appropriate provision for purposeful play, talk and direct enquiry, together with opportunities for child-initiated activity. It should provide pupils with experiences that lead towards the National Curriculum programmes of study.

What should schools do to translate these requirements into practice? What will inspectors look to see? Let us begin with the children under five.

We know the full extent of the curriculum to which under-fives are entitled. Ofsted defines it in the handbook; the School Curriculum and Assessment Authority and Ofsted have set out the areas of learning in more detail, together with the desirable outcomes for children on entry to compulsory schooling. The process has in effect prescribed the early years curriculum to an unprecedented degree, but along lines that seem to be largely acceptable to early years educators. Schools therefore must simply do everything possible to provide that curriculum in a way that helps children realize the desirable outcomes.

But schools also need to ensure the following:

1 That teaching and provision of the prescribed curriculum – a national curriculum in fact – exist in contexts and circumstances necessary for young children:
  - a wide variety of carefully organized play opportunity;
  - contexts and resources designed to foster talk as a main constituent of the learning process;
  - opportunity to learn through meaningful first-hand experience, through exploration, enquiry, problem-solving; through experimentation, investigation and construction;

- a major emphasis on active learning in which children's control, self-discipline and autonomy are developed;
- the chance for children to use their acquired skills and competencies and to build on them;
- contexts in which children feel emotionally secure and involved;
- opportunity for children to work at their own pace, to observe and reflect;
- a rich variety of story, song, poetry, music and dance;
- opportunity for adventurous play;
- contexts and resources that develop the ability to respond imaginatively to particular experiences;
- opportunity for practice and repetition done at a pace appropriate to the learner;
- that specific skills are being developed within the main areas of learning.

Examples in the areas of **language and literacy** include:

- reasoning, and putting things in a logical way;
- communicating with a range of people and expressing a variety of intentions, needs, requests, responses, descriptions, feelings;
- listening and responding to making story, poetry and song;
- reading and writing.

Examples in **physical development** include:

- developing skills of co-ordination and manipulation;
- developing body awareness;
- acquiring a sense of balance and agility.

Examples in **social and emotional development** include:

- learning to share;
- learning to be appropriately independent and assertive, to express feelings and needs, to form relationships, to begin to make sense of the world.

Examples in **mathematical development** include:

- learning to count, sort, conserve, measure, sequence, compare and order;
- learning to have a concept of shape;
- beginning to match and classify; to understand one-to-one correspondence.

Examples in **scientific and technological development** include:

- being able to observe, pose questions, hypothesize, set up tests, come to conclusions, communicate them;
- to begin to appreciate the properties of things;

- to predict;
- to construct and invent.

2 That the resources that will underpin such learning contexts are available.

3 That partnerships are formed with parents and carers in relation to their children's learning. We refer elsewhere to parents as the first and most important educators in young children's lives and the home as an important learning environment. Children come to school endowed with a wide range of competencies and skills. Schools need to identify these quickly and build on them.

Partnership that is informative to both parents and the school is critically important for children's continuing development and learning. Parents need to understand the nature and purpose of their children's experiences at school, and how they can continue to support that learning at home; schools need access to parents' peerless knowledge of the children, and their co-operation in maintaining a bridge of continuity between the learning experiences of home and school. In practical terms, such partnerships will be nurtured by carefully organized home visits, by regular reviews and consultation, by sensitively managed settling procedures, by displays and exhibitions that are informative about teaching and learning, by an informal and welcoming environment.

4 That careful assessment and record keeping are an integral part of the children's learning. Consistent observation of children's learning and behaviour patterns, of their responses to the whole range of experience, opportunity and stimulus provided in school, is at the heart of teachers' planning in the early years. The existence of a National Curriculum and desirable outcomes for young children provides teachers with valuable maps for learning and targets to aim at. But careful identification and mapping of children's attainment, progress and development and planning of learning based on the National Curriculum is absolutely essential at this stage. Anything else runs a risk of children missing out on the proper development and mastery of vital skills and the acquisition of important concepts.

Schools need to ensure that children under five years of age who are already in mainstream classes have access to the prescribed areas of educational provision. It is a matter to which inspectors will pay marked attention.

Ofsted will apply the following criteria in judging the strengths and weaknesses of the primary curriculum. The first three set out here can be considered as a unit:

- Is the curriculum balanced and broadly based: does it promote pupils' intellectual, physical and personal development and prepare for the next stage of education?
- Does the curriculum meet statutory requirements to teach the subjects of the National Curriculum, religious education and sex education where these apply?
- Is the curriculum planned effectively, providing continuity and progression of learning?

The other criteria are these:

- Does the curriculum provide equality of access and opportunity for pupils to learn and to make progress?
- Does the curriculum meet the curricular requirements of all pupils on the school's code of practice special educational needs register?
- Are there effective systems for assessing pupils' attainment? Is assessment information used to inform curriculum planning?
- Is the curriculum enriched by extra-curricular provision, including sport?

Let us first consider the combined criteria, which are in fact about the breadth, balance and coherence of the curriculum and how it is organized.

The organization of the curriculum, appropriate teaching methods and classroom practice have always been challenging issues for primary schools in particular. The advent of the National Curriculum has exacerbated the problem. It is easy to forget how radically different the situation was for schools less than a decade ago. Then the schools could be remarkably selective about what they taught. Pupils moving between schools could encounter significantly different curricula. Even more significantly, there was no external testing – and reporting – of pupils' attainment until well into the secondary sector. Schools were remarkably autonomous, in many cases and in many ways, in relation to the curriculum. But a National Curriculum allied to standardized testing has transformed the landscape of primary education, at least. It has also created significant difficulties in terms of curriculum delivery and management, especially for primary schools.

There are a number of reasons for the difficulty schools are experiencing in managing the curriculum, especially at Key Stage 2. They include: the sheer extent and volume of the orders; the introduction and development of IT and design and technology that were almost unknown in schools, at least in their existing form, a decade ago; major new requirements in connection with special educational needs; the problem of providing adequately for very complex subject demands at the upper end of Key Stage 2; the impact of the growing pressure of SATs that is resulting in certain subjects, such as history and geography and aspects of the creative arts, being sidelined for older pupils in the summer term.

The focus on subject provision in the inspection process is one of the elements that primary schools find hardest to cope with – indeed ,possibly the most difficult of all. The full significance of the fact that all subjects will be exhaustively inspected and reported on as separate entities does not come home fully to many primary schools until they hear the first oral feedback at the conclusion of the inspection. In a sense, primary schools are being literally scored out of ten here; the incidence of more than one subject being judged unsatisfactory can blemish a report; more than a couple and there is a cause for concern. It is not helpful for schools to be under a delusion about this matter. Surprisingly, in all that has been said and written about the inspection of schools, in all the helpful advice available from various sources, there has been relatively little emphasis on the importance of subject provision and the extent to which judgement of its quality in a school will flavour the final report. It seems as if little distinction is being made between the situation of secondary schools, which are literally constructed round subject departments, and primary schools, which, in many cases, are obliged to hand responsibility for the teaching of eight, nine or ten subjects to one class teacher and the co-ordination often of a number of them to one class-based co-ordinator.

What can primary schools do to satisfy the inspection requirements in relation to all the subjects? Perhaps they should begin by accepting that few schools be may yet at a stage where they can be confident about meeting all the requirements of the National Curriculum in relation to all ten subjects. It would probably be unrealistic to expect otherwise in a context where the Dearing Review itself insisted on a five-year moratorium on change or further development, to enable schools to take stock of where they were and to settle into the new curriculum.

Schools can usefully do the following: make a review or audit of the current position of subjects in the school. Begin with the core curriculum. Review then, perhaps, information technology – because of the growing significance being attached to its implementation – and design and technology. Review the subjects in relation to the orders and the programmes of study and establish how far each one is satisfying National Curriculum requirements. The audit could be undertaken by LEA subject advisers (whose expectations as individual subject experts may tend to be over-rigorous, however) together with the school's curriculum co-ordinators; there are no reasons, of course, why such a survey could not be conducted very effectively by co-ordinators alone, but the necessary time is unlikely to be available for this, especially where individual teachers may carry responsibility for a number of subjects.

Use the information provided by the audit to make a plan for subject development. Obviously such a plan should be reflected at least in some respects in the school development plan (it may well be that the outcomes of a subject audit will modify the development plan in some respects anyway). Whatever the outcome of the audit, there is little point in trying to transform the greater part of a curriculum in the months immediately prior to an inspection. Select those subjects – and certainly not more than three initially – where the need for development or amendment seems necessary. Prioritize any core subjects.

Decide, possibly with the help of an LEA adviser or a subject consultant, what needs to be done in terms of organization, teaching, resources, assessment and so on, to bring the subjects in question at least to sound standards. Confirm the role of the co-ordinator in this, and the support in terms of non-contact time, consultancy and advisory input that will be required by him or her. Establish what training and resources will be needed by staff and can be reasonably provided by the school. Keep governors informed of developments. Establish a timetable for implementation. Make information about the steps you have taken, together with a rationale for your plan of subject development, available to the inspection team. Try to establish detailed schemes of work for the subjects involved (see Appendix 4.1) and decide what can be done in the time available to build up support materials for teachers' use.

The second large concern faced by primary schools in relation to subjects is their efficient implementation and organization. In 'Primary Matters' Ofsted has this to say about the organization of the curriculum at the primary stage:

Almost all the schools in the survey continued to use topic work as a major mode of curriculum organization. Only one school taught every subject separately. Since the publication of the discussion paper, however, many schools had begun to review the balance between broad-based topics and those with one subject as the major focus. Some had considered more carefully the benefits of teaching certain subjects or parts of subjects separately. At Key Stage 1, numeracy and reading skills were nearly always taught separately as well as through topic work. At Key Stage 2 mathematics and some aspects of English were usually taught separately, as were music, RE and PE at both key stages.

The trend, particularly at Key Stage 2, towards topics with one subject as the major focus, helped to redress some of the long-established weaknesses in topic planning. Most of the schools had agreed two-, three- or four-year cycles for topics. The topics focused mainly on history, geography or science, with a different emphasis each half term. There was some evidence to show that this brought about more systematic teaching of the 'lead' subject and a general improvement in the quality of topic work. A few schools still employed broad-based topics which led to superficial subject coverage and tenuous links between subjects. Except for the schools which used broad-based topics, criticism of topic work planning centred mainly on those schools which did not ensure consistency of work between classes, or whose planning referred only to the knowledge teachers expected pupils to learn rather than referring also to the skills or understanding to be developed. In the criteria relating to effective planning of the curriculum, providing continuity and progression of learning, Ofsted indicates a focus for evaluation.

Inspectors should evaluate whether curriculum planning takes account of what has gone before and what will follow. The

> need for continuity and progression applies between years, between key stages and between schools. Evidence is needed of whether, as pupils move through the school, the curriculum builds systematically on existing knowledge, understanding and skills.

Curriculum planning in primary schools needs to make effective provision for the programmes of study, whatever type of organization is adopted. Many primary schools use topic work as a major mode of curriculum organization. Topics may be broad-based or have one subject as the major focus, particularly at KS2. If topics are broad-based, inspectors will evaluate how effectively they are planned to cater for the intended programmes of study and whether they provide a clear structure and sufficient progression.

It is vital therefore for primary schools to remember that no matter in what form the curriculum is presented, individual subjects will need to be clearly identified and provided for in the fullest sense possible according to National Curriculum programmes of study.

How can primary schools organize so formidable a curriculum burden; how can they convert from a situation where, until quite recently, they could afford to be selective about the extent to which subjects were taught, and, indeed, could minimalize the presence of some subjects? History and geography were good examples of this tendency. Though contributing to and servicing many projects and topics, their inclusion was often arbitrary, even idiosyncratic, with the result that their treatment as subjects lacked coherence, continuity and progression.

It is unlikely that primary schools will teach the whole curriculum through single subjects, for practical reasons, apart from the ideological one that young children do not view the world from, nor learn effectively about it through, a single subject perspective. How therefore can they manage and organize in ways that will serve National Curriculum – and inspection – requirements and avoid what many still regard as a prematurely and artificially demarcated curriculum?

The best guidance on the matter to date is provided in the SCAA document 'Planning the Curriculum at Key Stages 1 and 2'. Schools are likely to find the material useful as a reference point against which their own existing forms of curriculum organization can be checked, even if they decide against the wholesale adoption of the plan. They will certainly find the advice on time allocation and management extremely useful.

In summary, the guidance suggests:

1 The school should consider its policy on assessment to ensure that it provides a manageable framework for promoting accurate and consistent assessment across the curriculum. *Time allocations at the long-term level of planning will need to reflect this.* Planning will also need to take account of the time required to carry out statutory tests and tasks at the end of each key stage.

2 Before the detailed business of whole school curriculum planning begins, schools should take the opportunity to review and refresh their thinking on the school's aims, objectives, policies and priorities, which will all inform subsequent discussions and influence decisions (a process which inspection preparation will have already initiated anyway).

3 Discussion will need to consider a range of issues, including:

● Statutory curricular provision.	The National Curriculum subjects; religious education and National Curriculum end-of-key-stage assessment.
● Areas where schools are required to have policies which may lead to additional curricular provision being made.	For example: special educational needs and sex education.
● Areas where schools have chosen to develop policies which may lead to additional curricular provision being made.	For example: health education; personal, social and moral education; community links; and additions to particular National Curriculum subjects.
● Particular school priorities within the curriculum.	For example: meeting the needs of pupils with English as an additional language.

4 The curriculum is organized in a simple way. The content is divided into **units of work**. There are two categories: **continuing** and

blocked. Both types of unit will draw in the first instance on work from a single subject or aspect of the curriculum. Two or more units from different subjects or aspects of the curriculum can be linked as and when appropriate.

5 **Continuing work** is drawn from a single subject or aspect of the curriculum which:

- requires regular and frequent teaching and assessment to be planned across a year or key stage to ensure progression;
- contains a progressive sequence of learning objectives;
- requires time for the systematic and gradual acquisition, practice and consolidation of skills, knowledge and understanding.

6 **Blocked work** is drawn in the first instance from a single subject or aspect of the curriculum which:

- can be taught within a specific amount of time, not exceeding a term;
- focuses on a distinct and cohesive body of knowledge, understanding and skills;
- can be taught alone or has the potential for linking with units of work in other subjects or aspects of the curriculum.

7 Once a framework of continuing and blocked work has been established, curriculum coherence can be established by linking together, where appropriate, units of work from different subjects or aspects of the curriculum.

8 There are three main reasons for linking work at this level of planning. Units can be linked when:

- they contain common or complementary knowledge, understanding and skills, e.g. developing reading and writing skills through work in history, or work on the water cycle in science linked with work on weather and rivers in geography;
- the skills acquired in one subject or aspect of the curriculum can be applied or consolidated in the context of another, e.g. work on co-ordinates in mathematics applied to work in geography on four-figure grid references.

9 The work in one subject or aspect of the curriculum provides a useful stimulus for work in another, e.g. creating music from a poem or picture.

The planning process has been summarized in six distinct stages:

- establishing the amount of time available for teaching and assessing the school curriculum; identifying all aspects of the school curriculum that will require specific time provision and establishing priorities for each year group;
- for each year group, discussing and agreeing the proportions of the total teaching time to be allocated to each aspect of the curriculum;
- identifying which aspects of each curriculum area, including National Curriculum subjects and religious education, to organize and teach as *continuing* work, and allocating them to year groups. Identifying which aspects of each curriculum area, including National Curriculum subjects and religious education, to organize and teach as distinct and cohesive *blocked* units of work and allocate them to year groups;
- allowing notional amounts of time to each of the units of work identified in the previous task;
- identifying and agreeing links between units of work established in the previous task and reviewing time allocations;
- completing the planning process by bringing together the outcomes of stages 4 and 5 and allocating work to the three terms of each year.

There is no question that this is a formidable task. Schools may understandably decide to persevere with their current arrangements for managing the curriculum rather than embarking on so large an enterprise prior to inspection. There are also some severe challenges implicit in the process: deciding on the composition of blocked and continuing units, resolving where different subject units may be most appropriately linked, for example. One of the most significant features of the process, perhaps, is the extent to which it limits possibilities of large-scale project approaches. This may simply represent a sensible recognition of the changes called for in curriculum planning at primary level, brought about by the National Curriculum.

However, while schools facing inspection may delay undertaking a curriculum review of this dimension, consideration of it, even briefly, will alert staff to important issues of curriculum management and time allocation that can be profitably discussed as part of the inspection preparation. In the space of a week, inspectors find it difficult to get a full picture of curriculum balance and it may consequently be an issue pursued less rigorously than evidence of all subjects being taught and of National Curriculum requirements being effectively met.

Does the curriculum meet the curricular requirements of all pupils on the school Code of Practice Special Educational Needs Register?

Special educational needs (SEN) provision is obviously a matter of enormous importance and one that inspectors will examine minutely. Lesson planning in every case should provide for special educational needs through differentiation, planned tasks, resourcing, and appropriate grouping. Curriculum co-ordinators should ensure that guidance in relation to SEN is built into schemes of work. In this case we are considering provision for pupils who have been placed on the school's special educational needs register because, as a result of assessment by the school, their academic, physical, social or emotional development – or, very often, a combination of these – is giving cause for concern.

Inspectors will pay particular attention to the implementation of the code of practice. Inspection of this aspect of school life tends to be extremely searching. The requirements of the code represent formidable new demands upon professional expertise, time and resources. Ofsted's survey of provision suggests, however, that schools are beginning to cope well. Equally, it pinpoints areas of weakness common to many schools. In reviewing the code of practice and special needs provision, schools can do no better than refer to the Ofsted guidelines arising from their survey. The guidelines provide clear and valuable advice on:

● the school's SEN policy;
● the duties of governing bodies;
● the role of the SEN co-ordinator;
● the position of parents;
● individual education plans;
● annual reviews.

It may be helpful to quote here what Ofsted regards as 12 key issues for schools to consider in relation to the code of practice:

● What is meant by a school's special educational provision at Key Stages 1 to 3 being 'generally available written existing sources'?

- What can be reasonably expected by way of Key Stage 3 external support when seen as 'immediately necessary'?
- What is a practical workload for class and subject teachers, particularly at Key Stages 1 and 2?
- How can governors, especially SEN nominated governors, become more involved and fulfil their legal responsibilities?
- What is a sound set of criteria for measuring the success of the school's provision for SEN?
- How can the school development plan ensure that the consideration of the needs of pupils with SEN is present across all years, all subject departments and all aspects of the school's life?
- How can and does a teacher formulate and review an appropriate number of targets?
- Are funds specifically identified in the LEA formula, for helping pupils with SEN, and how are they distributed to the pupils for whom they are allocated?
- How can the partnership with parents become more effective?
- How can IEPs (Individual Education Programmes) be integrated into the school's general arrangements for assessing and recording the progress of all pupils?
- How can pupils with SEN become more involved in reviewing their own progress?
- How can the school assist the different educational, health and social service providers to become more of a united service?

Schools will respond to these very much according to individual circumstances. There is no doubt that the demands of the Code fall far more heavily on some than on others. In my opinion, few areas of school life exemplify more vividly the fact that schools will be constantly aspiring to perfection rather than attaining it. Where the immensely important matter of SEN and the new legal requirements attached to them are concerned, many schools are still at various stages of development. What they must demonstrate is genuine commitment, a comprehensive awareness of what is required of them and processes in place to achieve provision.

Is the curriculum enriched by extra-curricular provisions, including sport?

In many schools, extra-curricular provision continues to enhance the education of pupils. Clubs, classes and organizations provide for sporting, creative, cultural, scientific, aesthetic and natural history pursuits. They sometimes involve shared activities and competitions with other schools. They are inspired by the interests and enthusiasms of teachers, pupils, parents and members of the wider community. They reflect an admirable side of school life: a concern to enrich pupils' experience; to initiate interests that may well endure as a source of rapture and recreation in later life; to compensate for deprivation and lack of opportunity; to broaden horizons and give a glimpse of what might be.

Extra-curricular provision enables pupils to work and play collaboratively, to do what absorbs them free of evaluation, to enjoy, manage and put competition in perspective. It can make a significant contribution to the spiritual, moral, social and cultural life of the school.

In the main such provision owes its existence to the enthusiasm and generosity of teachers. It can be therefore a telling indicator of the spirit and ethos of a school, of its determination to go beyond mere obligation in the interests of the pupils.

It is easy, in time, for all that wide additional provision to become, save for those who participate in it, a little-regarded routine in the busy life of a school. Schools should ensure therefore that inspectors have adequate evidence of the programme of extra-curricular provision. Inspectors should have:

- a detailed programme of all activities, including those that will occur during the inspection week;
- a description of aims, purposes and rationale; the benefits and gains for pupils;
- invitation and encouragement to observe the programme in action and opportunity to discuss it with the participants. Inspectors will welcome the chance to do this.

It is also important that schools give a full account of the provision for sport outside of formal lessons, especially the steps that are taken to promote traditional team games, the numbers of pupils for whom this provides, the teachers involved and any competitions with other schools. Stress improvements and developments that the school may have brought about in providing curricular and extra-curricular games.

Are there effective systems for assessing pupils' attainment? Is assessment information used to inform curriculum planning?

Formative assessment is now commonly accepted as integral and absolutely essential to effective teaching and learning. It will be central to inspectors' evaluation in terms of the school overall policy and arrangements and in relation to every subject. They will wish to establish that:

- there is continuity of practice secured through a school policy;
- the policy provides for practical strategies that will make the demanding requirement for continuous formative assessment operable for the class teacher;
- arrangements for regular formative assessment of the core subjects are clearly defined;
- there is an economical, efficient system of recording and flagging up crucial stages of pupils' learning, progress and attainment to receiving teachers and those who need to know. (It is important to stress that this would not call for elaborate and complex systems, demanding prolonged and time-consuming analysis and investigation. It would be a systematic summary, at particular stages that indicated cumulative achievement of important skills and concepts. It would be linked to the kinds of profiles of achievement that are described here a little further on.)

Formative assessment provides for a systematic check of attainment and development in the foundation subjects, but on a significantly less detailed basis than the core subjects. One of the functions of such assessment will be to amass information for annual reports to parents. Information about core curriculum subjects will be gathered on a much more regular basis. Sometimes this will comprise no more than mental notes for teachers, gained from passing observations that are used to determine a response to an individual, group or class need, that will help with immediate planning but do not demand formal recording.

On other occasions teachers will set up assessments, tests and checks, with the intention of documenting necessary information.

Inspectors will wish to confirm that:

- assessments are related to the National Curriculum programmes of study and take account of the level descriptions;
- teachers match their assessments against national assessments – the SATs, for example – and any standardized testing used by the school or required, for example, by an LEA or outside validating body;
- perhaps most importantly of all, that teachers can demonstrate that the information obtained from assessment is being used to inform planning and to ensure continuity and progression in pupils' work.

How can schools translate these requirements into practical and effective action?

- Time for formative assessment of aspects of the core subjects needs to be built into every working week, though obviously not necessarily into every lesson; sometimes important information will emerge incidentally.
- Assessment needs to be a constant feature of teachers' planning.
- It is necessary, as part of whole school policy, to decide which aspects of the programmes of study need to be included as essential components of the assessment programme. However, many teachers will settle, of course, for additional activities and outcomes that they wish to take account of.

Attainment and progress can be assessed through a range of methods:

- assignments and tasks devised especially to test aspects of the programmes of study or to determine the extent to which particular units of work have been mastered. These may be given on an individual, group or class basis;
- observation of the response of groups of pupils to particular activities or on-going pieces of work that may yield information which teachers decide is worth taking account of;
- the use of graded worksheets;
- the use of the assessment materials increasingly provided by commercial schemes of work – mathematics schemes, for example;

- the observation and noting of common mistakes and misunderstandings by classes or groups of pupils and gearing teaching to provide for these;
- maintaining evidence from pupils' work that exemplifies assessments of levels of attainment. It is very important that schools are clear about this matter. The practice of using samples of pupils' work to compile sequential records of attainment has become common in schools. In fact Ofsted stresses that teachers are required only to collect samples of work carefully assessed and annotated to exemplify attainment at each level. Schools are increasingly doing this, especially in the core subjects (with written work often exemplifying achievement across a range of foundation subjects) and maintaining the evidence in pupil profiles or folders. Samples from such assessments are also kept in schools as exemplars of attainment at various levels for teachers to refer to.

The maintenance of such profiles can be a demanding and cumbersome task. Ideal as a basis for informing individual parents about their children's progress, they are not always, because of their cumulative volume, easily accessible to receiving teachers who wish to inform themselves of pupils' current attainment and cognitive development.

It is suggested therefore that schools give consideration to the use of a particular strategy for maintaining formative assessment, that has a number of advantages. It works in this way. All pupils are given a 'profile book'. Teachers indicate to pupils that at particular times pieces of work in the core subjects – and, where appropriate, in the foundation subjects – will be entered in the profile book. It is made clear to pupils that such work will be assessed and annotated, that the outcomes will be treated as a formal record, that it will be discussed in some detail with them and that it will be sent to parents for their consideration and written comment. There is no suggestion that this is 'better' than normal work or that it has to be accorded more care and attention than their work customarily receives. Any suggestion of that kind would only be likely to undervalue what pupils produce and achieve from day to day. What is important for pupils to appreciate is the purpose of documenting their efforts in this particular way: to maintain a continuous record of their achievement and development gathered together in a readily accessible source which remains their possession and about which they can comment.

Entries to the profile book can be made on a regular basis or concentrated during particular weeks. The value of such a profile book will be obvious to teachers:

- it makes pupils conscious of the process, makes them aware of the purposes of assessment and evaluation, develops their ability to be reflective and analytical about their work, and provides both an impetus to improvement and ways of achieving it;
- it involves parents in the process in a meaningful way;
- it reinforces assessment as an integral part of teaching and learning;
- it gathers work together in an organized and methodical way and presents it for examination in a manner that allows individual pieces to be viewed in a wider context;
- it allows for samples of work to be easily selected and photocopied.

The growing national emphasis on the promotion of pupil progress, the raising of standards through target setting and the identification of 'value added' has been accompanied by the development of a wide range of measuring and assessment procedures. In relation to the *formal* measurement of pupils' progress, schools are strongly recommended to refer to and consider at least some of the recommendations of the DFEE/Ofsted publication *Setting targets to raise standards*.

Sources of evidence used by inspectors: a checklist for action

Before the inspection
- the head teacher's form and the school prospectus;
- curriculum policies, guidelines or schemes of work;
- school curriculum audits or analyses (if available);
- discussion at pre-inspection meetings with head, governors and parents.

During the inspection
- observation of lessons;
- observation and analysis of extra-curricular activities;
- a scrutiny of samples of pupils' work and records, including National Curriculum assessment;
- discussions with teachers, support staff and pupils;

- examination of individual education plans, statements and annual reviews.

The inspection report will include judgements on the following matters:

- breadth, balance and relevance of the curriculum;
- match to satisfactory requirements (National Curriculum, RE and sex education) where these apply;
- equality of access and opportunity;
- curriculum provision for all pupils with SEN;
- planning for continuity and programme of learning;
- enrichment through extra-curricular provision, including sport;
- quality of careers education and guidance for pupils of secondary school age;
- the extent to which there are effective systems for assessing pupils' attainment; assessment is used to inform curriculum planning.

Schools are recommended to review and consider action of the following kind where feasible:

- Ensure that the areas of learning stipulated by Ofsted are being provided for all pupils under five, whatever the setting. Ensure that teachers are relating their planning to the desirable outcomes for children when they enter compulsory education.
- Review your arrangements for involving the parents and carers of young children in a partnership with the school.
- Ensure that regular formative assessment is central to the planning of teachers working with children under five.
- Make a careful survey of the coverage being achieved for National Curriculum subjects.
- Decide on a priority list for any corrective action that needs to be taken.
- Use the SCAA planning suggestions for reviewing the organization of the curriculum at Key Stage 2.
- Review your provision for pupils on the SEN register, taking particular account of the advice provided by the Ofsted survey.
- Review the provision made for pupils in relation to extra-curricular provision. Ensure that it is drawn to the attention of inspectors.
- Review the system for assessing pupils' attainment.

Primary schools need to consider carefully whether there is a need for standardized testing of pupils' attainment in reading and numeracy at stages in Key Stage 2 other than what is provided for at the end of the key stage. There is reason to believe that teachers need to have more precise information available about pupils' attainment and progress at certain stages of Key Stage 2 (for example, year 4) than can be provided by reference to the level descriptions in the orders.

The following questions to the TES column 'An Inspector Writes' highlight some areas that schools have expressed concern about.

Q The Office for Standards in Education has recognized the need for a 'level playing field' when making judgements about schools in contrasting circumstances. But how can inspectors make allowances, in socially disadvantaged schools, for the demands of the special educational needs code of practice and its overwhelming impact on other areas of school life and management? Will inspectors be satisfied with evidence that a school is doing its best to meet the requirements of the code, even if it cannot practically apply them to all targeted pupils?

A I might have delayed an answer to this, since I am not wholly confident of my reply, had not the question reflected a growing concern on the part of many schools about their capacity to meet the needs of pupils as defined by the code.

The code makes heavy demands in terms of the entitlement of registered pupils. There seems to be little doubt that some schools are wilting under the strain of making proper provision. Many claim that insufficient account has been taken of the likely repercussions of the code. How then should an inspector react in a situation where, as the question suggests, a school is not meeting the code's requirements in relation to all the registered pupils because it claims it is not practicable to do so?

I think an inspector should seek assurance that:

- governors are using their best endeavours to secure appropriate provision for their pupils who have special educational needs;
- the processes set out by the code are in place, inform the school SEN policy and are understood by all teachers;
- the special needs co-ordinator is provided with the authority, time

and resources to discharge the role and the means to support staff;
- the detailed requirements for pupils whose special educational needs are pronounced and severe are met, including formal statementing where appropriate;
- provision accompanying such statementing is properly implemented.

Finally, I think the inspector should take account of the statement in the inspection handbook: 'The degree to which pupils require additional help lies along a continuum and should be considered in the context of the provision normally available.'

Perhaps mistakenly, I take this as a faintly enigmatic plea for discretion, a reminder that a school can not only do the best it can, but must do the best it can. I believe that one of the justifications of the inspection cycle is that it illuminates areas we have been squeamish about looking at and raises issues we have been reluctant to cover. The plight of disadvantaged schools in providing for SEN is surely one of these. Inspectors will help by considering their circumstances with particular care. But in the end Ofsted may just confirm for us that we have here a problem too large to solve at a purely local level.

Q   The new inspection framework no longer calls for judgements about achievement in relation to ability. This was almost impossible to do in such a short timescale. But is its replacement – judgements about children's progress – likely to be any more reliable, or easy? For example, how can an inspector judge whether children in a large junior class are making progress in geography on the evidence of a single lesson?

A   It will be particularly important for inspectors to understand and establish what schools in disadvantaged circumstances are achieving in terms of children's progress, especially where evidence about their attainment in National Curriculum subjects will probably make disappointing reading for parents and cast misleading reflections on teachers' work.

Inspectors evaluate and report on what pupils are achieving in relation to national standards – and the progress they make in relation to their earlier attainment. As you suggest, this judgement about progress is extremely important, because it is a key indicator of the effectiveness of the school or subject area, and a difficult matter to get right. Inspectors are required to decide not merely whether there are gains in knowledge, understanding and skill, but whether they are sufficient, good or poor in relation to prior attainments. Clearly to base such judgements on the evidence of individual lessons, or even collections of lessons alone, would be unrealistic and unacceptable. Inspectors are required to employ various methods:

- frequent and systematic lesson observations are important. For example, in the geography lesson you allude to, an inspector might be seeking to pinpoint children's ability to recognize and apply patterns, to use appropriate geographical vocabulary, or to use and interpret globes, maps and plans at a variety of scales, and to determine whether that knowledge or skill has been extended or developed to any recognizable extent during the course of the lesson. The inspector will take account of children's ability to cope with, respond to and comprehend the lesson and will listen to their incidental talk and comments, the contributions they make, their responses to questions and the questions they raise for themselves.

  He or she will examine all work they do and the manner in which they tackle problems and deal with tasks – attempting as far as possible to relate all this to their previous understanding and attainment and to previous achievement;
- examine samples of children's completed work to compare achievement, to look for evidence of progress in specific knowledge, developing skills, more fluent descriptions and accounts and better presentation of information at different times;
- find out the levels, skills and techniques achieved through looking at the work on display;
- look at other forms of display and information, visual records, photographs, evidence of projects, out-of-school activities and similar educational initiatives;
- look at all forms of recorded assessment so past and present attainment can be compared;
- compare the work of different age groups in the same subject and the work of pupils of similar ability in different age groups;
- discuss the perceptions and evidence of teachers and other adults about children's progress;
- judge the progress of under-fives by observing the same children, taking account of whether they return to activities, showing what

they can do and how much further they can take them; practise, consolidate and extend their skills; solve practical problems.

In the area of children's progress, schools can offer useful information and valuable advice to inspectors. The advances pupils are making, what they are learning, how well they are getting on, have always been central preoccupations of teachers.

Schools monitor children's attainment and progress through formative assessment; profiles of work and the moderation of levels of achievement; national tests; the application of the special needs code of practice; entry profiles and baseline assessment.

This knowledge of children's progress can contribute significantly to inspectors' insights.

Q Inspection requirements have encouraged us to be more thorough about the evaluation of children's work. However, we are finding it more difficult to cope with the monitoring and evaluation of teaching and learning. Can you suggest practical strategies that will also satisfy inspectors?

A You have already made a positive start by setting up processes for monitoring and evaluating the children's work, because that will provide you with important information about the quality of learning and possibly teaching as well. But, as you suggest, the evaluation of teaching and learning is a larger, more complex and sensitive task.

Whatever strategies you decide upon, ensure that:

- monitoring and evaluation are part of the school planning cycle and the school development plan;
- all staff understand and accept its purpose: to broaden their experience and understanding, extend their expertise, and help them assume some responsibility for colleagues' development, create general agreement about teaching and learning processes and enhance the quality of work and achievement;
- evaluation is developmental, i.e. that the information it yields is used to underpin judgements about future development;
- your strategies are practicable: manageable in terms of expertise, time and resources;
- expectations of and demands on teachers are sensible and realistic;

- everyone is clear about who observes, the form it will take, the time to be allocated, the criteria employed, the way the information will be used;
- that feedback is supportive and developmental.

Establish:

- what the criteria for observation are;
- who will do the observing: senior staff, co-ordinators, key stage colleagues;
- the time allocated to the process and how that is provided for;
- the form of feedback.

Which strategies might you use? Here are some suggestions:

Classroom observation
- Decide the aspects of teaching and learning to be observed, e.g. time management, SEN provision, organization of groups, forms of differentiation, pupils' attitudes to learning, levels of attainment and progress.
- Decide how far the observation is related to the SDP and the whole school, key stage or year group issues.
- Decide what the criteria for observation are, e.g. quality of match between learners and activities; pace of work; degree of learner independence; nature of pupil response and behaviour; level of achievement and quality of progress.

Review of teacher planning
In reviewing teachers' planning you will wish to ascertain how far it provides for:

- statutory requirements; the coverage of National Curriculum subjects and programmes of study; other aspects of the school curriculum;
- broad levels of learning ability and forms of differentiation;
- appropriate styles of organization – whole class, groups and individual;
- the SEN code of practice;
- systematic formative assessment;

- the use of resources.

Any review of planning has to be closely related, of course, to school policy – the range of planning timescales used, the curriculum models favoured by the school and the forms of classroom organization employed.

Review of teacher assessment

As with planning, your evaluation of assessment will be significantly determined by the school policy and the lead it provides on issues such as the frequency of teacher assessment, the range of subjects to be targeted for review (all curriculum areas, core or on a rota basis); the forms of evidence acquired and how documented and recorded, the moderation of work, the use of standardized assessment and the employment of any form of base-line assessment.

In your evaluation you are likely to want to establish whether assessment is:

- providing reliable information about progression and achievement;
- contributing to and supportive of the planning of teaching and learning;
- enhancing rather than impeding teaching;
- helping children to monitor and understand their own achievement;
- promoting achievement through the compilation of profiles of work of high quality and standards.

Review of pupils' work

You are already engaged in this, but may wish to ensure that your evaluation criteria include:

- evidence of outcomes matching ability;
- high but realistic teacher expectations;
- the matching of SEN individual learning programmes to developmental needs;
- appropriate presentation of work;
- evidence of improvement and progress;
- consistent, constructive interactive marking.

There are other ways, of course – staff discussions, the nature of the learning environment, the quality of displays – that can all contribute significantly to the evaluation of teaching and learning in a school. But it is important that you are selective about the range of strategies employed. The combination of some of those referred to will provide you with a substantial basis, while avoiding the danger of teachers and children being overwhelmed by observation and measurement.

7

Leadership and management

The inspection focus in this section is on the extent to which leadership and management produce an effective school. The effective school is defined as one that promotes and sustains improvement in:

- educational standards achieved;
- the quality of education provided.

Judgements are based on the extent to which:

- strong leadership provides clear educational direction for the work of the school;
- teaching and curriculum development are monitored, evaluated and supported;
- the school has aims, values and policies which are reflected through all its work;
- there is a positive ethos which reflects the school's commitment to high achievement, an effective learning environment, good relationships and equality of opportunity for all pupils;
- the school, through its development planning, identifies relevant priorities and targets, takes the necessary action and monitors and evaluates its progress towards them;
- statutory requirements are met.

The inspection report will make judgements about:

- effect of leadership on the work of the school;
- monitoring and support for teaching and curriculum development;
- reflection of school's aims, values and policies in its work;
- development planning, implementation and evaluation to achieve targets and priorities;
- how well the school's ethos reflects commitment to high achievement, an effective learning environment, good relationships and equality of opportunity for all pupils;
- whether statutory requirements are met.

There are three key points about the evaluation:

- The focus is on the impact of leadership rather than leadership intentions, though obviously inspectors will wish to know what the latter are.
- Account will be taken of the quality of leadership and management, rather than style.
- Style and pattern of leadership are not judged for themselves but for their effectiveness.

Leadership and management will be judged as a whole. Judgement will take into careful account the part played and the contribution made by governors and staff.

One of the features of the contemporary school is the more inclusive and wide-ranging view that is taken of leadership and management. This is no longer seen as confined to a small coterie of senior staff. Heads of department carry the main responsibility for the quality of teaching and learning, of performance, progress and achievement in their subject domains; beneath them, post-holders at a variety of levels are accountable for managing aspects of the departmental work. Subject co-ordinators in primary schools are responsible for the overall quality of curriculum areas through the school, for monitoring the quality of teaching and learning, the levels of achievement and the progress being made, for leading on INSET and staff development. As the handbook points out, in primary and nursery schools, most teachers and some nursery assistants hold responsibility for aspects of the school curriculum and organization, and in some cases more than one area of responsibility.

Even class teachers, with no designated responsibility outside the care of their particular class – rare indeed now, in primary schools – are encouraged to think of themselves as managers of their pupils' learning, using time, resources and data to the very best extent in carrying out the task.

Inspectors, therefore, in evaluating the leadership and management of the school, will focus on three groups:

- the governing body;
- the head teacher;
- all other staff.

Governing bodies have important statutory responsibilities. They are accountable to parents and the wider community for the overall performance of the school. They are responsible for the secular curriculum policy, a policy on sex education, for the making and management of the school development plan, for managing, monitoring and reviewing the budget and for monitoring the school's progress, achievement and general effectiveness. They must ensure that there are school policies on pupil discipline, admissions and collective worship. They are required to fix the times of school sessions and dates of term and to produce the annual report to parents.

Ofsted identifies three main tasks for governors:

- to provide a strategic view of where the school is heading;
- to act as a critical friend to the school;
- to hold the school to account for the educational standards it achieves and the quality of education it provides.

Schools cannot stand apart from this element of the inspection and take the line that it is the business of the governors to cope with it as well as possible. The fortunes of school and governing body are inextricably bound up together; they are accountable to each other and have mutual responsibilities that should be reflected in an agreed and comprehensive agenda, that on occasions may well have been forged out of compromise and contending views and beliefs.

Schools need to do these things for their governing body:

- Keep them fully informed about the life and work of the school. This will include the knowledge they need to have on the school budget and development plan, the curriculum and extra-curricular provision, how the school is staffed, organized and managed, and school policies on major issues.

● Enable them to carry out the statutory responsibilities already referred to.

● Enable them to have a strategic view of where the school is heading. This will be most effectively done by genuinely involving them in the making of the school's development, business and financial plans.

● Encourage governors to play a monitoring and evaluative role in relation to the work of the school and the education it is providing. The position of critical friend is one of the most valuable and important that a governing body can exercise. Few things are less helpful in the end than a collusive relationship that seeks to resist or deny the need for consistent and rigorous review. The whole welfare of the pupils in the long run is significantly affected by the clarity, detachment and integrity with which the governors carry out the monitoring aspect of their work. Schools can help them by providing access to essential curriculum planning, data about pupils' achievement and progress, opportunity for individual governors to be associated with particular curriculum areas and support for the development of governor sub-groups.

In terms of financial management, the Ofsted and Audit Commission document 'Keeping Your Balance' provides essential advice. The questionnaire given in the document's appendix is designed to help governing bodies quickly assess the areas of financial management in which they need to take action. 'Adding Up The Sums', published by the Audit Commission, suggests a basic financial report that enables governors to monitor the budget effectively.

In relation to the two major responsibilities of drawing up the school development plan and monitoring the effectiveness of the school, the Ofsted publication 'Governing Bodies and Effective Schools' suggests certain key issues to be focused on:

● in *development planning*: where the governors are intending to get to and their key priorities; their current position and how they can move from that to where they want to be; whether they have the necessary resources to achieve their objectives; the identification and allocation of specific responsibilities, together with timescales for completion; the application of success criteria.

- their *evaluation of school effectiveness*: the key issues include: analysis of performance indicators, including: National Curriculum assessments and tests and/or secondary examination results; pupil attendance and exclusions, pupil involvement in extra-curricular activities; number of applications for admissions; destinations of school leavers.
- evaluation of more subjective indicators, including pupils' behaviour and attitudes, staff morale and commitment, the perceptions that parents and the community hold of the school and their attitude to it.
- whether parts of the school are more effective than others and, if so, the reasons for this. Governors are urged to examine the performance of different year groups, different departments in secondary schools, or different curriculum areas in primary schools.
- whether different groups of pupils are doing better than others and if so, why. Whether the school is more effective for different types of pupils, depending on gender, ethnic background and level of ability.
- how the school's achievement now compares with its previous achievement. How the school's performance compares with other schools. National assessment arrangements and examinations now provide information on levels of attainment in schools that allow for comparison of individual results with national and local results.
- what the school has contributed to pupil performance, focusing on the progress made by the pupils in comparison with other similar schools.

These are extremely serious and demanding responsibilities. They weigh heavily on governing bodies. However, when it comes to inspection, while inspectors will be anxious to have as extensive a dialogue as possible with governors, constraints of time will probably confine them to discussion of governors' involvement in determining the policies and management of the school in relation to:

- efficiency (finance/budget);
- management and administration, including the annual parents' meeting;
- staffing and accommodation;

- behaviour and discipline;
- the curriculum, particularly RE, special educational needs and sex education.

The handbooks stress the role of the head teacher as one who leads the school and is responsible for its management and organization. It places particular emphasis on his/her accountability for the quality of work achieved by teachers and pupils, for the standards of attainment, for maintaining improvement in outcomes where this is called for, and for ensuring the proper use of systems and resources towards these ends. The monitoring role is seen as extremely and increasingly important. Head teachers will be expected to have an informed and accurate picture of the quality of teaching and learning throughout the school, how outcomes compare with national standards, whether standards of attainment are adequate or could be higher, and whether teaching is contributing as effectively as possible to that. Their perceptions will have to be based on substantial objective evidence, rather than surmise or wishful thinking. Head teachers need to remember that inspectorate judgements about all the main aspects of a school – the teaching provided by staff, the learning resources and materials, the use of accommodation, the financial planning, the communication systems and administration – will relate to the effectiveness with which these contribute to and help secure satisfactory attainment and progress by pupils.

It is not uncommon now for head teachers to be referred to as 'inspectors in residence', a description not always palatable either to teachers or the heads themselves. Nevertheless, the phrase serves usefully to remind heads of the need to know exactly what is happening in the school, to have a clear picture, for example, of what pupils experience in terms of teaching and learning over any particular period of time; to be confident that achievement is as good as it could be; not only that pupils are doing things 'better than they did a term ago' but that the improvement is adequate and will be maintained. This in a sense, perhaps, represents the greatest change brought about by Ofsted: a main emphasis on outcomes, with a factor as central as teaching assuming its importance from the effectiveness with which it contributes to these outcomes.

Similarly, the whole environment of the school will be evaluated on the extent to which it contributes to 'core purposes of teaching and learning', and not, for example, on its inherent aesthetic appeal. The leadership and management provided not alone by the head or the head and senior staff, but by the whole staff, according to their carefully defined areas of responsibility, will be evaluated according to the contribution they make to the school's achievement and attainment.

Obviously the ways and means by which such leadership and management are carried out will vary according to the nature and size of a school. The part-time or full-time teaching head of a small primary school is clearly not going to be able to exercise, for example, the evaluation and monitoring of colleagues or provide to the same extent the practical support in classrooms for them that head teachers in larger schools could. However, there are other things such heads could do to ensure a proper focus on standards and progress and to ensure effective support for teachers' work and professional development. In common with schools elsewhere, the head and staff of a smaller school will need to be sure that everyone is working to common goals and purposes, have identified the strengths and weaknesses of the school in the broadest sense and at classroom level, have developed or be in the process of developing strategies for maintaining strengths and rectifying shortcomings, and to have clear priorities for improvement and ways of evaluating their progress and success.

Now let us look at the inspection criteria in these main areas and consider what schools can do, in terms of leadership and management, to meet their requirements.

Does strong leadership provide clear educational direction for the work of the school?

In this context the leadership of the school needs to provide for a clearly defined working relationship with the governing body. The leadership needs to support governors in having a long-term strategic view of the school in determining what its goals and targets are to be over the forthcoming two, three or four years. They need to arrive at a shared understanding of how all available resources will be used to implement a development or business plan designed to provide for the highest quality of education possible. They need particularly to match their planning for curriculum development to the finances available to them. It is not sufficient for a governing body to ensure that proper financial control and systems are in place and that actual expenditure compares with budgeted expenditure. These are, of course, very important matters and inspectors will want to know about the arrangements for their management; but they are only part of the story. Even more important will be the decisions about expenditure priorities and the grounds on which they are made, whether the importance of proposed major development is reflected in budgeting that provides adequately for them over extended periods of, say, a few years, especially at a time of financial unpredictability and uncertainty. There needs to be assurance that provision for staff appointments, now and in the future, ensures the acquisition of staff qualified to implement the development plan.

It is likely that governing bodies will establish a sub-group to manage financial matters. It will be important for the school to be represented on and contribute to the work of such a group.

Governors need to have sufficient clear and reliable information about the nature and quality of education provided by the school. This will be done by enabling them to become broadly familiar, at least, with the nature of National Curriculum subjects, about the significance of levels of achievement, and what pupils are expected to learn and master by different stages.

They need to know:

- how achievement and progress are monitored;
- about special educational needs provision for pupils at all main levels and stages;
- how assessment, formative and summative, is organized and how the information obtained from it is used to identify strengths and weaknesses in pupils' learning, to build on one and rectify the other.

In practical terms, this can be done by:

- making relevant curriculum documentation – possibly summarized – available to governors;
- by giving staff, co-ordinators, post-holders, heads of departments, senior staff opportunity to formally present to governors evidence of their curriculum planning, practical work and evaluated achievements;
- by inviting individual governors to link with departments or co-

ordinators and make themselves the governing body's experts/
consultants on specific curriculum areas;
- by regular provision and interpretation of objective evidence about
  pupils' attainment and progress;
- by establishing with governors ways not merely of monitoring the
  implementations of the main elements of the development plan, but
  of *evaluating* the extent to which these have been successfully
  implemented and the degree to which they provide value for money.
  In some cases both the school and the governing body may require
  external analysis and evidence in relation to the issue of value for
  money;
- by setting up a curriculum steering sub-group that would receive
  evaluation evidence, consider proposed curriculum developments,
  and act as a mediating and interpreting group for the parent body.

This particular criterion stresses that evaluation of the role of head
teacher will focus on the extent to which his or her leadership and management are influential in the quality of provision and the educational
standards achieved. In consequence, the head teacher will need to be
able to respond accurately and authoritatively about the following
issues:

- how the school plans for the pupils' education translate into practice,
  and what this eventually means in terms of pupils' regular classroom
  experience; whether provision matches National Curriculum
  requirements and any other statutory demands, e.g. provision of
  equal opportunity, the requirements posed by special educational
  needs;
- the means by which pupils' achievement and progress are
  monitored;
- whether the pupils' attainment is satisfactory; whether it matches
  national averages and, if not, whether the school can provide
  acceptable explanation and justification of that;
- the steps that are being taken to raise the standards of attainment;
  whether these are the result of careful analysis of work and the
  diagnoses of formative and summative assessment;
- how the school measures pupils' progress and achievement: through
  regular assessment and testing; moderation and the maintenance of
  profiles of work; reference to the National Curriculum levels of
  achievement; the consistent involvement of pupils in analysis of their

work; through target setting for improvement with them, through reference to and communication with parents;

- the quality of classroom teaching. This will call for agreement in the school about what constitutes effective teaching, which will mean in turn resolving dilemmas such as the correct balance of teaching and learning in lessons, effective ways of grouping and organizing pupils for work, provision for differentiation, the management of formative assessment, how effective discipline, pace of work, and acceptable outcomes can be achieved. It will require, especially, attention to ways in which extended interaction between teachers and pupils can be managed.

The realization of these objectives, in their turn, will be assisted by attention to schemes of work and good resourcing; through coherent whole school planning, monitoring and evaluation of classroom practice by heads of departments and co-ordinators and through the provision by them of practical classroom support.

The observation and monitoring of teaching performance by colleagues is a sensitive matter in schools. More schools are following the lead provided in this area by appraisal, and enabling senior staff and co-ordinators to observe and comment on colleagues' teaching performance. Some schools have initiated the practice through observations and evaluations by self-elected 'pairs', or within year groups or by 'neighbouring' teachers or by systems such as the 'triangles' suggested by Bernard Clark (Appendix 7.3). It is often most effectively done where there are clear criteria for observation, where specific aspects or areas are identified for attention, where observers are well informed about the context and where observations are closely linked to lesson planning. A particular concern for heads and of considerable interest to inspectors will be how senior staff, heads of departments, co-ordinators and all teachers with management responsibilities are enabled to carry them out. They will hope to find:

- clearly defined agreement about the role of staff carrying such responsibility, set out in job descriptions which define the aims, objectives and range of the task. Post-holders themselves will have a clear line of accountability and direction within a management framework;
- the regular availability of teachers' planning to the co-ordinators;

- opportunity and necessary resources to monitor and evaluate pupils' attainment, performance and progress through access to their work and outcomes of assessment;
- opportunity for designated staff to monitor and evaluate the work of colleagues in classrooms;
- either direct control over funding for a subject or curriculum area, or at least opportunity to make representation and bids for what the post-holders establish as necessary;
- an obligation to produce a subject development plan that takes account of the school development plan;
- opportunity to set up appropriate INSET for colleagues;
- access to appropriate INSET and to support from the school leadership in the interpretation of the role;
- an obligation to devise means of evaluating the effectiveness of their role.

This leads us naturally to the next criterion.

Are teaching and curriculum development monitored, evaluated and supported?

The perception of schools as self-evaluating organizations and the consistent monitoring and evaluation of curriculum and teaching by schools themselves are relatively new developments. It is now generally accepted that schools should know how far their objectives and targets are being achieved, what their strengths and weaknesses are, the extent to which pupil attainment and progress relate satisfactorily to national averages, how far the deployment of budgets and resources are justified by outcomes, whether teaching is successfully measured against widely accepted criteria and how far the school can be said to be providing value for money.

How can schools go about this and what evidence do they need to offer inspectors? First of all, schools need to consider what evidence is necessary and how it can be gathered. Evidence of attainment and progress will be gathered from regular assessment, from the grading of samples of work, and matching those with National Curriculum requirements and levels of achievement, from standardized testing, from the moderation of work samples against National Curriculum criteria, from consistently matching pupils' levels of attainment and performance against previous levels, from the establishment of baseline and entry levels of achievement as means to help determine value added by the school and from any evaluative information held by the LEA.

Schools need to identify strengths and weaknesses in whole school performance, both in teaching and learning, and to identify, as far as possible, the causes of these. They then need to decide what can be done to maintain strengths and to correct weaknesses. Out of such analysis and the information it provides schools can:

- devise plans for attending to weaknesses;
- implement developments and strategies that may be needed on a whole school basis, e.g. measures in all year groups for supporting pupils to develop literacy skills as quickly and efficiently as possible;
- manage change;
- set targets for improvement in pupils' attainment and progress;
- identify necessary INSET, related to skills and capacities that teachers must develop;
- pinpoint where review, change and development may be needed.

Does the school have aims, values and policies which are reflected through all its work?

In an important sense these are the elements that define a school, that give it its particular quality, that help to make it unique. They need to be thoroughly worked out, to be based on a clear and firm rationale, to be set down and articulated, to be understood, accepted and committed to by all who are required to implement them. Staff sometimes express surprise at being questioned, in the process of inspection, about areas that may seem the responsibility of colleagues. This is often a result of inspectors seeking to establish whether purposes, aims and intentions are commonly understood and shared by all staff.

Schools, in responding to this criterion, would need to review their aims and values and give colleagues an opportunity to contribute to the process. Outcomes would be documented and made available to staff, governors, pupils and parents.

If values are to be genuine and worthwhile, if they are to inform the work, attitudes and conduct of the school, then they have to be based on a recognition of the following:

- the rights and needs of pupils and their entitlement to the best and most fulfilling lifestyle possible;
- the need for pupils to develop moral sensibility, positive codes of behaviour and integrity, a capacity to relate to others, whether they be individuals or groups; to contribute usefully to their community and society at large;
- the need for equality of opportunity to be available to all;
- the entitlement of pupils to the whole of the National Curriculum and to all those additional areas of learning, development and achievement that the school deems appropriate;
- the chance for pupils to acquire skills and competencies that will enrich their lives, e.g. the ability to speak a modern language, to play a musical instrument, to have access to and knowledge of the wider world;
- the necessity for pupils to develop positive awareness of self and the capacity to have equal regard for others;
- the importance of providing for pupils' special educational needs;
- the need to cultivate in pupils a confidence in their ability to learn, intellectual curiosity and the ability to persevere against setbacks.

Staff, of course, are more likely to be committed to such aspirations where they have opportunity to contribute to their formulation.

Aspirations are relatively easy to define; too often, however, they can be grandiose and unrealistic. It is possible to bring them back to earth by matching them against the ostensibly simple but searching questions that Ofsted asks of parents in the official questionnaire. The most eloquent aims in the world will not stand up to such enquiry if they are not substantially founded and are not accepted and valued by staff.

The difficulty is to translate such aims into practice. Schools can only know if they are happening through regular evaluation of the extent to which, for example, the development plan is implemented, of the quality of spiritual, moral, social and cultural development, by review of pupils' perceptions, by constant monitoring of their behaviour and attitudes, by reference to attendance and punctuality.

We can, therefore, link this to the criterion which refers to a positive ethos.

Is there a positive ethos which reflects the school's commitment to high achievement, an effective learning environment, good relationships and equality of opportunity for all pupils?

No one will dispute the importance of positive ethos in a school. Some heads see it as a first priority. A school's ethos, whatever its nature and quality, is soon discernible. It cannot be misrepresented, long concealed or quickly altered to ensure immediate demands. It takes a long time to root itself. As the criterion suggests, certain things are essential to its make-up. They include good relationships: a state where people strive to be positive about each other, treat others well and fairly, use their power and status – whatever these may be – to cherish and encourage those less strong or less privileged than themselves, respect other beliefs and views, including those that may be alien to them, observe an agreed code designed for the good and welfare of all. Like ethos itself, good relationships cannot just be willed or wished into existence. They are nurtured, supported and encouraged by leadership and management, that set a personal example by the treatment of those in their care and service and by the creation of a positive moral, social and spiritual climate. Such systems, qualities and values will not grow by edict but out of a curriculum of high quality, especially in the creative arts, the humanities, RE and literature and drama, and the formulation and monitoring of explicit rules for the good of the school community. The leadership which provides for this will be motivated, in its turn, by positive perceptions and expectations of pupils, and by a clear-headed sense of their ability, potential and capacity.

Schools need to ask themselves these questions and to seek evidence that substantiates their answers:

- Does the school provide an effective learning environment? In what ways can the environment be shown to contribute to a positive school ethos, to achievement and progress?
- Are there characteristics that make the school memorable and contribute to the achievement of excellence?
- Are pupils' special educational needs provided for?
- Can the school be confident that characteristics of gender,

background and ethnicity are respected and provided for?
● What evidence is there of a tranquil and harmonious environment in which pupils feel valued, secure and confident? How does the school monitor this? Do pupils and parents have opportunity to express their views about this aspect of school life?

Does the school, through its development planning, identify relevant priorities and targets, take the necessary action and evaluate its progress towards them?

In this context inspectors will want to establish whether:

● the school's priorities are the right ones for the circumstances;
● the school's programmes of action, the use of staff time and the ways in which curriculum and staff development are funded, will achieve these priorities in the necessary time and whether the school has established sound procedures for monitoring the outcomes of work.

This requires schools to justify why they are working in particular ways, why they have set targets and what it is in their recent development that has influenced them to follow certain directions.

The new Framework and the manner in which inspection will be implemented seeks to provide schools with opportunity to define and justify the reasons for their planning and decision making. This criterion brings us back yet again to the practical implementation of the development plan, to how far a school has set up its funding and resources to achieve its aims. There is little point, for example, in asserting that the school has intentions of extending and enhancing its early years provision or enlarging opportunity for additional modern language learning, or access to IT, if steps have not been taken to ensure that the necessary staff time and resources are available to bring about the development.

Summary

In assessing the quality of leadership and management, inspectors will range over the following areas:

- the efficiency with which the school is managed; the way in which the budget is made and organized to meet the school's main educational aims and curriculum objectives;
- the extent to which the school provides value for money;
- the nature and quality of resourcing in the school, the ways in which it contributes to pupils' attainment and progress, the extent to which it matches and meets the school's educational priorities and programmes;
- the measures the school employs for evaluating its general effectiveness and efficiency: the effectiveness with which it monitors and evaluates pupils' standards of attainment and educational progress and the strategies employed to evaluate the progress of the school development plan;
- the ways in which the governing body is involved in policy and decision making, in the monitoring and evaluation of school effectiveness;
- the nature and quality of leadership provided by head, governing body, senior staff and middle management;
- the effectiveness of the routine administration and management of the school;
- the quality of school communications, both internal and external; the nature of public relations and partnership with parents;
- arrangements for the professional welfare, training and development of staff;
- the nature and quality of appraisal in the school and the extent to which it contributes to staff development; standards of attainment and effective teaching and learning;
- the educational rationale underlying the staff structure and the use of incentive points;
- the effectiveness with which accommodation is used to promote teaching and learning;
- the spiritual, moral, social and cultural life of the school and how they contribute to pupils' development and learning;
- the provision for equal opportunity and special educational needs.

Equal opportunity is not accorded a particular place in the inspection schedule and guidance, but is referred to throughout. This is an attempt by Ofsted to ensure that concern for equal opportunity permeates the whole life of the school and is a responsibility for all members of staff.

Inspectors will need to establish that the leadership and management of the school is complying with relevant legislation including the Sex Discrimination Act and the Children Act.

Schools need to ensure, through constant monitoring, that no pupil is denied access to the full range of opportunities for achievement that the school provides. In monitoring equal opportunity provision inspectors will consider how well the school:

- reflects equality of opportunity in its aims and objectives, curriculum and organization, including the grouping of pupils;
- monitors pupils' achievement by gender, attainment, background and ethnicity to ensure fairness of treatment;
- offers relevant role models to all pupils in its distribution of teachers and others within its staffing and management structures;
- provides appropriate support for pupils for whom English is an additional language in order to give them access to the whole curriculum.

Leadership and management: a checklist for action

Before the inspection
- the head teacher's form and statement, school prospectus and school development plan, and policy document;
- a staff handbook (if available);
- job descriptions (if available);
- minutes of the governing body meetings;
- pre-inspection discussions with head teachers, governors and parents.

During the inspection
- observation of lessons and the daily routines of the school;
- discussion with teaching staff, including subject and year group co-ordinators;

- discussion with support staff;
- discussion with pupils.

Schools are recommended to review and consider action of the following kind where feasible:

- Ensure that the governing body is fully informed about its responsibilities, especially legal requirements, and its role. Build a strong professional relationship with the governing body; provide them with the information they need to carry out their responsibilities.
- Establish with the governors their responsibilities in relation to inspection. Devise a plan with them for their practical involvement. Decide how they can best contribute to the preparation phase of the inspection process.
- Review fully the roles of the leadership and senior management of the school; consider using expert external intervention to support the review.
- Review all individual posts of responsibility and the contribution they make to the education provided by the school. Establish the part they will play in the inspection preparation phase. Draw up with the teachers concerned a practical plan for the implementation of all such roles. Ensure that support will be available to post-holders.
- Review all provision for monitoring the extent, and quality, of the school curriculum, especially including the part played in such monitoring by senior staff, heads of departments and curriculum co-ordinators. Consider whether the ways in which data about the curriculum is recorded and evaluated provide the leadership of the school with the information required to sustain and improve curricular provision.
- Review processes for monitoring the quality of teaching and professional development.
- Review the quality and effectiveness of staff training, development and support.
- Gather evidence from a range of sources – curriculum, staff, pupils, formative and summative assessment, analysis of pupils' work, lesson observations – about the extent to which the aims, values and policies of the school are reflected in all its work.
- Consider the ethos of the school, as exemplified in relationships,

quality of learning environment, high achievement, equal opportunity. Call, where feasible, on the perceptions of a range of people and observers with knowledge of the school from an 'outside' perspective.

Appendix 7.1: Preparing for inspection. A headteacher's view

The success in classrooms had to be paramount

Our problems in the classrooms stemmed from classroom management issues. Therefore we revised the discipline policy to ensure that there was a clear structure known to all which included a parallel SEN register for behavioural difficulties. Having created a system which acknowledged that some children did have behavioural difficulties, the next stage was to highlight deficiencies in the curriculum – too often these had been hidden, with behavioural difficulties being the excuse.

Clear standards of work were set; the word 'excellent' was removed from our vocabulary, and staff were encouraged not to collude with children regarding academic non-achievement. The school stressed more discussions on academic progress.

Planning was given a high profile and staff discussions on lesson planning meant there was considerable INSET in this area. Greater structure of lessons also led to an increase in the quality of work produced, and children's self-esteem was thus raised.

There is still much work to be done in this area.

A strong deputy is essential

… who is respected by the staff for her professionalism, obvious good teaching practice, and extensive knowledge of the whole school curriculum. An internal critical friend.

Head teacher working in the classroom

In retrospect, I believe my standing with the staff was heightened when I took a year 6 class, full-time, during the summer term – one of the most difficult classes in the school – and still ran the school. The benefit to me was that I could check systems we had put in place, it made me learn the minutiae of the National Curriculum, and reinforced the view that keeping discipline in classrooms is much harder since the popular media enjoy ridiculing teachers. There is a danger that when you have been 'out of the classroom' for some time, you can forget the daily and nightly pressures on class teachers. Having just renewed my own experience of their pressures enabled me to action-plan with greater empathy – especially knowing when to back off!

A strong administrative team

I was trained to be a head teacher in the days when the head and deputy spent a great deal of time doing administrative tasks. I very quickly realized that many of the administrative elements could be done more efficiently and effectively if I increased the school's administrative hours. This need not be an expensive process – in fact by enabling the head and deputy to spend more of their time teaching, this can be a saving to the budget.

The most important management task was to ensure the calibre of the new members of the team. I set out to find people who had taken early retirement from the education service. Why? Having been inculcated with education practice there would not be the long period of training, they would probably not be looking at a position with a view to career prospects, but because of their previous experience might have skills and knowledge which they would enjoy sharing as members of the team. (Highly proficient people, self-motivated, part-time, very cheap!!)

I had to be very honest with myself about my shortcomings and my strengths. I made a critical analysis of my administrative tasks, and set out to find people who could fulfil those parts of my role which were not my strengths. Each member of the newly appointed administrative team was linked initially solely to me in order to strengthen my management.

The part-time administrative contracts are for minimal hours. This allows me to be more flexible with their hours as the budget allows – of course, dependent upon the willingness of the staff concerned.

This has now set a precedent in the school and changed perceptions. I believe that there is a great danger with delegation in that good classroom teachers could feel that it is more important to gain administrative skills in order to get promotion. I disagree with this theory. I think the future must be that schools look more professionally at using good administrative staff to fulfil some administrative roles. That is not to say that teachers should not understand the principles and importance of administrative work.

When applicable, staff now have access to the skills of my administrative team (still through me). This is a learning process for them. (Nearly gone is the old idea that only teachers in the building do the important work!)

A strong chair of governors

… who is clear and decisive and able to give strong leadership, and who ensures that key procedures are in place. We discovered that some of our procedures were highly complex and utopian, and could not be adhered to. We sought advice from other authorities and have now simplified our systems.

We have used Lincolnshire material for standardizing our curriculum policies. The governors find the format most helpful, as, indeed, do the staff.

The budget

Unlike many businesses, who spend a great deal of time making money in order to pay for ideas, in education we start with a set amount of money. This enables managers to formulate a basic framework for the year. It is imperative to keep a 5 per cent contingency so that, should there be a major catastrophe, there is money in hand. Obviously, as the financial year progresses, this contingency can be reduced and allow greater flexibility. I believe it is important to remember that the money we get through the budget is for the education of the children who are in the school now. We allocated money in our school development plan with Ofsted in mind.

There must be very clear procedures with public money. I think it is very important, therefore, that head teachers like myself who have not had formal financial training ensure that there is someone with such training available for advice. We have managed this by co-opting an accountant on to our governing body (a very cheap option!).

I see my role as setting the budget and devising checks to ensure that the school fulfils financial regulations. I have never seen it as part of my role to spend hours with minutiae – less expensive people than I can do this far more efficiently! However, I found it important to devise a simple overall balance sheet so that I could allocate money quickly, should the need arise.

A strong shared ethos

We use the idea of a clear, simple and brief mission statement. This gives a focus to everyone in the school, which they all know and can talk about at their own level and in relation to their own role – children and adults.

Trust

My staff trust me. On many occasions when the going has been really rough, I have actually stood amongst them and asked them to trust me. Although they have known that I haven't all the answers, they also know I value them as colleagues and as people, and I will fight for them.

The openness of the staff regarding their professional capabilities continues to amaze me. But I believe we have achieved a secure atmosphere where the adults feel able not only to ask for advice, but to act upon it.

Outside consultant

Following a pre-inspection report my deputy and Identified a need for an outside consultant.

Professionally I don't have a problem with inspection. On reflection, without the iniquitous Ofsted procedure, I doubt whether we would have moved so far so fast. A bit like the war: a common enemy unites the school! However, for the future, I am planning to highlight specific areas, possibly using the Ofsted handbook; action-plan using success criteria; and then 'buying in' outside consultants to monitor the plan and its outcomes. This way I believe we shall be able to continue on the road of improvement without the horrendous stress.

Other educational establishments

The outside consultant introduced us to materials produced by other authorities. This has proved to be very stimulating and helpful to staff. It has also saved a great deal of time. Instead of starting from 'scratch', curriculum post-holders now have a starting point. Being able to use materials from other authorities is exceedingly helpful – only ever using one's own LEA can become incestuous and actually it can mean that the issue of raising standards is not addressed.

Ms J. Askew, Headteacher,
Ridpool Infant and
    Junior School,
Birmingham

Appendix 7.2: Points to be considered in preparation for Ofsted inspection. A headteacher's advice

- **Monitoring of teaching.** Monitor with specific criteria in mind, e.g. (i) do children clearly understand the objectives of the lesson as identified in the teacher's lesson planning? (ii) independent learning – does the children's independence grow as they move up the school?
- **Planning.** Ensure that long- and medium-term planning (post-Dearing) is in place for as many subjects as possible – certainly core subjects. Ensure that short-term planning (weekly) is done for at least the core subjects.
- **INSET.** Check past experience and recent INSET for all staff to see if it matches their responsibilities. If there are gaps, identify relevant INSET in the school development plan.
- **Senior management.** Involve senior managers in all decisions/concerns at weekly meetings. They need to have a clear overview when being interviewed by inspectors.
- **Subject co-ordinators.** Provide all co-ordinators with a clear list of criteria which will be examined by inspectors. Carry out mock interviews with staff if they are anxious.
- **Assessment /evidence.** An assessment policy is a must! Provide as much formative, as well as summative assessment – particularly baseline assessment – as possible. A collection of measurable evidence of children's work to show progress is a good idea.
- **Targets.** Identify clear targets for improvement in core subjects in the school development plan.
- **Continuity and progression.** Take all of the work from three children in each class, above average, average and below average and, along with senior managers, check for continuity and progression throughout the school.
- **Monitoring and evaluation.** Develop a monitoring and evaluation policy. Provide evidence that the monitoring has been evaluated!
- **Moderation.** Provide INSET time for all staff to moderate children's work in core subjects initially. Start with 'writing'. Develop moderated portfolios of work.
- **Ethos.** If head teachers have concerns about behaviour, they should invite their LEA adviser or an independent consultant to monitor

this and report back (children's behaviour often changes when the head teacher walks into the classroom).

Mrs Sylvia Gravensteed,
Welsh House Farm Infant
and Junior School,
Birmingham

Appendix 7.3: A commentary by a secondary head teacher on inspection

Bernard Clark, Head teacher, Peers Upper School, Oxfordshire

It is essential to create a sense of proportion and proper perspective among the staff about inspection, to avoid any suggestion of over-anxiety or frenzy. This was possible for us because departmental leadership, our training generally, the measures we take for professional development, the particular focus we put on the quality of our teaching, all combined to make teachers assured about their work. They did not expect to be surprised or disconcerted by the inspection findings, and certainly not in relation to teaching; they expected that, in the main, judgements would mirror what they themselves had learned through organized, reflective analysis of their own practice.

There is no point in pretence. It is the business of a school to know what its weaknesses and areas requiring development are. So, for example, we anticipated concern from the inspectors about absenteeism; we pre-empted things by inviting them to discuss the problem with us. We possessed the information and insights about the matter that inspectors needed in order to make proper judgements. We made clear, without in any way trying to minimize the matter, how seriously we regarded absenteeism, and the measures we had taken, and continue to take, to deal with it. We did not entertain any notion of trying to cover, to dress up the situation, to make it look better; improving things matters too much to us to see any advantage in concealment. We don't believe that inspection is about that.

Part of our calm and confidence about inspection was rooted in our early contact with the RI. We went out of our way from the beginning to arrange detailed and, we believe, mutually supportive dialogue; it was the foundation of a partnership that would achieve the main aims of inspection: to recognize our strengths, to confirm what we were doing well, to give us a plan for future development and to throw light on what we needed to improve and do better. We feel that the partnership remained entirely professional throughout and, if anything, more searching on their side, because we never left them in doubt about the concerns we ourselves felt about the things that had to be done in the school.

We made ourselves constantly available to talk with inspectors; we denied them nothing in terms of information and perception. They let nothing go; we had to justify all we said. In the end the inspection report came up with what we felt were accurate, genuine, fair findings; they affirmed, even more, they exhilarated us; they confirmed for us the quality of our work, enhanced our standing with pupils, parents and the community. At the same time they set us targets about weaknesses and areas that needed development.

Our confidence was rooted most strongly in the preparation we undertook. We kept it within reasonable bounds, but what we did was in relation to the important and critical things in the life of the school – what any reflective school should be concerned with anyway. We set out, for example, long before the inspection, to create a culture where teachers were routinely looking, as critical friends, at each other's teaching. We devised a system that we called 'Eternal Triangles'. Teachers were grouped in threes. The trios represented a balanced diversity of age, experience, gender, subject specialization, teaching style, e.g. 'formal' and 'informal'. They observed each other teaching, using the Ofsted observation form, supplemented by our particular criteria, and analysed and discussed their findings. This was an extensive process. What teachers found particularly helpful was not only the chance to watch other teachers teaching – which hasn't been that common a feature of schools – but to reflect upon other approaches and styles, to consider, for example, why a style completely at variance with their own could be very effective in a way they had not envisaged. They were constantly obliged to ask why some things worked very well, why some approaches were apparently more effective than others.

What this process did in fact was to help teachers extend their repertoire of professional skills, to become more competent, to reflect very hard upon their own teaching.

We were very determined and rigorous about focusing on areas of concern and weakness. Inspection sharpens your thinking about such things, makes you look at them again in a fresh light. For us, for example, absenteeism is a cause of concern: we have to keep working at it. Sitting down with outsiders helps you to look at problems and shortcomings from other perspectives, to consider other possible strategies.

One of the things we constantly try to do here is to look for causes and connections, to put things in context. Something like absenteeism, for example, is part, we believe, of a much wider issue; it is tied up with issues of behaviour and discipline and needs to be considered in that wider framework. But discipline and behaviour, themselves, have to be considered in the light of an approach to spiritual, moral, social and personal development. We believe as a staff that if these are not right then the curriculum won't be effective; we worked hard to make inspectors understand the emphasis we put on this particular matter, on ethos, on spiritual, moral and personal development, the vital importance of a civilized and orderly school community. Our ethos and expectations are very clear; students know that requirements about just and fair treatment of people apply to everyone – not just pupils but staff as well. Students have a right of appeal about any treatment they receive, but equally they know that unacceptable behaviour on their part will have consequences for them in every case. Ours is a system based on concerns for others and fairness; establish that and the sanctions need not predominate.

The heads of departments are vital to successful inspection simply because they are vital to the success of a school. They are the critical force. They are expected to create a reflective professional ethos within their departments, to maintain constant debate about education and teaching. We hold them accountable, but give them the support they need; they are expected to be very clear with me about the provision they make for students in their subject area, the expectations they have for them and the support they, in turn, offer them.

Delegate fairly and appropriately the detailed planning and preparation for the inspection, and provide what people need to carry it through. But trust them to get on with it, to let you know how it is going and to ask for help when it is necessary.

Get your governing body with you; we are particularly fortunate in the quality of our governing body. They represented tremendous support for us, in a number of important respects:

- we were assured by the confidence that so powerful and insightful a group of people felt about our work; in a sense, if it was good enough for people so informed and involved, then it seemed likely to satisfy any examination;
- they have made us very used to responding to scrutiny and enquiry, to being accountable;
- they endorsed, in a very credible way, the view we presented of the school to inspectors;
- they represented, impressively and convincingly, another view of the school as a dedicated educational community.

Inspection was good for us because we took it seriously, as we do anything concerned with the pupils' education and welfare. What it told us did not surprise us; it affirmed us as a good school. We feel better for it, reassured and confident, confirmed in the favourable opinion of the parents, and the wider community. We know there are things we have to do and attend to; they are already being done. We are moving forward with fresh heart.

We would say to colleagues: it is in your hands what happens so far as the outcome of inspection is concerned – as it usually is with most things that befall schools.

8

The efficiency of the school: staffing, accommodation and resources

The efficiency of the school

The inspection focus for this section states that an efficient school makes good use of all its available resources to achieve the best possible outcomes for all its pupils – and, in doing so, provides excellent value for money.

This section of the report provides a summative judgement on the basis of the findings on all aspects of the school's work. Inspectors will be required to evaluate and report on the extent to which:

- educational judgements are supported through careful financial planning;
- effective use is made of staff, accommodation and learning resources;
- there is efficient financial control and school administration;

- the school provides value for money in terms of the educational standards achieved and quality of education provided in relation to its context and income.

In addition to the criteria for the evaluation of the efficiency of the school, which we shall consider presently, Ofsted emphasizes certain points that schools need to treat very seriously:

- Whatever their financial constraints and the need for hard choices to be made, schools will be assessed on the consequences of their decisions, on the way in which total funding is used by them to secure educational objectives and to achieve improvement.
- They will be evaluated on the effectiveness with which staff are deployed, accommodation used and resources employed to support and enhance learning. In many cases primary schools will have minimal flexibility in these respects. Their choices may be confined, for example, to deciding between making limited non-contact time available for two core subject co-ordinators or allocating it instead to create some extra classroom support in years 4 and 5 to facilitate structured whole class reading sessions. Management of accommodation may call for no more than an acceptance that rising numbers demand the return of the school library to a classroom, with the central stock of books being relocated in a converted cloakroom. Resourcing may involve a choice between providing for geography or history textbooks or other learning materials for the coming year. Secondary schools, on the other hand, may be called upon to make larger choices: about the location of the most advantageous staffing provision; the balance of post-16 vocational and non-vocational provision; the relocation of resources or funding to enable the introduction of new course elements.

Inspectors' judgements of these choices and decisions will be based not on educational or management theory and certainly not on personal preconceptions, but on the nature of their impact on the quality of education offered by the school and on the standards of attainment and pupils' progress, on whether they have enhanced the learning opportunities and advantages available to pupils. They will evaluate staffing and resource allocation designed to enhance post-16 provision, not merely on the evidence of commensurably improved outcomes, but upon the discernible consequences in learning terms for those areas of the school from where the staffing benefits have been secured.

Funding for special educational needs is devolved in different ways by various LEAs. Ofsted will evaluate the way in which schools manage this funding and, indeed, all other special grants such as GEST (Grant for Education Support and Training).

Particular attention will be paid to budget planning that allows for significant surplus or deficit on current budgets. Inspectors will require explanation of the reasons for such budgeting. Ofsted accepts that schools have to budget carefully for the future and for unseen contingencies. The need for such prudence has become more pronounced since the advent of LMS and, with it, the ending of LEA capacity to come to the aid of schools in financial difficulty.

However, a surplus exceeding 5 per cent will be regarded as a matter requiring careful evaluation. Inspectors are required to look at large deficits in the 'light of the school's likely budget prospects and the LEA's policy on planned overspend'.

In this section of the report a judgement will be made about the extent to which a school provides value for money. Many primary schools, in particular, find unpalatable what they see as the commercial connotations of such judgement. However, schools need to treat the matter very seriously. Apart from the undesirability of an adverse judgement here, e.g. 'inadequate' or 'fair' value for money, it is an area of evaluation, tersely expressed, that is likely to attract the particular attention of parents and to which they will attribute considerable significance. Schools occasionally confuse value for money with the notion of 'keeping the books balanced'. Evaluation will be about more than a matter of accurate book-keeping. It is a large judgement about the efficiency of a school as an educational institution. It weighs up contextual factors such as socio-economic circumstances and pupil attainment on entry; the main inspection outcomes, such as pupils' attainment in relation to national averages; pupils' progress; provision, e.g. teaching; expenditure; and then goes on to make a value for money rating on a seven-point scale (see Table 8.1).

This will be one of the most important judgements made about the school. In the course of their preparation for inspection schools would be well advised to use the key judgement recording statements, to gain at least an impression of where they stand in this respect and to identify areas where improvement seems necessary.

Table 8.1   Evaluating value for money

The table uses key judgement recording statements. A school giving the very best value for money would have judgements on contextual factors coded as 7 and judgements on outcomes, provision and expenditure coded as 1, and average unit costs.

Judgement recording grade		1 2 3 4 5 6 7	
Contextual factors The socio-economic circumstances of pupils are:	Very favourable	• • • • • • •	Very unfavourable
The attainment of the intake on entry is:	Very high	• • • • • • •	Very low
Outcomes Pupils' attainment in relation to national averages or expectations is:	Excellent	• • • • • • •	Very poor
Pupils' progress is:	Excellent	• • • • • • •	Very poor
The attitudes, behaviour and personal development of pupils at the school are:	Excellent:	• • • • • • •	Very poor
Provision The quality of education, particularly teaching, provided by the school is:	Excellent	• • • • • • •	Very poor
Expenditure Unit cost for a school of this type is:	Very low	• • • • • • •	Very high
Value for money judgement The value for money provided by the school is:	Excellent	• • • • • • •	Very poor

Now let us consider the criteria and how schools can respond to them.

Are educational developments supported through careful financial planning?

In making evaluation here inspectors will also take account of Section 6.1 Leadership and Management and 6.2 Staffing, Accommodation and Learning Resources.

Inspectors will review the funding available to the school in the previous and current year. They will examine how this funding is used for different purposes, including provision for teaching and support staff, curriculum development, learning resources and premises. Schools may find it helpful to have an indication of the average pattern of expenditure in locally managed schools.

Inspectors will also be able to arrive at some comparison of pupil costs and the percentage spent on different items from the pre-inspection context and school indicator (PICSI) report. The PICSI report gives information on the range and median levels of expenditure. However, inspectors are advised about the need to regard such comparisons as tentative and to interpret them in the school context, because of particular factors. Schools need to be aware of the extent to which such factors impinge on their particular circumstances and be able to cite them authoritatively where they are relevant. They include the difference between LMS schemes throughout the country, differences in other income, the ways in which school circumstances will vary, particularly in relation to teacher staffing and premises costs, and other factors outside schools' control, e.g. changes in LEA spending and pupil numbers. Inspectors will examine the school development plan for evidence of forward planning. They will note the aims and objectives you have set for the school based on your audit of your current educational position, your predictions and intentions, and the developments you aim for over the next three years or so. They will expect detailed planning to be well under way for the forthcoming year, with further planning set down in outline. They will make judgements about the nature, balance and appropriateness of your planning and determine how far it seems to match and meet what they perceive to be the major educational needs of the school. They will then consider the match between the targets of your development plan and your budget plans and how far your planned expenditure is likely to provide, economically and effectively, for what your hope to achieve.

Inspectors will look for evidence that such budgeting is the outcome of strategic planning to achieve desirable educational goals and that financial allocation on, say, additional staffing or particular resources arises from careful analysis of school needs. However limited the funding available or the room for manoeuvre, schools need to demonstrate that their decisions are the outcome of an intention to achieve worthwhile educational objectives rather than merely relying on previous patterns of expenditure.

Inspectors will evaluate how the governing body is carrying out its responsibility for planning the use of resources. Such financial planning must be based on 'good current data and sound projections'. Governing bodies and schools will need to have:

- the best possible up-to-date information on expenditure and income under various budget needs for the current year from the LEA;
- estimates of what the costs of current planning are likely to be;
- sources of increased expenditure and what these are likely to amount to: general maintenance costs, salary increases, inflation;
- information about what needs to be put aside for contingencies and emergencies including staff illness, changing pupil numbers, breakdown of large-scale equipment and so on.

It will also be helpful for schools to take account of how they compare with schools of similar circumstances in relation, for example, to the number of administrator's hours, pupil–teacher ratio, teacher non-contact time, head and deputy teaching commitment and unspent balances.

Governors will have to provide evidence that:

- the school is meeting legal curriculum requirements, including the teaching of the National Curriculum;
- special educational needs are satisfactorily provided for;
- additional grants such as GEST are properly applied;
- all statutory obligations are discharged.

Is effective use made of staff, accommodation and learning resources?

This matter is dealt with in more detail in another section. Judgements will be largely based on evidence of how effectively all three aspects are utilized to achieve effective subject provision. In this context of school efficiency inspectors will examine rigorously the use that is made of additional teaching and support staff. They will look at the issue from two perspectives:

- additional staff appointed from school resources;
- additional staff appointed out of specific earmarked grants.

In the first case, inspectors will want to know:

- why the school opted for additional and support staff in preference to other resource options;
- why they are being employed in particular capacities, e.g. in specific age groups or in connection with particular aspects of curriculum;
- the aims and objectives of their work and the contribution they are expected to make to raising standards of attainment;
- their line of accountability and management and the professional support and guidance accorded to them;
- the steps that are taken to monitor and evaluate the effectiveness of their work;
- the steps that are taken to evaluate their contribution in terms of value for money.

Schools, especially primary schools, on modest and largely committed budgets, are apt to become agitated about this particular issue. They are sometimes at a loss to understand why there could be any doubt about value for money being achieved in contexts where any additional staffing is regarded as fortuitous, anyway. However, inspectors are not questioning the notion of the value of any extra support, but attempting to clarify whether the best possible use is being made of the relevant funding. For example, they might wish to determine whether the manifest benefits of reading recovery provision in a school might not be exceeded by the careful planning and resourcing of a detailed reading and language policy throughout the pre-school and early years; or whether releasing the deputy head on a part-time basis to support implementation of the special needs code of practice could be regarded as obtaining best value for money in terms of educational opportunity for pupils where history, geography or IT were inadequately resourced. Such an issue very often becomes a matter of fine judgement for head teachers and staff. What has to be borne in mind is the need for such judgements to be based on a sound rationale, together subsequently with clear evidence derived from consistent monitoring and evaluation of significant gains in terms of outcomes.

In the case of support staff financed through specific grants, inspectors will be concerned to ensure that the arrangements referred to earlier in relation to additional staff paid for out of school funding are similarly observed. They will be most concerned, however, to ensure that staff employed for earmarked purposes devote their time fully to them and have every essential facility and support available to them.

It needs to be clearly established how support staff operate, how their work fits in with whole school and class planning, how they relate what they are doing with pupils to their normal class-based programmes of work, how they share with class teachers essential information about the substance of their lessons and the progress being made by the pupils, whether any elements of the work are conducted on a full or partial withdrawal basis.

Is there efficient financial control and school administration?

Inspectors' concerns in this context are not numerous. They are:

- that the school has acted on the main recommendations of the latest audit report;
- that financial administration is sound, finances are kept in good order, adequate information is provided for the head teacher and governors.

Detailed advice is given in the DFEE document 'Keeping Your Balance: Standards for Financial Administration in Schools'. This is required reading for both schools and governing bodies. Schools are also required to complete the financial questionnaire which is part of the head teacher's statement. This can serve as a useful check for the school on the efficiency of its financial control and school admin-istration. Checkpoints include:

- procedures for the administration of personnel matters, including the payroll where this applies;
- that purchasing arrangements achieve the best value for money;
- the school properly controls the operation of bank accounts and

reconciles bank balances with the accounting records;
- school voluntary funds are administered as rigorously as public funds;
- the school has established sound internal financial controls to ensure the reliability and accuracy of its financial transactions.

Inspectors' evaluation of the school's administrative procedures will focus on the way they contribute to the smooth routine running of the school and to efficient day-to-day organization. The handbook suggests that administration is best where it is unobtrusive, but gives 'clear support to the central purposes of the school, keeping the way clear for teachers to focus on their work with pupils and supporting their endeavours'. Effective administration will ensure that the following matters are dealt with punctually and efficiently:

- internal and external communications;
- responses to official requests, e.g. from LEAs, government or DFEE departments, for essential information;
- the maintenance of the school diary;
- the ordering of essential supplies;
- the production of learning support materials for teachers;
- the reception and management of new or 'enquiring' parents;
- the reception and management of visitors;
- the management of day-to-day business with administrative and support staff;
- the efficient maintenance of all school records;
- the organization and management of the school office.

Does the school provide value for money in terms of educational standards achieved and quality of education provided in relation to its context and income?

This criterion summarizes a major intention of this section of the schedule, that is, to establish the value for money provided by the school. It seeks to put a school's achievement in a proper context by identifying and weighing up complex and important factors: whether, for example, higher-than-average costs may be caused by factors over which a school has little control, or are balanced by higher levels of achievement than those achieved by schools in similar contexts. This aspect of the report is therefore extremely important and, as we suggested earlier, is likely to be of particular interest to parents.

It is important therefore for schools to establish:

- with substantial evidence, that the quality of outcomes justifies major expenditure;
- that the contribution of staffing, accommodation and learning resources to teaching and learning outcomes is evident, substantial and cost-effective;
- that progress by pupils is consistent and satisfactory and can be demonstrated by reference to outcomes and some form of baseline assessment;
- that the school makes all possible provision to ensure and support high-quality teaching;
- that particular financial emphases can be justified by enhanced outcomes;
- that the allocation of any additional staffing resources can be demonstrated as contributing significantly to raised attainment.

Schools are recommended to review and consider action of the following kind, where feasible:

- Do your budgeting and planning reflect the intentions of the school development plan? Is the deployment of the budget likely to contribute effectively to the realization of the school's aims and objectives? Does the development plan have attached budgets?
- Be ready to describe and explain to inspectors any recent major budgetary decisions.
- What is the nature and extent of carry-over from last year's budget? Be ready to explain and justify this in educational terms.
- Review the level of resourcing in the school. What would you regard as the current emphasis and how would you justify this in educational terms and in relation to the school's main aims and objectives?
- Which areas are under-resourced? Why is this? What policy has the school for dealing with the matter. Is there a planned rolling programme of provision?
- Does the accommodation and the way in which it is used support

the implementation of the curriculum?
- How effectively are staff using accommodation?
- Does the way in which accommodation is organized provide effectively for different forms of study? Are pupils able to work, for example, independently, in small groups, to be taught occasionally in larger than class-size groupings? Does accommodation provide for the effective use of various forms of teaching and learning technology?
- Is adequate learning space available to pupils?
- Is current staff deployment effectively matched to curriculum and management needs?
- Is the school providing value for money? Can you justify this in relation to major areas of expenditure and main curriculum initiatives?

Staffing, accommodation and resources

The inspection focus will be concerned to evaluate the extent to which the school is staffed and resourced to teach the curriculum effectively, and whether there are any clear features which contribute to or detract from quality and standards.

Judgements will be based on the extent to which:

- the number, qualifications and experience of teachers and other classroom staff match the demands of the curriculum;
- arrangements for the induction, appraisal and professional development of staff contribute to their effectiveness;
- the accommodation allows the curriculum to be taught effectively;
- learning resources are adequate for the school's curriculum and range of pupils.

Staffing
With the issue of staffing provision – and the related matter of pupil/ teacher ratios and class size – we come to one of the most sensitive areas of school life. This is particularly so now when, as a result of significantly reduced funding, many schools are struggling to maintain existing and recent provision. Inspectors themselves will approach the matter acutely aware of how little flexibility is available to many schools for inventive deployment of staff and, indeed, how limited

choice is, in the first place, in some areas when it comes to making appointments. For some schools the highest aspiration at present may be to prevent the loss of staff, to maintain class sizes and to retain non-teaching and support staff. However, the issues are not always clear-cut or simple. Many schools still have choice and room to operate.

Whatever the particular circumstances, inspectors will want the following matters clarified:

- The amount of underspent budget and the implications of it for staffing levels. It is not uncommon now for schools to retain a significant budget element against emergency, for heavy costs arising from salary increases, serious damage to school fabric, extended and unprovided-for staff absences and so on. Such caution, of course, can be indicative of good housekeeping, desirable and laudable, but it is a different matter when, economy becoming parsimony, staff and resources are curtailed, to the detriment of pupils' education. Schools will need to offer convincing arguments for an underspend exceeding 5 per cent and to be able to demonstrate that it is having no adverse effects on the quality of education provided.
- The proportion of school time, at various staff levels, that is non-class contact in type; how such time is allocated among staff and the extent to which duties extraneous to direct classroom purposes occupy senior staff, especially.
- Inspectors will be concerned to find:
  - detailed information about the objectives that non-contact time is being used to achieve; evidence that such objectives are being realized and are contributing more substantially to the raising of standards of attainment and the quality of education than if the time had been used directly for teaching purposes;
  - assurance that there is no marked disparity between the teaching loads of experienced and inexperienced teachers. Teachers in the early stage of their careers should be regularly afforded time for continuing professional development and should not be required to bear disproportionate burdens of teaching time;
  - that primary schools where deputy heads are free of class teaching duties to enable them to discharge other responsibilities are able to demonstrate that such responsibilities are adding tangibly and valuably to raising pupils' educational standards and/or supporting staff development;

- that *the staff as a whole* has sufficient knowledge and expertise to meet the requirements of the school curriculum, including the subjects of the National Curriculum, RE and the areas of learning for under-fives;
- whether teachers and support staff working with pupils with special educational needs or with pupils for whom English is an additional language have the necessary experience and qualifications for such work; or, at the very least, will have the necessary training and support made available to them immediately;
- that schools are treating the appointment of appropriate staff as a matter of the highest priority. Increasingly schools must consider appointments not merely in terms of the quality of the individual teachers – obviously a decisive matter – but in the context of the needs of a whole team, required to deliver a wide and complex curriculum and to command sophisticated forms of assessment. Inspectors will consider whether the qualifications and skills of staff newly appointed to fill positions of special responsibilities complement and supplement, rather than merely reflect, those of other senior colleagues;
- that primary schools can justify requiring inexperienced teachers, and especially newly qualified teachers, no matter how able and willing, to assume the increasingly high-profile and demanding responsibilities of teaching classes at the end of Key Stages 1 and 2 – 'the SATs classes' – and can demonstrate that, where this occurs, substantial support is provided for them;
- that schools can justify, on the grounds of expertise, competence and qualification, rather than financial expedience or economy, the appointment of newly qualified teachers in preference to more experienced colleagues;
- that teachers working with children under five are fully informed about their curriculum entitlement and the desirable learning outcomes for them at entry to statutory schooling;
- that all support staff who work in similar contexts are qualified by experience and/or by training to carry out their responsibilities satisfactorily.
- Inspectors will pay close attention to the measures that schools take to induct all staff who are new to the school. In the case of newly qualified teachers they will require the school to carry out the induction arrangements required by the DFEE.

Properly organized provision on the part of the school is necessary to ensure that all new staff are made aware of school policies, of the ways in which teaching and learning are organized, managed and provided for; of the ways in which new staff are helped to appreciate the school ethos and aspirations, gain an insight into the school development plan and their part in it, to understand especially their particular teaching responsibilities and the support the school will provide in carrying them out.

They will need mentorship, moral support and practical guidance about their teaching responsibilities and classroom practice, about the preparation of lessons, the structuring and organization of learning tasks, about effective and constructive relationships with pupils and the statutory obligations they are required to observe.

Teachers new to the school, or already on the staff who are assuming new responsibilities, will in most cases need induction and training to prepare them for this. They are most likely to benefit from the mentorship that a relevantly experienced member of staff can provide, together with opportunity at regular intervals for shared evaluation of progress against agreed targets. Such INSET and support are rooted in the belief that:

- individual professional development and institutional growth and advancement are inextricably bound up together and unlikely to flourish apart from each other;
- the identification of strengths and weaknesses in their teaching, together with appropriate training for the development of the first and the elimination of the second, represent an entitlement for teachers that will enable them to flower professionally;
- a significant element of mentorship and training will comprise observation and evaluation of and commentary on individuals' teaching;
- training and most aspects of professional development are directed essentially to the raising of the quality of pupils' education;
- all staff have a vested interest in supporting the professional development of colleagues.

Inspectors will require information and evidence about the progress of appraisal in the school and whether it is proceeding in line with legal requirements. (They will, not of course, have access to individual appraisal records.) What they will look for is evidence that appraisal is contributing significantly to raising the quality of teaching. Schools need to consider what such evidence might be; while information about the intention and processes of appraisal will be helpful, schools should seek to provide more substantial evidence of outcomes – about ways, for example, in which classroom practice has been enhanced.

Inspectors will take careful account of provision for in-service training and staff development. In their preparation for inspections, schools will need to review the following:

- How the staff INSET/development programme is decided upon and arrived at; how far it is linked to the school development plan, to legal requirements, to the development of teachers' capacity to teach effectively the National Curriculum order.
- The nature and form of the five mandatory INSET days, and in what ways they are designed to:
  - enhance the professional expertise of staff;
  - advance the development of the school;
  - contribute to the implementation of the National Curriculum;
  - form part of a coherent pattern of INSET.
- How the training days are organized, implemented and evaluated.
- The means by which all INSET is evaluated in terms of its contribution to staff development, to the promotion of the school's aims and objectives and, crucially, to enhancing the quality of education provided for pupils and the standards of attainment they achieve.
- The ways in which individual professional development is managed and linked to institutional intentions and growth.
- The quality and effectiveness of training provided for all other school staff.
- The nature and quality of training provided for others who make a direct contribution to education in the school; for example, parents who help in the classroom.

Accommodation

As with staffing, accommodation and resources are liable to evoke defensive if not heated responses from schools. This is understandable where, in many instances, schools are obliged to provide for rising numbers of pupils in unchanged accommodation; to resource in a short time what have been revolutionary changes in curriculum and school management, without commensurate financial input; to make, for example, often in grievously straitened circumstances, appropriate outdoor provision for children under five, whose needs in this respect may be particularly urgent. There is little doubt that inspectors will appreciate and be sympathetic about the difficulties with which many schools contend. However, as with the attainment of pupils from disadvantaged circumstances, inspectors are there not to make futile attempts at balancing achievement in comparative contexts but to evaluate how effectively the teaching, the general management and organization, the use of existing accommodation, are contributing to raising attainment and maintaining progress. So, in relation to accommodation, inspectors will evaluate whether the accommodation is adequate for the existing curriculum and for any future developments envisaged; for example, the expansion of nursery provision, additional modern language facilities, the enlargement of science and technological provision. Obviously, so far as existing accommodation is concerned, there may be little or nothing that schools can do to improve matters. However, they will also need to be able to demonstrate that where the size of intake they permit is concerned, ambition does not exceed realism at the expense of the pupils. Equally, developments, however potentially valuable, can only be seriously considered where adequate accommodation is assured rather than merely wished for. In such circumstances precious time spent on planning may be merely wasted.

But schools are directly accountable for the use and organization of existing accommodation whatever it may be, and how they do that will be judged by inspectors. In their inspection preparation schools need to review the following aspects:

- Whether the current use of accommodation is the most effective possible; whether it best serves the learning needs and the whole development of pupils.
- The adequacy of accommodation in terms of health and safety.
- Whether accommodation and furniture meet the needs of pupils with physical or sensory disabilities.
- Most vitally, the quality of classroom accommodation. This is where pupils spend the greater part of their time. It is necessary for schools to do all they can to ensure that it is safe, attractive, comfortable, effectively organized, well maintained, suitably resourced and equipped; that appropriate provision is made for pupils with special educational needs, the needs of teachers are met, even if only

temporarily located there, and in general that a decent, appropriate and civilized environment for teaching and learning is established. A useful, if homespun, criterion for review of accommodation is whether it would satisfy teachers' wishes in relation to provision for their own children, and whether it could be displayed at any time without embarrassment or discomfort to parents. Perhaps a less ambitious but essential criterion is whether all teaching areas are adequate for the particular purposes for which they are being used, or whether in any respect they are impeding or restricting pupils' learning.

- The quality of the learning environment within the available accommodation. The days are long gone when inspectors and advisers might have been inclined to make decisive judgements about the quality of education provided on the basis of an attractive environment and alluring displays. These remain, however, even now, when the nature of pupils' attainment and progress are at the centre of focus, very important in so far as they contribute to pupils' education. Schools, in considering the qualities of the learning environment, need to ask themselves whether display material:
  - is engaging, attractive, linked to pupils' work and related to programmes of study;
  - is labelled, captioned and amplified by writing, both pupils' and teachers', designed to enlarge pupils' understanding and extend their literacy;
  - is interactive, in that it stimulates and challenges pupils to extend exploration, investigation and study generally, by judicious and interesting questioning and by highlighting particular aspects;
  - is likely to excite pupils' curiosity, enlarge their horizons, inspire their imagination;
  - celebrates their work and encourages them to do better;
  - is sometimes devised, organized and constructed by pupils themselves;
  - is changed at intervals that guarantee the maintenance of pupils' interest;
  - receives the care and attention throughout the school, in public areas, halls, resource centres and dining areas, that it does in classrooms.
- That the school has a common policy and guidelines about the management of classrooms for teaching and learning. Guidelines

would include advice on the following:
- organization and provision for effective group work;
- organization – including the use of flipcharts, chalk boards, overhead projectors – likely to ensure the most effective delivery of whole class lessons;
- provision of appropriate resources for pupils, at all key stages and whatever the subject, in terms of literature support – word banks, dictionaries, thesauruses and appropriate reference materials;
- provision of appropriate concrete and structural materials in mathematics;
- organization and provision to support individual work and quiet, uninterrupted study;
- the provision of proper working space for each pupil, and the training of pupils to use accommodation and space as effectively as possible;
- the management of noise levels;
- the provision of the most appropriate furniture possible;
- provision that will ensure proper and comfortable access to all aspects of the curriculum and all learning opportunities for pupils with learning and physical disabilities;
- how far the whole school accommodation can contribute most effectively to pupils' education; make them feel welcome, comfortable and valued; provide a civilized and enriching environment; convey in the most positive way possible the ethos and aspirations of the school; demonstrate clearly the things that make it memorable and most worthwhile.

Schools need to take account of the outside environment and the contribution it makes to pupils' education. This, for many schools, becomes an increasingly disheartening matter. Enormous effort on their part is often defeated by vandalism, undermined by the difficulty of creating something attractive and worthwhile in the context of a larger blighted environment. But schools can do their best to ensure the following:

- that grounds are free of litter, and walls of graffiti;
- that pupils are trained to take responsibility for maintaining the outside environment as well as possible; that any grounds or areas, however small, that are suitable for the purpose are used for planting

and growing;
- that possibilities for trails of various kinds – mathematical, geographical, even natural history in apparently unpromising situations, provision for orienteering – are considered;
- that pupils are given opportunity to produce their own guidelines to the school environment.

Resources

Possibly (and sadly) one of the things one can say with some certainty about schools – though inspectors, of course, could not bring such preconceptions to bear – is that their resources are never as much as they would wish or – in some cases – need. Teachers and pupils could always do with more – and for those who would contest that notion one would merely need to cite the case of fiction and reference material.

Whatever their circumstances, schools are advised to consider the following action:

- Make a review of existing resources, probably subject by subject, and identify major shortcomings. Very often this task will be the responsibility of the subject co-ordinator or a designated member of the department.
- Decide where shortfall needs to be most quickly corrected.
- Make a rolling programme for the building up of resources, based on most urgent needs, linked to the school development plan, curriculum development plans and National Curriculum requirements.
- Encourage subject co-ordinators and heads of departments to establish a book provision policy. Ensure that both fiction and reference material are provided for as well as possible.
- Clarify how book provision compares with general subject resources provision and decide whether the balance seems appropriate.
- Establish what audiovisual and multi-media material is most likely to raise the quality of pupils' education and attainment. Devise a rolling programme for its provision.
- Ensure especially that provision for information technology meets the requirements of the National Curriculum. This is particularly important for primary schools, where many pupils at Key Stage 2 are not receiving their proper entitlement (and where many schools advance convincing arguments that it is not possible to do so in present circumstances). Primary schools may wish to consider the value of concentrating IT provision and timetabling for group work.

- Review library provision. The handbooks offer specific advice (see Inspection Schedule in relation to this).
- Ensure that resources are appropriate as far as possible for SEN and provide for equal learning opportunity.
- Consider whether as much as possible is being done within budget constraints to give pupils experience of environments on a larger scale: museums and art galleries, great public buildings, the built environment, environments that contrast with the local environment.

Staffing, accommodation and resources: a checklist for action

Inspectors will take account of evidence from the following sources:

- the head teacher's form and statement;
- a sample of job descriptions;
- a staff handbook or staff development plan (if available);
- meetings with governors, head teachers and parents;
- observation of lessons;
- a scrutiny of timetables;
- an examination of planning documents;
- a survey of all the available accommodation on the school site;
- a scrutiny of school class libraries, reading materials, textbooks, resource collections, outdoor play equipment, museum/art galleries, national and historical artefacts.

The inspection report will include judgements on the following matters:

- match of the number, qualifications and experience of the teaching and other classroom staff to the curriculum;
- effects of induction, appraisal and professional development arrangements;
- adequacy of accommodation and learning resources, including books, materials and equipment.

Schools are recommended to review and consider action of the following kind where feasible:

- implement a comprehensive programme of support and induction for newly qualified teachers; ensure that this matches DFEE requirements;
- provide mentorship and practical guidance for teachers assuming new responsibilities in the school;
- provide an induction programme for teachers new to the school;
- provide appropriate guidance, together with reference to resources, school regulations and routines, for temporary or supply teachers;
- review and evaluate the nature and progress of the appraisal programme;
- review the school INSET and professional development policy and evaluate the value for money it provides, its impact on curriculum and staff development and on the quality of teaching and learning;
- review and evaluate the outcomes of mandatory INSET days.

Accommodation
- Evaluate:
  - how far accommodation indoors and outdoors for children under five is adequate;
  - the extent to which existing accommodation is providing for whole school curriculum needs;
  - whether envisaged curriculum development can be provided for in terms of accommodation;
  - whether accommodation satisfies health and safety requirements;
  - whether accommodation provides for equal opportunities and matches the needs of pupils with special educational needs.
- Provide guidance on the most effective use of classroom accommodation.
- Review the contribution of displays to the quality of pupils' education.
- Review the quality of the outside environment and the contribution it makes to the pupils' education.
- Review existing resources in all subjects. Make a rolling programme to provide for shortcomings.
- Review all aspects of book provision.
- Review IT provision.
- Consider how the wider outside environment is used to extend pupils' education.

The following questions to the TES column 'An Inspector Writes' highlight some of the aspects of efficiency and resourcing that schools have expressed concern about.

Q   We know of two schools that have been judged as not 'providing in part value for money'. Short of being judged as failing, we can't think of a comment more injurious to a school in the eyes of parents. We also feel that judgements about value for money are more suited to shops and shipyards. But to prepare for such judgements, what issues should we be considering?

A   Educationists naturally distrust what they see as a mercantile approach to a process concerned with children rather than goods, with things of the mind and spirit as opposed to profit. They rightly argue that the most laudable and enduring things about school are often those most difficult to quantify: memorable, illuminating teaching, the capacity to nurture disadvantaged children's sense of worth and potential, the unyielding struggle to make relationships with intractable communities.

Nevertheless, the question about value for money is a legitimate one when we think of schools as publicly-funded institutions.

It is not that they are asked merely about balancing the books, about maintaining regular profiles and showing planned and regular budget spending against each budget head, as the current jargon puts it. Rather, it explores more subtle and complex areas, what the Office for Standards in Education describes as the efficiency and effectiveness with which resources are deployed to maintain the school's aims and obligations and to match its priorities.

I suggest that the following are the kinds of question you need to be asking when you consider value for money. They derive from the obvious but challenging requirement that you have evidence that your spending is producing the results and the outcomes you had hoped for. So, for example:

- Does the organization of teaching and non-teaching staff represent the most productive balance? Is the employment of non-teaching staff justifiable in terms of benefit to the children (or is there any possibility of expensive support staff, unsupervised and loosely directed, being allowed to work in a desultory way with uneconomically small groups of children)?

- Are there manifest gains from expenditure on in-service training and staff development; is teaching performance enhanced, achievement raised and systematic monitoring brought about by the allocation of non-contact time to co-ordinators?
- Can you justify any emphasis, reflected in disproportionately favourable funding, on particular areas or elements of the school, or on particular curriculum aspects? For example, did the children's gains justify the release of the deputy from class responsibility, the major emphasis on special needs, the significantly increased early-years provision, the introduction of reading recovery or the after-school French clubs? Did such gains compensate for any consequential reduction of other elements of school life?
- Does your policy ensure that, as far as possible, pupils are not disadvantaged for want of essential books, equipment, materials and technology? Are there areas in which allocation of funding is disproportionately generous?
- Is time being profitably used: what returns for the school does the release of teachers on extended courses yield? To what extent do daily routines expand to consume precious learning time?

But, of course, in considering value for money, neither you, nor indeed the inspectors, will confine themselves to these areas – to what I think of as the book-keeping genre. Don't forget the even larger matters; providing for a broad and balanced curriculum that incorporates the full National Curriculum entitlement, for special needs, for classroom organization that guarantees appropriate differentiation, for equal opportunities. Where arrangements for any of these are seriously deficient then a school may indeed be judged as failing in part to provide value for money.

I have some sympathy for those teachers who feel that it amounts to impertinence to demand of meagrely funded primary schools proof that they are giving value for money. Equally, it now seems undeniable that, at least in some cases, schools and their pupils would benefit from more systematic and rigorous attempts to consider how the money available is most likely to bring about what they wish to achieve.

Q   Our recent inspection report is quite good, but the gloss is taken off it by repeated comments that resources in many subjects are limited or unsatisfactory. Governors – and some parents – have already been critical of us because of this and, as a result, seem to have ignored the report's generally favourable tone. But as a small school we have a massive struggle to find the necessary resources.

Do inspectors really understand what it is like to provide for the National Curriculum?

A   Your disappointment is understandable. The concerns caused by such criticisms will extend beyond individual subjects to matters of management, general efficiency and value for money.

There can be no question that it is much more expensive for schools to manage curriculum implementation now than it was before the Education Act. There are now ten prescribed subjects that have to be properly resourced, where, in the past, schools could afford to be more selective in their subject emphasis. The detailed definition of the orders forced a concomitant emphasis on resources, especially where junior children are engaged in levels of learning usually associated with the secondary stage.

The renewed emphasis on history and geography has created heavier demands, such as the need for atlases, and the emergence of information technology and design technology has created highly-expensive subjects at the heart of the primary curriculum.

Few areas remain unaffected. Concept keyboards and sophisticated construction kits are more common in the early years. In English, emphasis upon small group reading calls for sets of books, rather than individual ones.

Yet no one at a national level seems to have made a serious attempt to estimate what the implementation of an ambitious National Curriculum was likely to cost – and no appreciable extra money has been provided.

Schools, complaining less about the resources element than any other part of the National Curriculum, have attempted to implement it.

In reality, however, many have been obliged to give up the struggle as hopeless.

But the fact that the issue of resourcing has been relatively low-profile has only led to the kind of misunderstanding and confusion, and possibly unfair judgements, that the question complains of. I suggest schools need to be more rigorous and business-like in estimating likely costs of implementing individual subjects, even if only to identify shortfall.

Provided with such information, they must decide on a strict order of priority for resourcing subjects, a rolling programme extending perhaps over a number of years, incorporated within the school development plan, and capable of being justified on educational grounds.

This information could be presented to Ofsted as important pre-inspection evidence and could be discussed during the inspection. Inspectors need to be well informed about resource implications for particular subjects, realistic in their aspirations, and as confident of the validity of their judgements in this respect as in curricular matters.

9

Spiritual, moral, social and cultural development

Evaluation of provision for pupils' spiritual, moral, social and cultural development links four aspects of personal development in which schools have an important part to play. In this section inspectors need to evaluate what schools actively do to *promote* pupils' development. Although each aspect of spiritual, moral, social and cultural development can be viewed separately ,provision is likely to be interconnected and evaluation should reflect this.

Inspectors are required to evaluate and report on the strengths and weaknesses of the school's provision for the spiritual, moral, social and cultural development of all pupils, through the curriculum and life of the school, the example set for pupils by adults in the school and the quality of the act of collective worship.

Inspectors will base judgements on the extent to which the school:

- provides its pupils with knowledge and insight into values and beliefs and enables them to reflect on their experiences in a way which develops their spiritual awareness and self-knowledge;
- teaches the principles which distinguish right from wrong;

- encourages pupils to relate positively to others, take responsibility, participate fully in the community and develop an understanding of citizenship;
- teaches pupils to develop their own cultural tradition and to respect the diversity and richness of other cultures.

This area of education, and pupil experience, is one where, as we have said before, schools, and primary schools especially, normally feel confident of doing well, of being favourably reported upon. Such confidence, not always common in the profession, may arise from the great importance teachers attach to the development of schools as caring and harmonious institutions.

The promotion of pupils' happiness, well-being and sense of contentment often ranks high in schools' aspirations and formal aims. This is particularly true of primary schools where there is a marked consciousness of the vulnerability of very young children who, in most cases, will be experiencing their first prolonged separation from the home. Many teachers feel that the care and concern afforded children in school, the interest in their personal development, the encouragement they receive to express themselves emotionally and physically, all contribute to their growth in spiritual and moral terms. Teachers hold strongly to the view that unhappy children whose self-concept is low, who may be the victims of adverse social circumstances are, from the outset, greatly disadvantaged as learners. Many believe that schools should represent, in a sense, a sanctuary for young people. This attitude may be particularly evident in areas of social disadvantage and economic blight. Teachers will often place the highest priority upon helping pupils to develop a perception of a finer and more decent world than they may be accustomed to in the reality of their lives.

There is ample evidence that for many pupils, and not only the very young, schools are attractive and inviting places where they feel valued, cherished and cared for.

It is perhaps understandable, then, that schools may be often both surprised and disappointed by reserved inspectorate treatment of areas of work and provision they personally regard highly. They will cite calm, harmonious atmospheres, attractive environments, friendly and encouraging relationships with pupils, equality of opportunity, and wonder why they may still be judged as falling short, for example, in relation to spiritual and cultural development.

The fact is that both these areas are extremely complex and difficult to encapsulate. Attractive environments and caring relationships will provide a powerful basis for social and moral development; but it can be too easily assumed that, as a result of such provision, more is taking place in terms of spiritual – and cultural – development than is actually the case.

It is, perhaps, this tendency to take certain things for granted that may cause schools to underperform in some, or even all, aspects of this section. Sometimes important opportunity for valuable development may be lost because certain events become routine and mundane. School assemblies are an occasional but conspicuous example of this, when they become run of the mill, and fail to inspire curiosity, interest or enjoyment. When that becomes customary it is difficult to detect purpose or value in the occasions. In the long run they are more likely to do as much harm as good.

The fact is that all four areas of spiritual, moral, social and cultural development have to be as scrupulously planned as any subject. Spiritual and cultural development in particular are unlikely to happen if left to chance. There is greater possibility for moral and social development if only because they are likely, at the very least, to grow out of the need for pupils to respond to school rules and codes of conduct, and the tendency to encounter and experience models for civilized and decent behaviour in the way in which adults treat them. Even here, however, true moral and social awareness develop only when pupils are helped to understand underlying principles and values, and to see reason, cause and purpose in things. Pupils might well be very willing to behave morally and go through appropriate motions in social terms, because it seems the safest thing to do in particular circumstances or because they wish to avoid sanctions. But such responses do not always constitute true moral or social understanding and may well not survive in other contexts and on later occasions. That, in truth, is what a school should be seeking to develop, a capacity on the part of pupils for appropriate behaviour because they have a clear sense of what it means in terms of civilized social behaviour, and because they value it not merely in the personal interest but the general as well.

Schools can take encouragement from the fact that growth or development in one area may be likely to enhance the quality of another. Where social development is nurtured, where pupils are encouraged to take responsibility for others, where staff provide models for pupils in terms of concern and respect for the less capable or less fortunately favoured, there is a strong possibility that a climate is being formed where moral principles are more readily comprehended, appreciated and adopted.

Now let us look at the various criteria and consider how schools might respond to them. As we have implied, we are likely to find the four areas inter-related in important respects.

Does the school provide its pupils with knowledge and insight into values and religious beliefs and enable them to reflect on their experience in a way which develops their self-knowledge and spiritual awareness?

This remains for schools one of the most difficult of all areas to provide for. Spiritual development, especially where young children are concerned, is a difficult concept to encapsulate and translate into satis-factory practice. Many teachers are uncertain about how to approach the matter, regard it as linked with elements of belief and divinity about which they are uncomfortable, and tend to treat it as an aspect of moral and social education.

But schools need to go further than treating spiritual development as an extension of moral and social awareness. They must seek to cultivate in pupils, and in younger children from the outset, a sense of the wonder of their existence, the extraordinary nature and quality of being human, their part in a complex and thrilling creation, their relationship to and interdependence with others.

Pupils need to be helped to think about the marvel of their own lives, how they are developing capacities to think, plan, act, assume responsibility, make decisions and choices. They must come to perceive themselves as part of a higher order of things in a world of marvellous diversity and beauty. Out of the experience that provides for that, and the vital capacity to reflect upon it, will flower, gradually, a sense of the wonder and beauty of things, a capacity for response, and a developing ability to formulate a set of values and beliefs.

The problem for teachers, of course, is that all this will seem alarmingly intangible and elusive. How do they go about translating it into a classroom reality? How far are they required to go in translating spiritual awareness into religious belief?

It needs to be remembered that evidence of spiritual development on the part of pupils is likely to be much more difficult to substantiate than outcomes in many other areas of the curriculum. The spiritual outcomes of pupils' early experiences may not flower until later in life, when they are able to reflect maturely and with hindsight on the things that have influenced and shaped them. The spiritual development of pupils generally, and young children especially, will grow primarily out of rich experience, well-ordered provision and the opportunity to engage with it and reflect upon it. The following are probably essential to this end:

- For young children, play that introduces them to a wealth of materials and artefacts, that excites curiosity, stimulates invention, enriches the imagination, encourages them to adopt roles and perform, to solve problems and resolve dilemmas, to make sense of what is strange and perplexing, to come to terms with aspects of human action and behaviour. Play takes children into the realms of the fantastic and wondrous, enables them to create, make believe and pretend, lifts them for a time out of the mundane and earthbound.
- Drama – whether it be improvisatory and 'problem-solving' and therefore in some respects an extension of play, or a studied consideration of plays as dramatic creations – has the power to illustrate, and clarify for all pupils, aspects of the human condition and behaviour, to illustrate qualities of heroism, resilience and generosity and the capacity to aspire to higher planes of existence. In a sense drama of all kinds enables pupils to put great issues under a microscope, to consider values and beliefs and to be reflective about themselves.
- Few things contribute more powerfully than story and literature to pupils' understanding of the nature of human goodness and aspiration. They enable them to identify with the perennial human struggle towards betterment, the effort to find solutions to great problems and people's extraordinary capacity for sacrifice, loyalty, courage and generosity.

Story and literature

From the very outset of their lives story is at the heart of children's learning; it gives shape, form and substance to spiritual issues. It offers ground for endless reflection, for argument, speculation and resolution. But schools have to plan and provide for such outcomes. Teachers will need a rich choice of literature available to them, to be familiar with specific texts, to have a keen sense of the possibility they offer, to understand how they can be most subtly and effectively used for a variety of purposes. Story and literature can permeate the life of a school in a variety of ways and influence and sustain its philosophy, ethos and style of life. It can contribute to assemblies, inspire drama, dance and the creative arts generally, underpin religious education, be at the heart of festivals and celebrations. It can provide solace, joy, enlightenment, inspiration and hope for pupils of all ages. It can lastingly illuminate and enrich the human spirit.

Art, dance and music

If literature, story and poetry offer a cerebral and imaginative path to spiritual development, the creative and aesthetic arts, dance, music and fine art do so in compellingly physical and sensory ways. It is well nigh impossible for pupils to resist involvement in them. In a sense music and dance are a universal language of young people, to which in many respects they have more ready access than to some other areas of the curriculum.

Their influence is two-fold for pupils. On the one hand, there is the inexplicable manner in which the creative arts appeal to and enrich all spiritual consciousness. Pupils' exposure to the fullest range of music and dance, their various encounters with great painting, sculpture and architecture, with the visually beautiful and compelling, generate not only delight, astonishment and pleasure but the likelihood of being touched and affected by great minds reflecting on the place of human-kind in the wider scale of things.

On the other hand, opportunity and encouragement to practise such arts for themselves, to express feelings and emotions, their personal response to experience, their perceptions of the lives and destinies of those around them, inescapably nurture sensitivity, insight, under-standing and a growing spiritual consciousness.

As with story and literature, this requires detailed planning and extensive provision on the part of schools, together with an awareness not merely of what can be achieved in learning terms, but of the possibility for development of spiritual, moral and humane sensibilities. Schools must strive to provide for pupils an experience of music, dance and the creative arts, and an opportunity to engage with them outside of formal classroom contexts. Schools must attempt to create visually rich and harmonious environments, tranquil in places, challenging and intriguing in others. Opportunity must be offered for pupils to see drama, music and the creative arts being performed and made by others. They must have a chance to explore the wider environment, natural, built and made. It is out of such experience and provision, and the sympathetic interest and expert support of teachers and informed adults, rather than through statements and edicts, that spiritual awareness will develop.

Other curriculum areas

Other subjects have major contributions to make to spiritual development, to understanding of the concerns of others, to empathy with their struggles and predicaments, aspirations and achievement – history, geography and RE, the humanities themselves are obvious examples. History is a subject that can be all too easily marginalized in curriculum terms, excluded to a large extent by circumstances of time and resources from pupils' experience. But the lessons and insights it has to offer are indispensable to an understanding of ourselves, of what we have grown from, of the essential commonality of human beings. History can be irresistible as a study, because it is built on story, tied up with investigation, search and detection, and affords the chance for vicarious involvement and for the espousal of causes. It allows us to make moral choices and decisions in retrospect. History gives pupils the material of dreams and visions. It helps them to understand at one and the same time people's capacity for greatness and man's inhumanity to man, and their own right to and opportunity for positive choice.

Geography in its turn, enormously enriched now by multi-media resources, provides pupils with unprecedented opportunity to know the world, to experience its diversity and beauty, to appreciate their links with it and the significant part they can play in enhancing it. The lives, beliefs, cultures, systems and values of other nationalities are put vividly before them. They learn that human freedom and liberal values are not universal, that people's lives the world over are blighted by oppression and disadvantage. They come to appreciate that in a contracting world what happens, for instance, in the Far East today may well impinge on their lives in one form or another in the immediate future. The strength of other people's beliefs, the ways in which faiths, cultures, philosophies and a search for truth influence their lives, is brought home to pupils.

A sense of awe and wonder is frequently referred to as central to spiritual development. From the moment children take their first un-certain steps into the environment, they are on the threshold of an unending, transforming source of richness to the human spirit. The marvels of the natural and animal world, the wonders of growth and regeneration, the incalculable diversity of it all can inspire and feed reflection of the most profound kind. It is vital that schools provide access to this from the small world play of young children, the opportunity to grow things, to observe and care for living creatures, to explore and know the immediate environment, to the opportunities for older pupils to chart a larger world, to understand its systems and economies, to come to know something of its varied languages and modes of living, to explore, in a practical way, ever expanding domains.

Very often such provision is most difficult to provide for pupils who live out their time in blighted areas and disenfranchised circumstances. It is understandable for teachers to feel defeated by such challenge. But the most apparently unremarkable of provision – a small wild garden, a study of the surrounding streets, the studies of parents' childhoods in other places, the occasional opportunity for an expedition further afield, access to attractive, high-quality textbooks, the opportunity to see museums, to meet interesting visitors, to correspond with children in other localities and countries by tape, letter and video – can enlarge pupils' vision and perceptions out of all proportion to the effort called for in the first place.

Although, as the handbook points out, religious education is not synonymous with spiritual development, it is an obvious gateway to it. This is the subject most immediately concerned with humanity's search for ultimate meanings to life and existence, for assurance of a guiding providence, of a shape and order to our destiny. It is a subject that calls for the greatest sensitivity and discretion on the part of teachers, and never more than now in a multi-faith country, where, for an increasing number of people, adherence to religious beliefs and worship is of central importance in their lives. Pupils need to be encouraged to understand and respect the importance of spiritual quest. They should be encouraged to learn and think about religious and spiritual matters, to understand their importance and sacredness to countless people and to reflect upon their importance for themselves.

Many teachers find religious education a difficult, even unpalatable part of their work. There is continuing controversy about the realism of teaching pupils about the major faiths. But there can be no question about the importance of the subject to pupils' wider development and to their spiritual growth, especially where so many of them are involved through their homes in religious observance.

Collective worship

Collective worship is legally compulsory; there are clear directions about its implementation in the handbook. Inspectors will be required to determine that what the school provides is in keeping with the law. But they will have a wider concern than this. They will want to discover the part collective worship plays in the whole life of the school, the contribution it makes to pupils' spiritual and moral development and, indeed, to their social and cultural development as well. Schools need to ensure that:

- the act of collective worship usually subsumed in assemblies has a religious flavour in that it is based on the recognition of a supreme being;
- the substance of the act of worship is relevant, understandable, attractive and positive for pupils; that story, drama, music, the creative arts enhance, at least at times, the interests and concerns of pupils, at their various stages of development;
- it is related to their experiences of life in school and not alien or remote and artificially separate from it;
- it seeks to enhance pupils' self esteem and dignity;
- it is conducted in attractive and carefully ordered environments;
- it is evaluated for the contribution it makes to the quality of life in the school;
- pupils play a significant part in it;
- the outside community has some opportunity to contribute to it;
- in the inevitable clamour and rush of large institutions and great buildings – and they are all large to young children – substantial opportunity is provided and maintained for reflection and tranquillity.

Spiritual development grows incrementally out of a rich curriculum and a good and civilized environment. But as important to it is the whole ethos and quality of school life, the models of living and behaviour provided by teachers, their relationships with pupils and with each other, their manifest attitudes, beliefs and convictions, the readiness of the school to look outwards to the wider world. It is not always easy for a school to evaluate its own position and quality in this respect. It may well be one of the areas where evaluation by 'critical friends' would be valuable. It need not necessarily require a formal 'inspection' type exercise. A request for the views and opinions of those outside the school but most familiar with it, couched perhaps in the form of a judicious set of questions, might well provide all the helpful information needed.

Does the school teach the principles which separate right from wrong?

Moral tone, the nature and quality of discipline, and the behaviour of pupils are among the issues that most influence pupils' perceptions of a school. Inspectors are no exception to this rule. And it is absolutely right, of course, that the moral issue should be treated so seriously. Any institution that is uncertain or ambiguous about the moral principles on which it is based and operates, or hesitant in the way it implements them, insufficiently concerned about the moral framework provided for the people who live and work there, is almost certain to court failure in important respects, if not totally.

Nowhere does this apply more than to schools, where young people, vulnerable and impressionable, at the very outset of their lives, sometimes exposed outside to harsh circumstances and influences, come to be educated. The purpose of schools in this particular context is to create secure environments, based on clear moral codes, fair, just, appropriate and at the same time supportive and compassionate microcosms of a desirable society, in which young people, in all their various stages of development, can grow eventually into mature, civilized and integrated adults. It is a formidable challenge, especially in contemporary situations, where there is evidence of social malaise, of the break- up of traditional family life, of indifference at best, and hostility at worst, on the part of many parents towards education.

Inspectors, while taking account of the many difficulties facing some schools especially, will look for evidence of:

- a clear moral code based on positive, civilized, decent values and principles and a concern for justice, honesty, truth and respect for individuals;
- the translation of the code into general rules and modes of behaviour that are comprehensible to and accepted by all;
- a climate where the spirit of the code predominates rather than an emphasis on rules and sanctions as a deterrent;
- an understanding by pupils that, in any society, deliberate flouting of the moral code has to be accounted for and that clearly established consequences have to be faced up to;
- the promotion of a rational appreciation on the part of the pupils of the nature and purpose of a moral code and the need for it, and the assimilation of its principles and values as an intrinsic part of their thinking, behaviour and general response to others;
- the readiness of pupils to assume responsibilities and obligations, as much as to assert rights;
- evidence, in the whole life of the school, of the practical realization of moral principles and values. This will be visible in:
  - the general concern for all individuals by all staff and pupils and a constant practical commitment to equal opportunity;
  - an absence of any form of bullying or intimidation;
  - a readiness on the part of pupils to support the less capable and less advantaged;
  - a respect for the concerns, pursuits and interests of others, for their culture, values and beliefs;
  - respect for the environment, for property and possessions, for those who come into the school from outside, for those who visit or work there on a temporary basis.

In practical terms, schools can do the following to ensure the achievement of such objectives:

- Use particular aspects of the curriculum to promote a moral climate; as we suggested earlier, some subjects will do this particularly effectively, story and literature especially, RE, history and drama all offer the means of nurturing true moral understanding more enduringly than expectations of reward or fear of sanctions.

- Consistently monitor the ways in which pupils treat each other and behave to particular groups and individuals outside the classroom.
- Establish appropriate sanctions for breaking of the code. Make the nature of these sanctions clear to pupils and parents.
- Make provision for pupils whose particular temperaments, attitudes and general life experiences result in unacceptable patterns of behaviour. This provision, often including reference to appropriate outside agencies and the use of specialized professional support, should be designed to enable pupils to become acceptable members of the school community, but should also be concerned with the rights of pupils and staff to pursue their work and interests in peace and security. Consider the value of 'contracts' with such pupils about behaviour over set periods of time.
- Be informed about the use and value of strategies increasingly used in schools to promote self-esteem and positive behaviour.
- Enable staff who are interested to become trained in counselling skills.
- Review and evaluate, especially in large schools, the staffing structures set up to promote discipline and pastoral care. Review with responsible staff the effectiveness of codes of behaviour and strategies for promoting moral behaviour.
- Review and evaluate the school's equal opportunities policy.
- Establish from the outset with very young children their awareness of what is acceptable and unacceptable behaviour.
- Make sure policies and practice in relation to codes of behaviour are quite explicit to parents and involve them immediately in cases of serious disruption of the code.
- Make the whole environment of the school as attractive as possible, give pupils a say in its development and make them responsible in significant ways for its maintenance and presentation.
- Encourage pupils to relate positively to each other, take responsibility, participate fully in the community and develop an understanding of citizenship.
- Provide opportunity for pupils to work co-operatively and support each other. This can be achieved through careful attention to the organization of group work in classrooms. Pupils are frequently organized in groups, but do not always have the chance in fact to work together in such contexts. Thought needs to be given to ways in which pupils can genuinely work together in ways that are

productive: as partners on various assignments, in mixed groups on particular creative activities, in conferencing groups to discuss and support each other's writing, as 'friendly critics' of each other's work, in ability groups for particular aspects of the curriculum, as members of teams dependent on each other for success and achievement, as members of extra-curricular clubs and groups.

Schools, in organizing groups, need to pay careful attention to their composition and structure. There will be times, for example, when the most effective way to organize is through ability grouping. Absolute adherence to this form, however, is likely to be perceived as a statement of philosophy not particularly conducive to the promotion of strong self-concept or to the development of harmonious relationships. Groups need to be set up and run in ways that will afford responsibility at some time, and as often as possible, for all in the group, the opportunity to lead, to take charge of some of the group business and affairs and to have the care of others. They need to be frequently organized in ways that represent the diversity of social groupings in the wider world. Schools need to provide opportunity for pupils themselves to decide upon the purpose and composition of groups.

- Give pupils responsibility for the management of some school business. This will range from responsibility on the part of very young children for the distribution of materials, the care of classroom areas, the maintenance of notices and labels, through situations where older primary children take a lead in the management and organization of aspects of assemblies, functions and festivals, are responsible for some of the care of visitors, make a significant contribution to the maintenance of the classroom, contribute at times to the care of younger children, to the secondary school context where pupils may gradually assume responsibility for the organization and management of societies, teams and clubs, of aspects of school organization and routine, of contributions of a charitable and voluntary nature to the life of the community. For many older pupils in secondary schools the nature of aspects of the curriculum they encounter, in vocational education, for example, is concerned with developing capacities for assuming responsibility and exercising initiative both in relation to the individual's work and the business of the wider school community.

Inspectors will look for evidence at the secondary stage that:

- the whole range of educational provision is contributing to pupils' developing maturity and self-awareness;
- pupils are developing confidence in their ability to relate to and interact with a widening range of people;
- pupils are developing an understanding of what constitutes appropriate behaviour;
- pupils are consistently encouraged to be reflective, to become aware of their capacity for constant development, for spiritual, moral and social growth;
- pupils are being helped to appreciate and value their personal qualities, abilities and attributes and their potential for learning and achievement;
- pupils are being helped to operate effectively in the wider world, to understand and respond appropriately to social conventions, to relate positively to people of different age, status and background;
- pupils are enabled to value what they themselves bring to that wider world while attaining and developing enthusiasm and eagerness to learn from it;
- pupils are being helped to acquire and · cultivate the skills of conversation, discussion, enquiry, debate, analysis, reflection and response;
- pupils are helped to master skills that will enable them to operate and be comfortable in a range of social contexts;
- pupils are helped to be wholly competent and confident in terms of their literacy. Few things are more likely to inhibit social development than a consciousness of being unable to share in this vital human activity;
- pupils are consistently given opportunity to assume care and responsibility within school for younger pupils and for those with special needs, and are educated in the necessary skills to do so;
- the whole ethos, life, daily business and management of the school consciously promotes equal opportunity and respect for individuals.

Schools should bear in mind that inspectors will discuss these aspects of their school experience with individuals and small groups of students. In some cases, especially in primary schools, this may be dealt with incidentally with the groups who are interviewed about work samples. In other cases, inspectors may prefer to discuss these aspects with new groups, or, indeed, schools themselves may decide that it would be more sensible and equitable to involve a wider range of pupils.

Does the school teach pupils to appreciate and develop their own cultural traditions and appreciate the diversity and richness of other cultures?

Many schools find this area a challenging one, possibly for a number of reasons:

- the difficulty of defining what a cultural tradition is, especially in relation to the diversity of cultural traditions represented in schools of rich ethnic diversity;
- the problem of providing for pupils access to and involvement in a wide range of cultural experiences;
- the difficulty of providing convincing evidence of such activity for inspections.

Schools might consider some of the following strategies for dealing with this particular aspect of school life:

- Place consistent emphasis upon the place of story and literature in pupils' education from the very beginning of their time in school. Develop a policy for the use and teaching of story and literature that extends across all the key stages, that builds consistently on pupils' experience, interest and developing insights, and guarantees diversity, continuity and progression.
- Build into the programme from the beginning a significant component of literature and story from other communities, cultures and countries.
- Encourage pupils and parents from other communities, cultures and ethnic groups to contribute their story and literature in various ways: through social occasions – often organized on a class or group level – in festivals and celebrations, in presentations to younger children, through taped and videoed recordings, through the making of books,

journals and personal written records.

- Build into library provision a representative component of international folk tales, story and literature.
- Make literature and story from a range of cultures an important part of book weeks.
- Make story and literature from different cultures a regular part of school assemblies.
- Invite storytellers and poets from different ethnic backgrounds and cultures to contribute to school occasions, festivals and celebrations.
- Use ethnic and religious celebrations and festivals to read relevant literature and tell stories from other cultures.
- Make music and song from different cultures and nations a regular part of school assembly. Teach pupils about its genesis, history and development. Build it in as a component of music education. Encourage pupils from different ethnic groups to demonstrate their knowledge of and skill in the music of their cultures.
- Invite musicians from different cultural traditions to perform on occasions in the school.
- Build up collections of taped music from a range of cultures and traditions.
- Build up and regularly display collections of musical instruments from a range of cultures.
- Make and display collections of art and artefacts from different ages, cultures and traditions. Help pupils to appreciate the vitality, beauty, complexity and significance of human creativity in all times and places.
- Use history and geography to help pupils to a recognition, understanding and appreciation of people's cultures, music, literature, song and dance throughout the ages.
- Help pupils to understand the interaction of different cultures, language, art, music, philosophy and literature and their influence upon each other.
- Focus regularly in assemblies on musicians and artists from different cultures and traditions and upon people from other nationalities who have contributed to and influenced the growth of human civilization.
- Build collections of artefacts, costumes and materials from different cultures.
- Create an ethos and ambience where pupils from different cultures

and traditions feel encouraged to contribute from their particular experience, knowledge and skills to the fuller life of the school.
- Make as much provision as possible for pupils to visit exhibitions, displays, museums, art galleries, concerts and events with a wide cultural reference.
- Use the occasion of educational visits abroad to promote pupils' wider cultural awareness.
- Make links with schools with ethnically diverse intakes and a wide cultural tradition.

Spiritual, moral, social and cultural development: a checklist for action

Before inspection
- analysis of the school prospectus, curricular documentation, staff handbook, model of behaviour;
- discussion with governors and the head teacher;
- discussion with parents.

During the inspection
- observation of lessons, of the daily routines; collective worship, extra-curricular activities;
- examination of the agreed syllabus for RE, curriculum guidelines and schemes of work;
- assessment of the range and quality of resources;
- observation of pupils' responsibilities; discussions with teachers and other staff.

The inspection report will include judgements on the following matters:

- provision for pupils to acquire knowledge and insight into values and beliefs and for the development of spiritual awareness and self-knowledge; teaching of principles which distinguish right from wrong;
- encouragement for pupils to relate positively to others; take responsibilities; participate fully in the comments and develop an understanding of citizenship;
- opportunities for pupils to appreciate their own cultural traditions and richness of other cultures.

Schools are recommended to review and consider action of the following kind where feasible:

1 Bear in mind the complexity of providing for spiritual education and remember that it will not be provided for simply through a rich environment. It has to be minutely planned for.
2 Similarly, cultural development does not always earn significant praise in inspections because there may be a tendency not to define it precisely enough and to believe it will emerge as an influence in an accidental way.
3 Treat assemblies as a powerful instrument for promoting spiritual and cultural development especially, and plan for this.
4 Ensure that pupils are constantly reminded of and helped to understand the principles and values that underlie the school's codes of conduct and behaviour. Reliance on codes alone is unlikely to promote moral and social understanding.
5 When planning for the four areas of development, keep in mind their potential to interact with, reflect and enhance each other. Bring this to the attention of inspectors.
6 Spiritual development is closely linked, for young children especially to growing self-awareness in the context of the wider world. This process is heavily dependent upon a range of experience and environmental encounters. Carefully structured play, drama, story and literature, the creative arts, the wonders of natural history and technology all play a vital role in the development of a sense of awe and wonder, a realization of the higher role and destiny of humankind.
7 Collective worship has an important role to play in spiritual development.
8 Inspectors' judgements of schools will be significantly influenced by the moral behaviour and moral development of pupils. Make sure there is a code of behaviour understood and committed to by all that permeates the life of the school. Relate the code to moral principle.
9 Provide opportunity for pupils to assume responsibility.
10 Encourage pupils to care for others; make this a manifest part of school life.
11 Be rigorous about curbing oppressive behaviour; make constantly clear to all pupils why it is unacceptable in a civilized community;

make opposition to it an institutional responsibility.

12 Establish a strong policy for equal opportunity and ensure that its influence permeates the school.

13 Develop in pupils a sense that the environment belongs to them by giving them some control over it and responsibility for its care and maintenance. Make sure it is an environment worth preserving.

14 Promote moral values through the curriculum, e.g. in history, literature, drama, social studies, history and geography.

15 Make your codes of behaviour and the principles that underpin them explicit to parents. Stress their obligation to support the school in their implementation.

16 Regularly evaluate with staff responsible for pastoral and social care for pupils' welfare and behaviour the effectiveness of the school policy and strategies.

17 Provide prolific opportunity to work in group contexts. Organize and structure such work to ensure collaborative effort and independence. Provide opportunity for pupils to exercise responsibility and to exercise a variety of roles.

18 Identify and cultivate in pupils the range of social skills and competencies required by them to operate effectively and positively in the larger adult world.

19 Prepare pupils for discussion with inspectors of the four main areas of development.

20 Give artists, poets, musicians and storytellers from various cultures an opportunity to perform in the school.

21 Encourage parents from various cultures to contribute their knowledge and expertise to the promotion of cultural development.

22 Invite all heads of departments and curriculum co-ordinators to build into their policies and schemes of work provision, opportunity and encouragement not only for cultural development but for the spiritual, moral and social as well.

23 Use assemblies to promote the literature, art and music of writers, artists and musicians from different ages and cultures.

24 Develop a cross-phase policy for literature, story, poetry and drama.

25 Promote a wide cultural and ethnic dimension in these developments.

26 Use festivals, social occasions and celebrations to promote cultural development.

27 Encourage pupils to perform, present and represent from their own

strong cultural traditions.

28 Build a wide range of artefacts, tapes, books and musical instruments representative of various cultures.

Appendix 9.1: Discipline policy: an example from Ridpool Primary School

1 Introduction

1.1   The basis from which the discipline of the school should stem is that everyone within the school, children and adults, should feel secure in an atmosphere which enables them to work; where no-one's happiness, safety or belongings are threatened by others; and where each treats the other with courtesy and kindness.

1.2   The first aim of the discipline policy is to help each child to grow in self-discipline. Emphasis is placed on:

- consideration for the value of their work and that of others;
- respect for the common good;
- recognition that their needs will be cared for;
- recognition of their need to care for others.

1.3   Whenever possible, it is the aim of the school to achieve the stated standard of discipline through positive promotion of good practice. Encouragement of public recognition of good behaviour is the first means through which discipline standards shall be achieved.

1.4   For those occasions when the preferred approach does not achieve the standard which the school finds acceptable, there is a clearly defined discipline structure.

2 The discipline structure

2.1   For this structure to be effective it is crucial that it is known, understood and adhered to by all adults who have dealings with children in the school. If the structure is short-circuited, in all but the most exceptional of circumstances, the effectiveness of the system is lost. The structure will be ineffective also unless there is a common standard to which all adults work, and which they are prepared to uphold consistently, without fear of favour within the classroom and beyond it.

2.2   The common standard, drawn up by the children in November 1991, is outlined later in this document. Whilst its wording seems negative, it is the language children understand and are comfortable with, and the underlying purpose of the statements is entirely positive and perfectly in keeping with the basis for discipline statement which begins this document.

2.3   We as a staff feel that it is our responsibility to establish and maintain discipline structures within the classroom. It is important that we reflect before we act. It is also important that all facts are known before action is taken or a discipline matter is passed along the chain. Third parties cannot give effective support unless they are appraised of the accurate, full facts.

3 The chain of responsibility

3.1   The chain of responsibility for discipline is:
1 Self-discipline
2 The class teacher or adult on duty
3 Support within the year group or other teachers
4 Head of phase
5 Deputy head
6 Head of school
7 Governing body, if asked by the head teacher.

3.2   The exceptional circumstances in which this chain may be short-circuited should be strictly reserved for issues of similar gravity to:

● witnessed acts of gross physical violence
● deliberate attempts to seriously risk their own or the safety of others
● serious injury to anyone (whether an accident, through carelessness or wild behaviour, or with wilful intent)
● extortion – deliberate physical or mental pressure on another (bullying)
● wilful acts of vandalism.

These are issues of such gravity that the parents should be involved at once, and the head of phase would need to be involved from the outset.

3.3   The chain offers support in above-average depth. The involvement of colleagues within the year group, or other nearby teachers, is very valuable because it contains problems 'within the family' before children are dealt with by senior managers who are in a position to impose more serious sanctions, and consult/involve parents and outside agencies. By adhering to the chain, the children and their parents will recognize the gravity of a situation when senior managers are called in to deal with it - and quickly see that the more senior the manager, the more grave the situation.

4 Dealing with parents

4.1   Most dialogue with parents is of a friendly nature, even when it is necessary to indicate that there is a problem. However, colleagues will be wise to consult a more senior member of staff before approaching parents over a discipline matter – just to make sure that:

- someone else knows of the proposed approach and supports your judgement, and
- someone can be near at hand should the meeting take a difficult turn.

5 Sanctions

5.1   Staff should avoid using sanctions which would be difficult for senior management to support.

5.2   Whilst a few parents resent any disciplining of their children, most parents welcome support when the punishment is reasonable.

5.3   Over-reaction when pushed to the limit (which, as we all know, children can provoke) is rarely effective. It is the time to distance yourself from the situation by using the discipline chain.

6 Disciplinary support already in place

6.1   Discipline procedure is in line with the special educational needs code:

- classroom management sheets
- daily report sheets
- heads of phases' discipline books
- deputy head's discipline book
- head teacher's discipline book.

All of the above should be used within the discipline procedure.

6.2   It is very important that colleagues accept that having handed on a problem to someone else in the discipline chain, then it becomes that colleague's decision to deal with the situation as s/he considers appropriate.

7 Some possible discipline strategies

7.1   Make an agreed set of class rules, and stick to them. It is wise to limit the number of rules to, say, five, so that the whole teaching time is not taken up in keeping dozens of rules. The children should also agree the sanctions for breaking these rules. These too should be graded and limited in number. When such a system is employed it is crucial that it is consistently applied. Such class arrangements should be approved by a member of senior management, who needs to be happy that they could wholeheartedly back up the arrangements.

7.2   Praise for those who do it right – and rewards – set the desired standards for all. Most children like to be liked – even those who pretend otherwise.

7.3   Avoid direct confrontation, where there is risk that the teacher may 'lose'. Verbal aggression forces children to react and is rarely appropriate. In this situation a teacher risks 'losing face' – which creates insecurity for all the other children (not to mention the teacher!).

7.4   At playtimes or when moving children from where they are to somewhere else (on whatever pretext), a simple 'Please could you help me by checking that the door is closed' can peacefully take the steam out of a perceived potential 'situation'. Asking a child to walk with you for a short time can also cool a potential hot spot.

7.5   If a number of incidents create a situation that the teacher feels no longer able to handle with safety, support should be sent for.

7.6   Few teachers enjoy playground duty, but it can be more bearable if it is filled with positive problem-avoidance rather than solely dealing with the negative issues that arise.

7.7   Since 'rules' have to be rigidly and consistently enforced, which can become more of a punishment for teachers than for the children, the aim should be to establish few, and win with those.

7.8   In everything, being fair and just is most important. No-one manages it all the time, but it should never stop being the aim.

School rules drawn up by the children (November 1991)

Based on the Ridpool empathy – *'First walk a mile in the other one's shoes'*.

1 Do not hurt others – fighting, kicking, name-calling
2 No gangs
3 Do not throw harmful objects
4 No bullying
5 No swearing
6 Do not damage property – personal or the school's
7 No running along the corridors
8 No stealing
9 Do not be rude to, or answer back to adults
10 Do not bring chewing gum to school.

The children's rules expressed as 'positives' (November 1991 and reviewed spring term 1996)

To keep the Ridpool empathy and first walk a mile in the other one's shoes we must:

1 Try to 'improve on our previous best'
2 Work hard at making sure everyone is safe and happy by not stopping others from working, not fighting, not kicking, not name-calling
3 Make sure groups of friends don't become gangs
4 Care for people and property by not throwing harmful things
5 Make sure we never bully with words or actions
6 Use polite language
7 Look after the school, and respect other people's property
8 Keep the school safe by not running along corridors
9 Treat grown-ups with politeness and respect
10 Help to keep the school tidy and not bring chewing gum.

There are further examples of good practice from Ridpool Primary School, including a behaviour modification booklet.

10

Partnership with parents and the community

Inspections will focus in this area on the extent to which parents support the work of the school and are informed about their children's progress. They will look at the way in which the school involves the local community and how this affects pupils' attainment, progress and personal development.

Inspectors will evaluate and report on:

- the effectiveness of the school's partnership with parents, highlighting strengths and weaknesses, in terms of (i) the information provided about the school, and about pupils' work and progress through annual and other reports and parents' meetings; (ii) parents' involvement with the school and with their children's work at home;
- the contribution which the school's links with the community make to pupils' attainment and personal development.

They will base their judgement on the extent to which:

- links with parents contribute to pupils' learning;

- the school's work is enriched by links with the community, including employers.

Partnership between school and home is increasingly accepted as a decisive factor in pupils' learning and educational success. Parents are now generally recognized and acknowledged as their children's first and most influential educators, and the home the most important learning environment, where young people spend about 80 per cent of their time. The pre-school years, especially, are regarded by educationists as crucial, the period of perhaps the most rapid learning and development of all. During this time children acquire skills, knowledge and competence and come to understand ideas that are essential to their growth as full people and to their learning in general.

Powerful support for children during these early years, the provision of particular desirable experiences, and contexts, underpinned by care and encouragement, together with rich language models and resources, ensure an educational start of incalculable value. Children, on the other hand, who are disadvantaged in these respects have a formidable amount of ground to make up.

Neither is the importance of the home in the children's education diminished in any sense when they enter formal education. It is at this time, when parents may feel that the major part of their contribution to their children's upbringing, in educational terms, is done with, that the vital matter of partnership begins. Indeed, a consciousness of the importance of the very early pre-school years in children's education and development, and the consequences for their lives subsequently, has led to a wide range of projects, nationally and internationally, designed to promote home/school partnerships even before formal schooling begins. In many cases these are directed at children denied access to forms of pre-school education. Some of these are large-scale projects funded and evaluated by major organizations, others are initiated and conducted on a less ambitious scale by schools themselves. Many set out to affirm parents in their role as educators, especially parents in adverse social circumstances with, perhaps, unhappy personal memories of school. The projects remind parents of the substantial contribution they have already made and will continue to make to their children's education. They offer the parents various forms of support, often comprised of opportunities for a range of shared pre-school experience with their children, of access to story, music and play clubs, to book and toy libraries; they may be offered practical workshops and seminars in attractive and unthreatening contexts about particular aspects of parenting and children's early learning.

Obviously these forms of partnership, initiated before children begin their formal education, are not commonplace and vary widely where they are provided. The need remains vital therefore for the home to be significantly and actively involved once the child enters the formal stage of education. It may never be more important than at this stage, when parents giving their children over, in a very real sense, to the care of others may also feel they are relinquishing responsibility for their education as well. Some parents, indeed, will welcome this for a variety of reasons – the necessity of caring for younger siblings, the need to obtain employment, resume a career, pursue study, or simply to have a break from the urgent demands of rearing young children. A significant proportion of parents may feel they are not equipped to educate their children beyond this stage and that it is now the business of professionals; some will assert that teachers are paid to do it and must get on with it, while others will shrink from being involved, simply because they feel unwelcome and excluded. One thing seems certain: whatever the cause of parents distancing themselves from their children's continuing education, it will be to the children's disadvantage.

The problem is that such divides, slight in themselves at first, grow wider with time; for various reasons, the older children become the more difficult it is for parents not merely to play an active role in their education, but, indeed, to be able to say with any certainty what it is about.

On the other hand, evidence suggests that the greater the interest retained by a parent in the child's education and progress – however unostentatiously that may have to be expressed at times in his/her development, and even where a parent does not feel competent to offer anything practical in the way of support – the more likely it is that the child will be encouraged to persevere and be successful.

Parents' continuing involvement is therefore important both to the child and the school. It is in everyone's interests that it is nurtured and supported.

Our concern here, however, is to consider how the inspection process will evaluate the issue of partnership and what schools can be realistically expected to do to provide for it.

First of all, schools are statutorily required to provide certain information for parents. This information comprises: details of important business such as the state and management of the school's financial affairs, curriculum planning and provision, examination outcomes, annual reports of pupils' attainment and progress, specific details about staff and governors (see 'The Head's Legal Guide', Croner Publications). Parents must be afforded opportunity also to discuss their children's annual report with appropriate staff.

The parents of pupils with special educational needs have to be closely involved in the formal review of their children's progress (see Chapter 6). Inspectors will be rigorous in determining how such requirements are carried out. But they will wish to go beyond the merely statutory; they will want to establish what the school does to secure the involvement of parents in their children's education. They will base their judgement largely on the extent to which such involvement and partnership have an impact on the pupils' education.

The following are examples of some of the measures schools adopt to promote partnership:

- Early contact with the parents of children likely to attend the school, and opportunity offered for involvement in a range of events designed for mothers and toddlers – music, story, movement, puppet and play sessions. Such sessions will often be underpinned by clear, simple and useful literature, underlining how much parents have already accomplished with their children, and suggesting ways in which the various activities can be taken forward at home.
- Regular story club for parents and toddlers waiting to collect older siblings.
- The provision of occasional sessions during the day for mothers and young children comprised of talks, demonstrations and discussions about parenting and aspects of early education.
- Setting up 'parent rooms' or spaces where parents can organize, with the school's support, their own activity related in various ways to their children's education. In some cases this may involve parents in making materials for use in school.
- Providing opportunity for parents to buy story books at reduced rates or through payment over extended periods of time.
- Organizing special assemblies for parents and younger pupils and

older siblings in the school.

Now to partnerships when children formally begin school. The kind of contacts referred to above obviously prepare the ground for this. But what schools – and inspectors – have to remember is that partnership, for reasons already suggested, is not something easily achieved. Schools have to proceed with sensitivity and caution; they need to recognize that it is a lengthy and demanding process, critical for children's success but not achieved overnight. There are certain things that schools have to do and others that are desirable. Let us consider some of these:

- Parents have to be provided with a school brochure. This gives schools an important opportunity to convey their ethics, beliefs and aims, a picture of their curriculum, their educational objectives and plans, the steps they take to provide for pupils' welfare and special needs, the total provision they offer, including measures for spiritual, moral, social and cultural education. Not least it provides an opportunity to assert the school's commitment to home/school partnership and to set out the ways in which they try to achieve this.

The initial period of children's formal education, when parents are especially concerned to respond positively to the school and to what-ever seems best for their children's education, is potentially a golden period for partnership and one that can create a secure platform for the future. Teachers will find it helpful to bear at least some of the following in mind:

- There will be considerable diversity among parents and this will be reflected in widely varying experiences, viewpoints about schools and expectations for their children. Quite clearly no institution can cater for every individual expectation; schools have to set out their agenda and programmes, have to define their parameters so that parents are clear about what they can expect and what is hoped for from them. But it is important to bear this diversity in mind and remember that absence of response may imply uncertainty about how to proceed; social or cultural constraints in relation to public appearance and speech; difficulty because of domestic circumstances in being free at particular times; timidity in relation to formal occasions, as much as apathy or hostility. Schools may need to review their public events and formal occasions and question whether their style or nature may sometimes exclude particular groups. Some parents, for example, may feel more confident about participating in class or tutor group occasions rather than larger gatherings. It is probably safe to assume that parents – and children and the school – will gain more from meetings with the class teachers rather than a large-scale occasion with head teacher, senior staff or teachers who have no direct knowledge of the child.

● Parents' true interest lies in the education of their children, what is being done for them and what they are experiencing. Matters of great importance to a school may be significantly less important to parents because they do not seem to bear upon the children's education. Parents are likely to find formal occasions more attractive and congenial if they include opportunity to see displays of children's work, video recordings, film or photographs of their educational experiences, or a chance to see them perform in music, dance or gymnastics, however briefly.

● However diverse their experience and expectations, parents are the unique authorities on their own children; they have a knowledge and an insight about them denied to anyone else. It is essential that schools and parents share as far as possible the unique knowledge of children gained from their respective perspectives.

● The need to take advantage of the frequent opportunity that occurs in the early stages of children's education for teachers to talk informally with parents as they visit the school each day. This is also a period when parents are more willing to attend particular events designed to inform them about the school's approach to education – especially where children are involved, as in assemblies – or to hear suggestions about how they might help directly with the children's learning. Such occasions may often be enhanced by the provision of consistently affirmative, easily assimilated practical guidelines.

But partnership must continue long beyond the early stages. What other aspects of partnership do schools need to bring to the attention of inspectors?

● Many schools provide regular written information to parents to keep them abreast of school news, development, and events, and to convey information about their children's educational experiences. In some cases these are provided in the form of regular newsletters to which parents themselves occasionally contribute. Most parents usually find such material interesting and informative. But, in common with all written communications between school and home, they need to be composed with care and sensitivity. No matter how friendly and positive the intention, written communications for some parents can be alienating, convey wrong impressions, or be simply inaccessible for a variety of reasons, including style of address – or simply because the parents do not command the language in which it is conveyed. Such communications may well distance parents from a school rather than bring them into partnership.

- Schools, of course, have to provide reports, annually at least, about individual pupils' progress. This is a crucial exchange; information must be presented in as informative a way as possible, with every opportunity for parents to discuss the report in person with the class or subject teacher. What makes this a particularly significant innovation for primary teachers especially is that they are required to provide information – and probably explanation – about pupils' relative positions and performance. Inspectors will seek assurance both at the parents' meeting and through examination of school documentation that such information has been properly and fully provided.

- The governing body is a lynch pin in the home–school partnership. They are responsible to parents for the education the school provides for their children and the care it takes of them. Parent governors are elected to represent the views of parents generally, to listen to and convey their concerns, to act as a conduit between them and the governing body, to canvas their views and opinions before meetings and report back to them afterwards.

- The governing body is legally required to provide parents with an annual review that describes how they have discharged their functions in relation to the school; to give, in a sense, an account of their stewardship. They are additionally required to hold a meeting for all parents for the purpose of discussing and amplifying the report.

- But many schools want to go further than the demands of legislation. They attempt to give parents an insight into the way they provide for the pupils' education, the methods and approaches they employ, the ways in which they teach reading and mathematics, their approach to 'new' subjects such as IT and design and technology and the purposes of the school expenditure.

It is now commonplace for schools to give parents a broad outline of the educational experiences their children will encounter over a half or full term, about the projects they will do, the main emphases in the core and foundation subjects. Apart from informing parents, it is felt that knowledge of this kind may enable and encourage them to support their children's work and contribute in various ways to the planned learning activities.

Many schools invite parents to become directly involved through participation in activities such as shared reading at home, with opportunity created for reciprocal information about children's progress. The most successful of such enterprises are based upon a common understanding of main methods and approaches, clarified for parents by the school. Teachers feel that such enterprises, apart from providing important support for children individually, create a 'climate of literacy' in which reading comes to be regarded as a valued activity. Similar schemes are run in some primary schools in connection with mathematics. In the latter case the process is often supported by guidelines and materials for interesting and relevant activities that parents can manage with confidence.

Such involvement, of course, is about what parents can do to support their own children's work. But for many years now, primary schools, particularly, have been involving parents on a wider basis, that is, in supporting the work of teachers within the school and in classrooms. In many cases such support is very much of a 'housekeeping' nature, tied up with the organization and management of classrooms, areas of the school such as the library, or the maintenance of equipment and materials. Parents help with school outings and expeditions, with the organization of swimming, games and similar activities.

Some schools go further and involve parents in supporting teaching. This is most often done by hearing readers, supporting young children's play activities and contributing to creative activities. In some cases parents are provided with broad school-based training to equip them for their involvement. Provided it is properly managed, that parents are clear about the task, and how it contributes to teaching objectives, such partnership can be particularly valuable in that it enlarges the possibility of extended interaction between the teacher and groups of pupils.

Formal parent–teacher associations are, of course, an important element of partnership. Such bodies often make considerable material contributions to the life of a school through financial support, the organization of social activities, and environmental enrichment. But their greater value may lie in the expression they represent of communal support for and involvement in the school. The additional work that parent–teacher associations can sometimes create for school staff and the time expended on careful communication are often well repaid, not merely in terms of material outcomes, but in the enhancement of relationships between school, parents and the wider community.

Parental involvement, especially of the kind related to pupils' learning, tends to become radically reduced at secondary school level. This is not to imply that parents are less concerned, nor schools less anxious to participate in partnership, but, for various reasons, there is significantly less direct access for them to their children's learning and curriculum experiences than they have been accustomed to at the primary stage.

Some secondary schools, however, have adopted a couple of potentially valuable approaches in supporting parents to maintain informed contact with their children's new educational experiences:

● Emphasis is placed on parents' involvement with their children's class or tutor group, rather than trying to generate interest on their part in whole school issues; something for which they may have little real feeling or interest. Parents meet with class tutors on a number of occasions through the year to receive general accounts and descriptions of the children's experience, presented through displays of work, film and video material and presentations by the pupils. There is opportunity for discussion of work, attainment and progress, on a collective and individual basis. Specialist teachers come to talk about their subjects, some of these unfamiliar in many respects to parents, and indicate ways in which they can be supportive of the children's learning. Opportunity may be provided for parents to accompany the class on educational visits, to support them in particular subjects, to organize occasional social functions for them. The intention is that parents follow the tutor group through their school life, building up a large body of knowledge about their education, development and progress, getting to know the group on a collective and individual basis, discovering constantly how they can contribute to their learning and general well-being. The potential of this approach through the secondary phase lies in parents' understandable inclination to be continually concerned about schooling as it relates to them as a family rather than about broad or general whole school issues.

- Partnering: secondary and primary schools are encouraging year 6 parent/class groups to link with year 7 parent/tutor year groups for a sharing of experiences, to induct parents and pupils to the new secondary scene and to ensure continuity of the parent/tutor group relationship.

Partnership with parents is one of the contributory factors that constitute the quality of education provided by a school and is judged on the contribution it makes and the impact it has on the outcomes — the educational standards achieved by pupils at the school. It is an element that has come to attain something of a sanctified position in recent times. The involvement of parents in their children's education is seen as a good thing of itself. But there is a need for questioning to take us beyond that position. What exactly is meant by involvement and what form can it most profitably take? How can it be most effectively and productively managed? What kind of training is necessary and can be provided for parents who support teachers in the classroom? How far can learning at home support learning in school? How much time can or should schools devote to a social partnership designed to foster closer links with parents? Is it necessary and possible to evaluate this in terms of value to the pupils' learning? How far should schools involve themselves in the domestic circumstances and problems of parents? How far can and should this be evaluated in terms of value to pupils' learning and progress? These are the questions that occupy and challenge many schools. For all the effort teachers expend on relationships with parents and the home, what will concern inspectors in this context is:

- how far schools support parents' involvement in their children's education by providing necessary information in its most comprehensible and accessible form about their children's attainment and progress;

- how parents are enabled by the school to become more involved at home in their children's education;
- how far information and involvement are positively supporting children's education;
- how parents are encouraged to become involved in their children's work at school;
- how the school's work is enriched by links with the community.

Many primary schools are enlarging pupils' involvement with the community. Apart from the more customary contributions to festivals, celebrations, concerts and other local events through performance and displays of work, pupils may have opportunity to learn about the nature, composition, characteristics and work of the local community, how it relates to the wider world, how it impinges on their lives. They will do this through community research projects, through particular aspects of the history and geography orders, through visits to and exploration of aspects of community life, through input from key community figures and through games, situations and projects that allow them to gain some insight into the complexity of community issues.

In similar fashion, some primary schools are beginning to forge links with the world of industry and commerce. These are intended to begin the process of helping children develop an understanding of the world of work and its crucial importance in their lives, now and in the future. This is done by enabling them to:

- gain an understanding, from the earliest stage, of the role of people who feature in their lives and form part of their experience, through talks, demonstrations, visits to work places and so on;
- learn about the work their parents do;
- learn something about the machines, tools, technology and equipment necessary for particular jobs;
- gain an understanding of the social and economic consequences of work, of its implications for community, national and international well-being;
- have opportunity to run creative and technical activities on a 'business' basis, simulating and applying commercial processes of design, manufacturing, construction, advertising and marketing and economic management. Firms, businesses and industries are sometimes invited to take an interest in such projects or to monitor

and sponsor them in a modest way.

Such developments, of course, are carried out on a much more ambitious scale at secondary level, where the world of work has more urgent and immediate implications for pupils.

What inspectors will wish to determine is not how spectacular or exotic such ventures are, at whatever age they are undertaken, but whether they extend and enhance pupils' understanding of the world of work, of the greater society outside the school and how it functions, of implications for their lives, and of the meaning and responsibilities of citizenship.

Secondary pupils' involvement in the world of work can be a critical and decisive part of their education, and their initiation into the adult world. An Ofsted report on careers education highlighted the following as important elements of effective work experience:

- it is effective for students of all abilities;
- it stimulates serious thought about the world of work and self-analysis;
- it prepares students well, provides for two-week placements and for periods of debriefing;
- it makes useful links with GCSE English courses;
- through contact with compact type arrangements (a partnership between schools and businesses to promote pupils' eligibility for the world of work), it helps students to an awareness of employment expectations and the ways in which good performance at school can enhance chances of success in the job market.

Partnership with parents and the community: a checklist for reflection and action

Inspectors will take account of the following evidence:

Before inspection
- analysis of the returns of the parents' questionnaire;
- discussion with parents at the pre-inspection meeting;
- looking at the prospectus, newsletter to parents and similar information; minutes of governors' meetings.

During the inspection

- the examination of annual reports to parents and arrangements for follow-up discussions;
- a scrutiny of reading diaries, logs and other means of maintaining contact with parents over pupils' work;
- discussion with governors, head, pupils and parent helpers;
- contact with local community.

The inspection report will include judgements on the following matters:

- contribution to learning through parents' involvement with the work of the school and with their children's work at home;
- information provided about the school and about pupils' work and progress;
- enrichment through links with the community, including employers;
- provision for voluntary service and work experience for pupils of secondary school age.

Schools are recommended to review and consider action of the following kind where feasible:

- What, if anything, can the school do to begin a partnership with parents about the education of pre-school children who will attend the school in the future?
- What does the school do to involve the parents in the education of young children beginning school? What support is offered, especially in relation to reading and writing?
- How does the school explain its approach to teaching and learning to the parents of young children?
- What advice and practical support can the school provide that will enable parents to contribute as fully as possible to their children's learning outside school?
- Review the processes by which you provide parents with information about their children's education, attainment and progress.
- Consider the use of pupil profile books that help not only to give parents a considerable insight into their children's work but allow them to comment on it and enquire about it in more detail.
- Check that parents are receiving the information which is their

statutory entitlement about the workings and business of the school.

- Ensure that parents have an opportunity to discuss their children's annual report.
- Ensure that parents of pupils with special educational needs are closely involved in the formal review of their children's progress.
- Review your forms of written communication with parents. How suitable and helpful is it for parents from different ethnic backgrounds? How informed and involved do these parents feel?
- Are the school's public events organized so that parents have an opportunity to see their children practically involved and to gain a direct insight into their educational activities and work?
- Do parents have a clear idea of the educational activities their children will engage in over periods of half a term or a term? Does the school indicate ways in which the parents can contribute to these activities?
- Do parents contribute directly to work in the school? Do they help in classrooms? Do you evaluate the value of this to children's learning? Do you provide training for the parents?
- What do you do to maintain parental involvement at key stages and beyond?
- How are history and geography being used to enhance pupils' knowledge of the community and the world of work?
- How does the school actively involve pupils in the community and the world of work? How do you evaluate the impact on their learning?

11

Support, guidance and pupils' welfare

The inspection will focus here on whether the school's support and guidance enables all pupils to take full advantage of the educational opportunities offered and to have high but realistic expectations of themselves; the extent to which these ends are achieved through monitoring of progress and personal development, through individual support and advice, and through a climate in which pupils' well-being is paramount.

Inspectors will evaluate and report on:

- strengths and weaknesses in the school's provision for the educational and personal support and guidance of pupils and its contribution to educational standards achieved, taking account of individual needs, and the steps taken to ensure pupils' welfare;
- the school's arrangements for child protection;
- any matters which, in the view of inspectors, constitute a threat to health and safety.

Judgements will be based on the extent to which the school:

- provides effective support and advice for all its pupils, informed by monitoring of their academic progress, personal development, behaviour and attendance;

- has effective measures to promote discipline and good behaviour and eliminate oppressive behaviour, including all forms of harassment and bullying;
- has effective child protection procedures;
- is successful in promoting the health, safety and general well-being of its pupils.

In ensuring that all pupils are able to benefit to the fullest extent from their education and that their health, safety and well-being are provided for, schools will need to pay particular attention to the following groups of pupils and the particular issues that relate to them.

Young children at nursery and reception stage

For a majority of these children this is likely to be their first prolonged separation from home. The change and the implications for them are immense. Many of them will be required for the first time to operate in unfamiliar, large spaces. They will be expected to come to terms with:

- relating to and working with hitherto unknown adults;
- facing up to new and demanding expectations;
- being treated as one of a large group;
- having to respond to new routines, to obey particular conventions;
- coping with the physical and mental demands of a longer day, and challenging learning activities and opportunities.

For many young children the differences between home and school may be large enough to be an impediment to their progress and development. Some children may be fortunate enough to come from homes where adult support, interest and the ability to intervene constructively together with access to learning resources and varied experience are at least as great as a school can hope to provide. In other cases children may find that teacher expectations, styles of address, questioning and information giving are so radically different from what they are accustomed to, and so difficult to come to terms with *quickly*, that personal confidence about their abilities and readiness to try things out may be eroded.

Schools are likely therefore at this stage to place major emphasis on the promotion of children's self-esteem and personal confidence.

Children will be given opportunity, within secure and ordered environments, with the support of familiar adults, to do things at a pace they choose, to learn through play, sensory and practical experience, encountered in various contexts, through access to diverse resources. There will be a constant emphasis on language and rich provision for its development.

Systematic observation of individual children's development and progress will be a critical component of teaching and support staff's work with young children. Observation will identify children's competence and achievements, their particular interests, concerns and needs. Out of regular observation, documented and analysed, will come carefully structured learning provision, geared to individual children, to their cognitive, physical, social and emotional development. Children's ability to learn, particularly at this early stage, is seen as closely related to and significantly dependent upon their emotional and physical well-being. Teachers will pay particular attention to the promotion of these.

Great importance will be attached to the experience, learning, knowledge and capabilities that children bring with them from home. Schools, in consequence, will do all they can to make a partnership with parents, the children's first educators and main authorities on their development and experience, to secure critical insights and knowledge and to ensure that the vital transition stage is safely and productively bridged.

Pupils with special educational needs

The Education Act has highlighted the requirements and entitlement of pupils with special educational needs and established extensive legislation to provide for them. Inspectors will wish to establish that schools adhere closely to the requirements of the Code of Practice. But the inspection schedule stresses the need for particular care in relation to pupils who may require regular medical supervision and therapy, pastoral support for pupils with emotional and behavioural difficulty, and the monitoring of behavioural objectives set out in individual education plans.

For many schools the demands of such pastoral care will be particularly heavy, a formidable drain on personal resources. The degree of 'return' and success achieved are likely to have large implications for the whole work of the school. Evaluation will need to provide solid evidence that such provision is 'paying its way', is helping measurably to raise educational standards and enhance the quality of life in the school.

To provide effectively for pupils' welfare, to ensure not only that they have appropriate personal guidance and support but are able to respond to them, schools must have clear policies and practical strategies for:

- monitoring the progress of individual pupils, academically, behaviourally and socially;
- the promotion of good behaviour, positive attitudes and a sense of personal responsibility among pupils;
- the elimination of aggressive and oppressive behaviour, of all forms of bullying, harassment and intimidation;
- the promotion of regular attendance and punctuality;
- the good health and well-being of pupils;
- enabling children to develop effective ways of protecting themselves and being able to contribute to the protection of others;
- effectively maintaining contact with, involving and securing the practical support, where necessary, of all appropriate outside agencies dedicated to pupils' welfare.

Let us now turn to the inspection criteria and consider how schools can best respond to them.

Does the school provide effective support, advice and guidance for all its pupils, informed by monitoring of their academic progress, personal development, behaviour and attendance?

This criterion takes us back to some of the important features referred to in Chapter 9 on the spiritual, moral, social and cultural ambience of a school and particularly to factors that contribute to good relationships between all the groups within an institution. Such relationships are founded on a concern for others and a respect for the rights and needs of the individual. They do not occur by edict. They survive and flower where there is professional integrity, concern to provide the best curriculum possible, a determination that all pupils will have equality of opportunity, will be expected to achieve their potential and supported in doing so, a genuine care for the individual which is informed and acted on, a refusal to go for the soft option, to turn a blind eye to the unacceptable for the sake of an easy life, or to accept their second best from anyone.

Positive relationships, like moral beliefs and values, cannot be conjured up spontaneously for a school. They have to be nurtured over time. But they are more likely to develop where the following are present:

- a set of educational values shared by staff and informing objectives designed to serve the needs of pupils;
- as comprehensive and objectively based knowledge as possible of pupils' achievements, interests and needs;
- realistic, firmly grounded expectations about what pupils can achieve at their best and a determination that they will do so;
- expertly devised programmes of study, matched to pupils' needs and development and backed by consistent assessment and diagnosis;
- a stimulating, civilized and harmonious working and living environment;
- strategies designed to monitor and provide for all pupils with special educational needs, whatever they may be;
- a particular commitment on the part of all staff to the total welfare of pupils for whom they have a specific responsibility;
- a readiness on the part of all staff to extend this professional concern to all pupils where they encounter them and to know them as well as possible.

In practical terms, such objectives and intentions will call for some of the following:

- early screening, consistent monitoring of pupil performance, scrupulous appreciation of the Code of Practice, provision for regular review (on a termly basis) of pupils' work, accompanied by individual consultation, feedback, advice and consultation; the extension of such review to include personal development;
- the establishment and maintenance of as close a relationship as possible with the parents;

- the development of systems for early identification, response and positive reinforcement for pupils with special educational needs;
- an agreed staff policy, underpinned by INSET and practical support within the school, on classroom management and organization in relation to pupils with special educational needs;
- the provision of resources, support and training required by teachers to enable pupils to meet the objectives set out in individual education plans.

Inspection has highlighted the matter of pupil attendance. There is no doubt that this is a cause of growing concern in some schools. The problem is not confined to difficult urban areas or to particular years in secondary schools. Many schools, both primary and secondary, in affluent areas, are increasingly faced, for example, with the problem of pupils removed from school by parents for additional holidays abroad.

The issue of attendance is one about which many schools are, uncharacteristically, tempted to give up, because their most determined efforts seem futile in the face of persistent pupil truancy, and indifferent, elusive or even hostile parents, reluctant apparently to exercise control. Some parents, indeed, have themselves given up the struggle. The problem is serious enough for some LEAs to initiate determined campaigns, including legal measures against parents, in an attempt to reverse matters.

Schools are obliged to persevere with their efforts to improve attendance, no matter how time-consuming or disappointing, for these reasons:

- unless absenteeism is seen to be resolutely dealt with, it may come to be regarded by pupils generally as an easy option;
- most obviously, persistent absenteeism will seriously hinder pupils' attainment and progress;
- pupils whose whereabouts and movements are unknown, because they are truanting or absent without cause, may be exposed to physical or moral danger;
- there may be serious factors concealed within the school that contribute to the incidence of absenteeism: bullying and intimidation; aspects of the curriculum that are inappropriately or ineffectually delivered. Schools need to consider the possibility of such factors, identify them where they exist and take steps to deal

with them:
- put in place systems for monitoring the recording and reporting by teachers of absences;
- follow the matter up with parents, make sure they are aware of their legal obligations, and offer support to them in improving their children's attendance;
- identify reasons and causes of absenteeism and deal with them;
- devise systems that will improve attendance, including reward systems and personal targets for pupils to aim at.

Obviously pupils who are persistently absent will fall seriously behind in their work and study. This in a sense contributes to a cyclical process: increasing absenteeism exacerbates regression in understanding and achievement, and, as a consequence, presents itself more and more as the only feasible option. It is essential therefore that schools act swiftly in the matter. They should, in addition, attempt to make provision that will support pupils in making up lost ground as quickly as possible and give them a sense of progress and achievement.

Does the school have effective measures to promote discipline and good behaviour and eliminate oppressive behaviour, including all forms of harassment and bullying?

In this context inspectors will look for:

- a climate that promotes good behaviour;
- the incidence of misbehaviour and provision for dealing with it;
- evidence of harassment and bullying and how these are dealt with.

Certain provision and circumstances are essential to a climate of good behaviour in a school. They include:

- rules that are perceived by the whole school community to be fair, desirable and relevant, designed for the welfare of the individual and the good of all;
- consistent application of rules and a clear understanding on everyone's part of the consequences of breaking them;
- a moral climate built on values articulated through the curriculum,

look at behaviour policy

the collective action of staff, assemblies, the social and cultural life of the school, the nature and quality of the environment;

- a strong emphasis on spiritual, moral and social development;
- a consistent recognition of good and mature behaviour; unfailing confrontation of misbehaviour, together with an explanation of why it is unacceptable;
- frequent opportunity provided in the curriculum, in social, sporting and cultural activities for pupils to develop a sense of personal responsibility and to assume care and responsibility for others;
- carefully monitored opportunity for pupils to have some responsibility for the care of younger pupils, for keeping living creatures and growing things where feasible, and for maintaining aspects of the school environment;
- opportunity for pupils who have transgressed to make amends and retrieve lost ground.

Probably the most effective deterrent to unacceptable and oppressive behaviour is a civilized and harmonious school community, where good behaviour is publicly admired and consistently acknowledged. But harassment and bullying can survive in hidden and unsuspected areas of a school, however positive the climate. Those who suffer as a result may well be the least likely to complain, because of intimidation. Schools simply cannot afford to ignore bullying or even to allow for its existence. They need to ensure that at least some of the following measures are in place to guard against it:

- ways of knowing of its existence. These will include the regular termly review/consultation interviews between teachers and individual pupils; consistent and careful monitoring of pupils' work and the extent and nature of their involvement in a range of school activities; their attendance, punctuality and general behaviour; alertness for indications of racism; disparagement of others, and name-calling, verbal abuse and individually directed graffiti;
- constant and rigorous attention to behaviour at break and lunch times, inside and outside the school, at the beginning and end of the day;
- teaching pupils to recognize that informing about bullying is positive, mature and supportive behaviour;
- creating a climate where bullying is confronted by the whole school;

- training staff to deal with the problem;
- devising and implementing strategies for dealing with oppressive behaviour once it is identified. These will include immediate confrontation of the problem, contact with parents, assurance and support for the victim, decisions about appropriate action for individual cases, involving, where necessary, governors and outside agencies, opportunity for the aggressor to acknowledge and atone and to be supported through whatever process of rehabilitation may be necessary.

Does the school have effective child protection measures?

The school needs to ensure the following:

- that all staff understand the local child protection procedures;
- that the school is in a position to implement the procedures;
- that a member or members of staff have co-ordinating responsibility for child protection procedures;
- that all staff are trained in recognizing and identifying indicators of child abuse and the responses appropriate to such situations;
- that the procedures are in place for monitoring the well-being of pupils on the child abuse register and providing, in every way possible, for their welfare and the development of a sense of personal worth;
- the provision of learning programmes and materials, matched to stages of development and maturity, that enable pupils to identify sources of threat or danger, and provide them with strategies for protecting themselves and others; that such programmes help them at the same time to maintain a proper perspective, and positive attitudes about adults who have their best interests at heart, and about personal relationships in general.

Is the school successful in promoting the health, safety and general well-being of its pupils?

In this context schools need to make careful provision for the following and to monitor their proper implementation:

- a written health and safety policy; agreements for the provision of first aid and other medical support given to pupils by the school. This will include provision for pupils with specific physical and medical needs, together with the administration of regular medication;
- the treatment of injuries and arrangements for dealing with accidents;
- the preparation, organization and management of school trips, visits and outings according to prescribed regulations for safety; the training of all staff in such procedures and in dealing with misadventures and emergency;
- the proper conduct and supervision of school meals and break times and the training of supervisory staff to deal with misadventure and emergency;
- the regular monitoring of features of premises, equipment and working practices of the school that may impact on pupils' well-being.

Ofsted provides in the handbooks specific advice on health and safety to which careful attention should be paid.

Support, guidance and pupils' welfare: a checklist for action

Before the inspection

Inspectors will take account of the following evidence:

- the pre-inspection meeting;
- the school prospectus;
- school documentation relating to policies and procedures on behaviour and discipline, bullying, pupils' welfare; health and safety and child protection; equal opportunities and SEN policies.

During the inspection

- observation and discussion with pupils;
- procedures for dealing with oppressive behaviour and for child protection;
- procedures for monitoring attendance;
- discussion with welfare officers and usual staff from other agencies;
- health and safety issues.

The inspection report will include judgements on the following matters:

- effectiveness of measures to promote discipline and good behaviour;
- effectiveness of child protection procedures;
- success in promoting the health, safety and general well-being of the pupils.

Schools are recommended to review and consider action of the following kind where feasible:

- Make special provision for the care and welfare of pupils entering school for the first time.
- Use the DFEE/SCAA advice on care and provision to evaluate your own provision and arrangements.
- Review the quality and nature of your partnership with parents of school beginners.
- Ensure that your arrangements for the care of pupils with special educational needs are compatible with legal requirements and the Code of Practice.
- Review and evaluate your procedures for monitoring pupils' academic progress, personal development, behaviour and attendance. Do you have a written policy and guidance for staff in relation to the monitoring of pupils' progress and the provision of advice, support and guidance for them?
- Check that staff are fully aware of the need for such provision and the processes for implementing it.
- Does the level of pupils' attendance in all areas of the school meet official requirements?
- Are you satisfied that processes for monitoring unauthorized absence are adequate and satisfactorily implemented?

- Are your efforts to improve the performance of poor attendees meeting with success?
- How do you evaluate the quality of behaviour and the effectiveness of discipline in the school?
- Do you have a policy for dealing with poor behaviour and oppressive conduct? Have you got evidence to suggest it is being satisfactorily implemented? Are all staff aware of responsibility for implementing disciplinary processes?
- Ensure that a member of staff has designated responsibility for co-ordinating child protection measures.
- Ensure that procedures for monitoring the well-being of children on the child abuse register are in place and being satisfactorily implemented.
- Teach pupils to identify sources of threat and danger and provide them with self-protection strategies.
- Ensure that staff are trained to recognize indications of child abuse and how to respond to them.
- Review and evaluate regularly your arrangements for the health and safety of pupils.
- Ensure that your health and safety policy and guidelines are kept up to date.
- Take careful account of Ofsted's advice, contained in the handbooks, on child protection and health and safety.

The following questions to the TES column 'An Inspector Writes' highlight some of the aspects of pupil welfare that schools have expressed concern about.

Q I am a former head teacher, still working in education, and a grandparent who attempts to support my grandchildren in their schooling. I would like to know how much account the Office for Standards in Education takes of the quality of lunchtime and playtime provision simply in terms of food and refreshment. Are factors such as inferior supervision, with children rushed through meals, restrictions on the refreshments that 'packed lunch' children can bring, ignored as simply not important enough to be part of inspection? I don't think there is any reference to the matter in the new 'improved' handbook.

A   There is, in fact, a passing reference to the 'organization of school meals' in the context of the promotion of the health, safety and well-being of the pupils. But the handbook leaves no doubt about the importance of children's welfare, their security, comfort and well-being.

School dinners, and their rituals, despite an occasional tendency to regard them with wry humour, play a vital part in children's welfare. For some, they may provide the only ample and nourishing food of the day. For many young children, experiencing their first prolonged separation from home, these meal times may well be daunting occasions. For all children they should be, ideally, a source of anticipation and pleasure, civilized and attractive times that provide not only nourishment and refreshment but opportunity for the cultivation of relationships and mature behaviour.

In some cases school meal times are anything but this: boisterous and rushed; characterized by variable catering; a source of conflict between children; the recreational aspect limited. Schools will rightly claim, of course, that they are often limited in what they can do to improve some of these circumstances.

In what is often, admittedly, a rather cursory examination, inspectors will endeavour to make as informed judgements as possible about:

- the nutritional value of meals;
- the hygiene, comfort and attractiveness of the environment in which the meals are prepared, served and eaten;
- the general pattern of menus;
- the extent to which supervision encourages children to eat as leisurely and adequately as possible and have sufficient drink available.

Considering the matter from the point of view of what schools might additionally do, reference to some of the suggestions you make may be helpful:

- Create a tranquil and harmonious atmosphere where children do not feel hurried to finish quickly.
- Make clear to supervisory staff the value of their work and their essential role in the school team – even if their wages do not always reflect this.

- Provide appropriate staff training that enables them to appreciate the importance of their relationships with the children and the ways in which these can be enhanced.
- Ensure that sufficient water is available and that children are not reduced to queuing up at a playground fountain or drinking from washroom taps.
- Give children who have packed lunches the opportunity to bring carton drinks.
- Consider whether children can have water available to them in the classroom throughout the day. For some children their first chance for a drink may not occur until morning break. Consider the possibility of children having hot drinks in winter.
- Lunchtimes can be an opportunity for developing children's concern and responsibility for each other.
- Give particular consideration to the recreational opportunities available to children when the meal is over.
- Provide, at least occasionally, a chance for parents and governors not only to sample the meals but to share the whole of the children's lunchtime.

It seems to me that this matter is every bit as serious as you claim. In most respects I believe schools are making significant improvements. School meals may be, in many cases, an exception to this, with significant repercussions for children's wider education.

Q   We are due for inspection within a term and feel that our work and performance generally are satisfactory. There is one serious exception: the attendance of our Year 9 pupils, despite all our efforts, has remained extremely poor – less than 83 per cent – for more than a year. This contrasts with general school attendance which is above the 90 per cent benchmark. Do we stand a risk of being ranked as a failing school because of this?

A   This is one of the factors that could cause a school to be seen as 'failing'. Whoever is to blame, such absenteeism is denying a sizeable proportion of your pupils the education they are legally entitled to, and is 'affecting their achievement and disrupting progress', as the inspection handbook puts it.

It is also likely to be conveying undesirable messages to pupils, parents and the wider community about your ethos and management. It must cause some doubts about efficiency and provision for the welfare of pupils, about the nature of the partnership with parents, about working relationships with the education welfare service.

Perhaps most worryingly of all, absenteeism on such a scale may mean that some pupils, unknown to home or school, are exposed to physical or moral risk.

Inspectors will want to know about the following:

- the nature and composition of the absentee groups, the likely degree of truancy, the way in which the problem has developed and escalated, the steps taken by the school to deal with it;
- the school's attendance policy, and how expectations about it are conveyed to parents and pupils;
- how absence is recorded, evaluated and followed up;
- the working relationship with the education social worker and the nature of your partnership with parents about their children's education;
- whether you have incentive or reward systems in relation to attendance;
- how you have reviewed the nature of the curriculum and general learning experiences of Year 9 pupils, the form and nature of teaching groups, to establish whether there are critical links between these and pupils' reluctance to attend school;
- the specific steps you have taken to deal with the problem: the identification of causes, targeting of particular pupils, consultation and joint action with parents, strategies for improvement.

How likely are you to be judged a failing school because of this problem? Well, there is no doubt that persistent absenteeism on such a scale, together with the associated concerns, places you in a category where you could be perceived as a cause of serious concern.

However, it appears from what you write that your Year 9 may represent a particular circumstance that entitles you to leniency, if not sympathy.

But while inspectors may treat this as a 'one-off', especially in the light of acceptable attendance elsewhere in the school, they will want substantial assurance that you remain rigorous, and in no way complacent, about the future of Year 9 as they move through the school.

12

Providing for a positive approach to inspection

This book began with a consideration of the importance of inspection to schools and teachers, and the pupils they educate, and a suggestion that it was worth treating it as something more than an unlooked-for trial to be merely survived.

We finish with a reminder of some of the factors that are inseparable from a positive and creative approach to the process.

In spite of the unrelenting criticism it has received, and its undeniable fallibilities, and however impermanent its status may be, inspection has infinitely more potential to benefit than diminish schools. An inspection that leaves a school poorer in any sense than it was before is, in fact, an aberration from the system and inimical to all that the system was designed to achieve.

Schools are likely to get the benefits that inspection is intended to provide if they take careful account of the handbook, and, we presume to say, consider seriously the relevant issues raised in these pages, and act upon them where necessary. The following are likely to be important for all.

The purpose of inspection

Teachers need first to be clear about the nature and purpose of inspection. Its purpose is to help improve the quality of education that schools provide and to raise the educational standards achieved by pupils. Schools need to come to terms with the fact that the process is essentially a judgemental one based on analysis of exhaustive evidence, as opposed to descriptive; the advisory element apparently craved by many teachers is, in an important sense, implicit in the report's recognition and acknowledgement of effective and successful elements in the work of the school, and in the 'key issues for action' defining the measures necessary to rectify weakness and to advance development and growth.

Schools need to treat inspection as a process designed to help them to better things – however fine they may be at present – and capable of enriching those who work and study there. The school's main concern should be to make the most of inspection and get the best possible from it.

Attitudes to inspection

It is important for teachers to recognize that no school, however low its fortunes may be, faces inspection from an irretrievable or hopeless position. No school is without the capacity or potential to come out of inspection with credit. For some, the process of self-review, the preparation and the action that has to be taken will be signally more painful and demanding than for others; but it need be futile for none. (I believe that in time, when inspection is long done and finished with, we shall come to recognize as an enduring value the definition it has provided of effective schooling and the suggestion that the way to it may be more direct, less obscure and convoluted than we had sometimes been led to expect.)

The large majority of schools will not need the comfort offered here. An analysis of what the handbook has to say about education and its management will serve to reassure most that they are further along the road in many respects than they could have envisaged. They can face inspection with confidence and see the issues for action as part of an enhancing process.

Nor, of course, are schools short of advice; this book, for one, has presumed to offer it extensively. But many schools are likely to find much advice redundant in their particular cases; it may serve most usefully as a reminder of what has already been achieved or implemented, or is in the process of development, or as a set of markers against which they may measure how far they have come.

Preparation

Staff, therefore, would be well advised to begin their preparation as a whole team by setting down formally, drawing on evidence co-ordinated by heads of department and subject co-ordinators, what they perceive to be worthwhile, valuable and substantial achievement within and on the part of the school, and matching that to the expectations implicit in the handbook. They are likely to be surprised and encouraged to find more than they had hoped for. It will make the next step – that is, the identification of elements of the life and work of the school that must be improved – easier both practically and psychologically. In setting about that task the staff will have begun the process of preparing the story they must tell, without pretence, contrivance or invention, of where the school has come from and what it has learned from the experience; even more importantly, where it intends to go and why, and how it plans to do so.

A preparation phase is vital simply because a school needs to present itself at its best, to secure the accreditation from which fresh impetus flows; which endorses the good opinion of the community and renews, exhilarates and encourages staff. The temptation to 'let them take us as they find us' is best resisted. Teachers would be most unlikely to take so casual a stance towards guests invited for a meal. Something of the same attention to preparation for inspection will have worthwhile and lasting repercussions for the whole school community.

Preparation for inspection needs to be planned with extreme care, based on reliable evidence and objective judgements, and should seek to be positive, affirming and encouraging for staff, but designed to identify critical targets for development or corrective action. Preparation is likely to be most effective if it replicates the Ofsted process, pinpointing strengths and weaknesses, according to objective evidence and applying the evaluative criteria of the Schedule. Judgements of informed, critical outsiders about specific aspects of the school will contribute valuably to the process. In addition, the perceptions of a range of 'critical friends' can be sought in relation to various features of the school: the general learning environment, the management of discipline, communications with parents, extra-curricular provision, arrangements for the care and welfare of pupils.

Pupils' educational attainments

In a realistic appraisal of the school's position, the main focus must be on the educational attainment of the pupils, and emphatically on their progress. The school has to be absolutely informed about these and what they reflect of the quality of education provided, its strengths and weaknesses. The matter of progress is particularly important. Circumstances difficult to contend with may militate against pupil attainment in relation to national standards; teachers and pupils may continue to be disappointed in their efforts to narrow the gap. But progress is a different matter; what schools do in respect of this through consistent monitoring and well-planned intervention can make a significant difference. Pupils' progress needs to be an article of faith with schools, whatever their circumstances, with the evidence that demonstrates it constantly sought for.

Of course, education is about more than attainment and progress, more than a matter of strengths and weaknesses. Schools must provide, for the full education of pupils, wide experience and richness of curriculum. In review and preparation no less attention must be accorded to the spiritual, moral, social and cultural development of pupils than the academic. These have to be treated as central to their schooling and not something merely decorative on the margins. There are head teachers who contend that until schools get those particular elements right, together with the ethos they generate, securing the curriculum is likely to remain a struggle.

Teaching

So far as the inspection process is concerned, the educational standards achieved by pupils come first; everything else follows and is judged on the basis of its contribution to these. Foremost among the contributory factors that comprise the quality of education is teaching. What happens when the classroom door closes on pupils and teachers, the nature of the educational interaction that takes place between them, the translation of planning into effective teaching and learning, will determine, above all, the quality of education provided by the school.

In its review and preparation a school needs to concentrate more on teaching and on its constituent features than on any other contributory factor: the specialist curriculum knowledge, understanding of child development, the ability to create conditions and circumstances for effective learning (in the new Framework Ofsted has backed away from attempting to assess learning; for schools with an infinitely greater knowledge of their pupils, and the extended timescales within which they operate, the quality of learning taking place is something that can and should be consistently monitored).

What has to be done in relation to teaching in general, and to individual teachers – together with some aspects of management and leadership – is likely to prove the most complicated and hardest part of preparation. In many cases it may require detailed examination of teachers' practice – the very core of their professional lives. There will be times when it will demand decisive and resolute action; sensitive but determined leadership by head and senior staff that makes the needs and rights of pupils the main priority.

Heads of department and subject co-ordinators

The matter of the evaluation of teachers' practice by colleagues brings us to a group of people likely to prove most influential of all in terms of the inspection outcomes – the so-called middle management of the school, the heads of departments/faculties and subject co-ordinators in primary schools.

Let us consider first heads of departments. No other single group of teachers is more decisive in determining the fate of a school. They shape and manage, contrive and secure – or in some cases, perhaps, don't quite! – the nature and quality of curriculum provision, of teaching and learning and the standards of attainment. They set targets and expectations. They are responsible for the leadership, inspiration and professional development of colleagues. Corporately they have the capacity to create a curriculum vision, to work across subject boundaries, to pool their peerless knowledge of effective pedagogy for the benefit of all. A school stands or falls by its heads of department. In any judgement of leadership, their contribution will be central. In practical terms, they will be at the heart of inspection preparation; they must play a major role in putting the house in order.

Curriculum co-ordinators in primary schools are often unfairly mentioned in the same breath as heads of departments in terms of responsibility; unfairly, since they do not command anything like the time, resources and power of their secondary counterparts, and may often be accountable for more than one subject. Yet few groups have exercised a more positive influence on the remarkable curriculum developments of the primary sector in recent years – the incorporation of IT and design and technology, the valiant efforts to manage the National Curriculum, the development of assessment, the increased focus on attainment, the notable advances in whole school planning and evaluation. Inspection will make heavy demands on subject co-ordinators; schools must give the most careful thought to the support needed by them to carry out their role before, during and after inspection.

In the case of both heads of departments and curriculum co-ordinators, a main emphasis will be on their monitoring role in relation to pupils' attainment and progress, curriculum provision and staff development. In this respect they have to hold constantly before them the following simple but crucial questions: 'Are the standards of attainment in the subjects for which I am responsible high enough? How do I know? If not, what can be done about it? How will we know things are improving?' What plans for improvement.

The head and senior staff

This brings us to the ultimate leadership, the head, senior staff and governors. The leadership provided by head and senior staff will be commented on in a specific section of the report: the management and efficiency of the school. It seems to be a fact that schools are generally efficiently managed; leaders of schools have learned much from the introduction of LMS; the area of management has been a prominent feature of training in the last couple of decades. Inspectors, however informed, expert and experienced in the various facets of education, may struggle to match heads' knowledge and command of the complexities of managing the contemporary school. But, of course, leadership is about much more than technical and organizational expertise, crucial as these are. It is about the capacity to formulate a vision and involve others in its realization; to get the best from people individually and corporately; to set high standards for all and provide the support to help achieve them; to ensure that the curriculum offered to pupils is not merely in line with legal requirements, but reaches beyond that to give them what they will need to meet the challenges and opportunities of a new century; to ensure that the rigorous planning necessary for all of that is attended to.

The leaders of schools are ultimately responsible for the quality of teachers' work, for the nature of the educational environment, for the welfare of the pupils, for their spiritual, moral, social and personal development. For them it is not enough to prove they can balance the books; they must ensure that the fullest value for money is provided in all of these aspects.

Heads must lead in managing the inspection process and especially the preparation phase. In fact much of the business itself will be carried out by others – heads of departments, senior staff, curriculum leaders, the governors, teachers, support staff, the pupils themselves. The school community they lead will speak for heads in the end. It is for them to control the overall plan and work with their agents in the field in managing it.

The heaviest burden for leaders through the whole of the inspection process, from the preparation to the aftermath, will be in providing the proper support for colleagues. The demands in this respect upon their resources are difficult to over-estimate; in most cases they will eventually feel drained by them. Heads must ensure their own sources of support; these will be in the family, in friendships, professional and otherwise, in the wider circles of leadership, in the experience of colleagues, in the practical help of LEAs, the governing body, colleges of education and so on. Above all they may need help to keep things in perspective, to bear in mind from the beginning that the story of a school, however difficult the journey may be from time to time, and whatever the ups and downs, is always worth the telling.

The governors

The main partner in the leadership of the school, the governing body, obviously has to be involved from the outset in the inspection process. Every head's relationship with governors will be unique, with its own distinguishing features. But whatever form the relationship may take and whatever stage of development it is at, few heads will need reminding of governors' immense significance for schools.

As for governors themselves, the Education Act and the massive responsibilities it heaped upon them will have dispelled long ago any doubts they may have entertained about the importance of their role. We have made reference elsewhere to the practicalities of their part in inspection and need say no more about that here. But heads, and governors themselves, may sometimes forget or not even suspect the attention that will be paid by inspectors to the governors' role in the school and the perceptions they have of it. Inspectors will treat them with circumspection; they are, after all, in the strictest sense, the managers of the school, the representatives of the community. No one will be more serious than the governors themselves about the responsibilities they bear. No matter how inexperienced they may be, no matter how much other demands upon their time reduce their active involvement, they bear an accredited responsibility and the trust of the community to ensure what is best for the school and the pupils. Heads need to ensure that the volume of that concern, insight, acumen and commitment to the school is conveyed to and shared with the inspection team in dialogue between them and the governors.

The pupils

Let us finish with the pupils. Inspection and all that it brings in its wake – the questions that discomfit, the need for painful evaluation and re-appraisal by schools themselves, the unearthing of uncomfortable truths, the requirement to admit to areas of weakness, even the stress caused to some teachers – will all be justified if it contributes to a significant improvement of pupils' education. That is what it was made for. For the schools that can accept it for what it is, keep its rigours in perspective, and make the most of it, the gains will be theirs as well as the pupils', to enrich them long after the trials and hardships are no more than a memory.

Index

INSET DAYS 4/5 BEFORE OFSTED

ATTENDANCE

TUTORS → YR COORDS → HD

EVIDENCE YR10/11 VERSUS YR7/8

ORGANISER

SYSTEMS

1. ENSURE STUDENTS FILL IN 'ATTENDANCE RECORD' IN ORGANISER
2. NUMBER OF O'S < NO. OF STUDENTS IN GROUP
3. ENSURE WE ARE USING THE NEW REGISTERS WELL
4. REGISTERS RETURNED EVERY DAY

STUDENT/TEACHER REPORT SCORES?

EQUALITY OF OPPORTUNITY is fundamental to all our efforts. We are not always successful but we always continue to strive for it.

EVIDENCE (PARENTS COMMUNITY ETC)

1. WORK EXPERIENCE COMMENTS ** (SL)
2. PARENTS (REPORTS) FROM REPORTS **
   COMMENTS
3. YEAR 7 COMMENTS

SAMPLE WORK

WORK OF 2 ABOVE AVERAGE
       2 AVERAGE
       2 BELOW AVERAGE
FOR EACH YEAR GROUP
} SELECT EARLY (EARLY OCT?)

BEHAVIOUR MANAGEMENT STYLE/STYLE/STYLE

EXPECT SUPPORT — USE SUPPORT — ASK FOR SUPPORT EARLY
  HAVE HIGH STDS — NOT CRITERIA COMPLETELY DISRUPTING
                       BUT NOT PRODUCING ENOUGH WORK
                          CHATTING TOO MUCH etc.
             HAVE
WE ARE HERE TO WORK TOGETHER
I AM HERE TO SUPPORT (& OTHERS ARE HOD/HOY/DEPS)
            YOU
IF YOU DO NOT USE THIS SUPPORT (1-7!)
   (3-6 OBSERVATIONS)

ON TIME TO REGS

POLICIES TO GOVERNING BODY (END OF SEPT MEETING
+ ANY NEEDING LARGE AMENDMENTS TO NOV MTG

FILE OF POLICIES FOR EACH GOVERNOR

AFTER SCHOOL INSET   MORE PETER MARTIN?

WHOLE STAFF   WHAT DO WE AGREE IS VALUABLE
AT OAKLANDS

DOCUMENTATION   p94

| HOD'S RESPONSIBILITY |

ROSEMARY TONG - SCHOOL SELF EVALUATION 1ST MTG
MINUTES OF

p233 - "MY RECORD BOOK"